HEGEL'S LOGIC AND METAPHYSICS

Kant said that logic had not had to take a single step forward since Aristotle, but German Idealists in the following generation made concerted efforts to re-think the logical foundations of philosophy. In this book, Jacob McNulty offers a new interpretation of Hegel's Logic, the key work of his philosophical system. McNulty shows that Hegel is responding to a perennial problem in the history and philosophy of logic: the logocentric predicament. In Hegel, we find an answer to a question so basic that it cannot be posed without risking incoherence: what is the justification for logic? How can one justify logic without already relying upon it? The answer takes the form of re-thinking the role of metaphysics in philosophy, so that logic assumes a new position as derivative rather than primary. This important book will appeal to a wide range of readers in Hegel studies and beyond.

JACOB McNULTY is Lecturer in Philosophy at University College London. He is the author of numerous journal articles and a Routledge Philosophers volume on Marcuse (forthcoming).

HEGEL'S LOGIC AND METAPHYSICS

JACOB McNULTY
University College London

CAMBRIDGE
UNIVERSITY PRESS

CAMBRIDGE
UNIVERSITY PRESS

University Printing House, Cambridge CB2 8BS, United Kingdom

One Liberty Plaza, 20th Floor, New York, NY 10006, USA

477 Williamstown Road, Port Melbourne, VIC 3207, Australia

314–321, 3rd Floor, Plot 3, Splendor Forum, Jasola District Centre, New Delhi – 110025, India

103 Penang Road, #05–06/07, Visioncrest Commercial, Singapore 238467

Cambridge University Press is part of the University of Cambridge.

It furthers the University's mission by disseminating knowledge in the pursuit of education, learning, and research at the highest international levels of excellence.

www.cambridge.org
Information on this title: www.cambridge.org/9781316512562
DOI: 10.1017/9781009067805

First published 2023

A catalogue record for this publication is available from the British Library.

Library of Congress Cataloging-in-Publication Data
NAMES: McNulty, Jacob, 1989– author.
TITLE: Hegel's logic and metaphysics / Jacob McNulty, Dartmouth College, New Hampshire.
OTHER TITLES: Logic and metaphysics
DESCRIPTION: Cambridge, United Kingdom ; New York, NY, USA : Cambridge University Press, 2022. | Includes bibliographical references and index.
IDENTIFIERS: LCCN 2022022789 | ISBN 9781316512562 (hardback) | ISBN 9781009067805 (ebook)
SUBJECTS: LCSH: Hegel, Georg Wilhelm Friedrich, 1770–1831. Wissenschaft der Logik. | Logic. | Metaphysics. | BISAC: PHILOSOPHY / History & Surveys / Modern
CLASSIFICATION: LCC B2942.Z7 M435 2022 | DDC 160–dc23/eng/20220815
LC record available at https://lccn.loc.gov/2022022789

ISBN 978-1-316-51256-2 Hardback

For Anna

Contents

Preface

Hegel's *Logic* is often thought of as a work in metaphysics, rather than one in logic. Whatever, exactly, is meant by logic – Aristotelian syllogistic, "formal" or mathematical logic – the concerns of this area of philosophy are simply too austere to capture Hegel's ambitions. Hegel's *Logic* has more often seemed to pursue some unique form of metaphysics, of transcendental idealist philosophy (or even of some unique combination of these). While I am sympathetic to this received interpretation of Hegel's *Logic*, I believe it is potentially misleading. Hegel's *Logic* is not a logic in any straightforward sense, but it does contain an interesting answer to an old question in the philosophy of logic.

That question is the following. What justifies a law of logic, for example the law of noncontradiction? What legitimates the use of some set of logical materials, for example the proposition? What case is there for laws and materials on which all, or nearly all, of our justifications (ultimately) depend? In the face of this problem, we seem to confront a dilemma. On the one hand, we may simply shirk the demand for an argument-based justification and treat their justification as a type of brute fact. However, this seems philosophically suspect. On the other, we may attempt to provide a rational argument for these laws. However, this risks vicious circularity. Most authors, historically and down to the present day, have preferred the former route. As I hope to show, this more sober approach is characteristic of both the Scholastic-Aristotelian tradition, on the one hand, and Kant, on the other. However, Kant's followers, the German idealists, opt for the latter, more ambitious, approach. Fichte and Hegel attempt the impossible feat of arguing for the laws and materials of traditional logic noncircularly. Since it is Hegel's attempt that will mainly concern me here, I argue that he sets out to achieve this ambitious feat with three sets of resources.

First, a set of principles whose content and justification are independent of formal logic. This is Hegel's ontology or theory of the categories.

Compared with traditional varieties, it (or the relevant part of it) is primordial in being independent of ordinary logic in this way.

Next, Hegel employs a method of rational argument, the dialectic, that dispenses completely with the laws and materials of formal logic. It concerns not concepts, judgments and inferences but a more primitively characterized subject matter. Though rule-bound, it obeys norms distinct from those of formal logic, even avoiding the strictures of such seemingly inescapable principles as the law of noncontradiction. It is neither a method of reasoning, in the sense that Kant and the tradition recognized under the head of formal logic, nor a form of nonrational insight, advocated as an alternative by Romantics, fideistic religious believers, aesthetes, mystics and others. It is intermediate between these.

Finally, Hegel avails himself of concepts that are *necessarily nonempty*, ones that could not possibly fail to be instanced. These are concepts like those that figure in classical versions of the ontological argument for the existence of God. As they figure here, however, their interests are mainly methodological, not theological or religious. These concepts are (or purport to be) inherently contentful, meaning they can figure in a system of thought forms, all of which are necessarily instantiated. In this way, Hegel avoids the risk Kant saw for any form of metaphysics that attempts to make do with concepts alone. I mean the risk that the result will be little more than a game that thought plays with itself, devoid of contact with reality.

In sum, Hegel noncircularly derives the laws and materials of traditional logic from protological ones contained in his ontology, and whose application to the world is secured by their self-instantiation, the template for which is provided by the ontological argument from the tradition of rational theology.

Some will object to the thesis that logic depends on metaphysics, pointing out (correctly) that Hegel's *Logic* is consistently logical and metaphysical throughout. I agree, but see no incompatibility between my project and this received view. I use the terms logic and metaphysics in the narrow, un-Hegelian senses of the term that represent their (then) received meaning. Hence, I focus on those parts of the logic that overlap with their traditional subject matter, specifically the part overlapping with formal logic and the part overlapping with general and special metaphysics. All of these are just so many parts of the broader enterprise Hegel called speculative logic. However, I prefer to approach the *Logic* with traditional conceptions of logic in metaphysics in mind and have the new Hegelian idea of a "speculative logic" emerge from the confrontation. Hegel held that there can be no satisfactory account in advance of the nature and method of our science. He further held that full insight into the nature of this science is only achieved at its close. I take my interpretation to be supported by these two tenets of the Hegelian method.

Though Hegel's logic is a not a work in "logic as commonly understood," the subject matter of this science does take up a proper part of the work. Hegel treats orthodox logical topics, albeit against the backdrop of much that is patently non–formal logical: the nature and forms of concept, judgment and those of inference, and even the fundamental laws of thought (contradiction, identity, sufficient ground and so on). Most of these discussions, though not all, can be found in the "Subjective Logic," which Hegel tells us corresponds with logic-conventionally-so-called. This division is itself preceded by an "Objective Logic," which Hegel tells us corresponds with the former metaphysics, in its general and special branches: in particular, ontology and theology.

While the relationship between the two is complex, and likely one of interdependence, I am interested in the dependence of subjective logic on objective. My argument is that it is this that expresses Hegel's resolution of the logocentric predicament. By treating the laws and materials of traditional logic taken up in this section as subordinate and dependent part of a larger metaphysical system, we can locate in Hegel's logic a noncircular argument for the laws and materials on which all rational argument depends.

The result is not simply the old principles of traditional logic on a new foundation but, rather, new versions of those principles. Only those that admit of being justified in this ambitious way survive the transition to Hegel's system – some are completely jettisoned. Also changed is the status of these logical principles, which were previously merely formal, that acquire a content through their intimate association with forms of ontology and rational theology: for example, affirmation and negation, the copula and contradiction through their relationship with being and nothingness, identity and difference. Approached in this way, Hegel's treatment of orthodox logical topics, for example contradiction, appears in a more sympathetic light. Yet while Hegel's approach is more revisionary than reconstructive, this does not mean his project is not addressed to traditional logicians. He is attempting to show that this is what their logic would have to become if it is to surmount the logocentric predicament.

Granted that ordinary logic is dependent upon the former metaphysics, the latter is in a sense logic again: "speculative logic." Indeed, both are "speculative logic," the name for the whole in which both these branches are encompassed. What is more, it is at the level of this broader enterprise

of logic in the broad Hegelian sense that we encounter the fiercest controversies over the nature of Hegel's metaphysics and its compatibility with
Kant's critical philosophy. In a different book, my focus on the two sub-
parts of speculative logic might have been a way of sidestepping controversies concerning this issue. I am describing the relationship among two
of the *Logic*'s parts, so it is possible that this account be compatible with
different conceptions of the whole. However, I do embrace controversy
to some extent by choosing a more traditional interpretation than is now
in favor, among either the so-called Kantian-idealist interpreters or "neo-
metaphysical" interpreters.

Here, I defend my decision to interpret Hegel's metaphysics in this
more traditional way not in general terms, as others have already done, but
rather in terms of the specific philosophical problem that interests me: the
logocentric predicament. What is needed is a set of laws and materials as
well as a method of employing them wholly independent of formal logic.
Hence, the success of Hegel's project will depend on his ability to convincingly cast ontological and theological principles of his logic as more primitive than any with which traditional logic would have been concerned.
That is not something any previous ontology or theologian sought to do,
so far as I know. Those who accuse my Hegel of regression will at least
need to contend with *this* original feature of his project.

Though I do not want to exaggerate the ecumenicism of my interpretation, I do reject an assumption often made tacitly in the debate over
Hegel's metaphysics, namely that Hegel's logic must be consistently one
thing throughout. I prefer instead to distinguish between prospective and
retrospective orientations toward the logic. The logic begins in a metaphysical mode, fundamentally un-Kantian, though always self-critical. Yet at its
close there is a turn to the standpoint of the self-conscious, knowing subject, though I disagree with the common idea that this is a version of Kant's
Copernican turn. What is more, the retrospective perspective does not
revoke the prospective but supplements it. There is a mutual dependence of
each of these components on the other. In retrospect, being will turn out
to be something thought of by a self-conscious knower, though this should
not be assumed from the outset. For this discovery to take place, a self-
conscious knower must be shown to be – unlike Descartes, Kant, Reinhold
or Fichte, thinkers for whom the first-personal knowledge we have of our
own capacities will suffice for ambitious philosophical purposes.

Interpretive issues aside, the main philosophical risk confronting such a
project should be obvious, and is that of attempting to explain the obscure
by the still more obscure: the grounds of formal logic by the categorial

structure of being and the nature of God. Yet I think this is to miss the point of Hegel's undertaking, which is to challenge the received Kantian view of these disciplines. On this view, formal logic articulates thought's default, uncontroversial employment, presupposed in all its subsequent employments (mathematical, scientific). By contrast, speculative metaphysics as a further extravagance is to be pursued with caution, if at all. As I understand it, Hegel's proposal is that the situation is very nearly the reverse. It is not excessive ambition that leads thought into impasses but undue humility.

A subordinate aim of the book is to suggest an account of the history of German idealism in terms of the philosophy of logic. Idiosyncratic as it may seem, this project in philosophical logic is one Hegel is compelled to take up by his engagement with Kant's critical philosophy. As I hope to show, Hegel and other idealists criticized Kant for his uncritical reliance on the logic of the day. They contend that Kant's ability to criticize mathematics, the sciences and metaphysics was purchased at the cost of an uncritical reliance on ordinary or formal logic. Hence a reconstituted version of the critical philosophy, more consistently self-critical, would require nothing less than a new orientation toward logic. Kantian critique must be radicalized, not only to include such putatively uncontroversial assumptions as the finitude of our knowledge vis-à-vis that of an intuitive knower, the two stems of our cognitive power and so on but also to include formal logic itself.

While the dilemma set out above, between treating the justification of logic as brute and arguing for it in a way destined to be viciously circular, emerges repeatedly in the history of philosophy and even today, I claim it arose for the German idealists as well. It did so at a decisive point in their reception of Kant's critical philosophy. Indeed, this very dilemma was laid out by Jäsche in his preface to the first edition of Kant's logic lectures in 1800. It is Kant who, Jäsche tells us, regards as primitive the justification for such fundamental logical laws as the principle of noncontradiction. Yet his idealist followers, Jäsche observes, were unsatisfied, and sought something more ambitious.

Hegel does not claim to be the first to attempt a noncircular derivation of logic's laws and materials, but he does regard his predecessors as having failed. Reinhold experiments with a form of virtuous circularity but fails to show it is not ultimately vicious after all. Fichte, in programmatic remarks on his system, contends that the laws and materials of logic, even the law of noncontradiction, can be derived from a unique post-Kantian version of the cogito: "I am I." Yet in the system itself he ends up showing only that ordinary logic and transcendental philosophy are equiprimordial, not that the former can be noncircularly derived from the latter.

Where Hegel finds inspiration for a superior approach is in Jacobi's version of the ontological argument, itself inspired by the precritical Kant and the version of the ontological argument in the Ideal of the first critique. Liberated from the form of syllogistic argument used by the Leibniz–Wolff School and the Romantic irrationalism of Jacobi, a new Hegelian version of the ontological argument emerges at the outset of Hegel's system. In an ironic reversal, the very argument necessary for a reconstituted, Hegelian version of general and transcendental logic is the one denounced by Kant as the epitome of precritical, dogmatic metaphysics.

In Chapter 1, I outline Hegel's conception of the logic that preceded him, the logic of the Aristotelian tradition, and explain his critique of it. Hegel's critique is essentially that this logic cannot meet a demand for justification through rational argument, *indeed the very demand makes of all other sciences*. Essentially, then, pre-Hegelian logic fails to overcome the logocentric predicament and is impaled on its first horn: complacency. An important historiographical point of this chapter is that Hegel, in all likelihood, treats both Aristotelian logic and Kantian pure general logic together as forms of traditional logic.

In Chapter 2, I describe Hegel's relationship to Kant's transcendental logic, specifically its theory of the categories, which I claim is implicated in his "swimming objection" (often thought to apply generically). As I argue, transcendental logic suffers from a problem parallel to the one that afflicts ordinary logic, an inability to self-justify without begging the question. Hence it too is incapable of providing the type of argument for itself that it demands of mathematics, the sciences and metaphysics. Worse still, transcendental logic incorporates ordinary logic, and therefore the problem that afflicted the latter as well. This occurs in Kant's decision to derive his table of categories from the table of forms of judgment. Hence the problem is not only redoubled with another related one but compounded. For Hegel, this is no coincidence. The two main problems are not only parallel but interconnected.

This raises the stakes of resolving the parallel dilemmas raised by ordinary and transcendental logic, and the resolution comes in the form of a revival of a well-known argument from the early modern period. Only with a concept that vouchsafes its own instantiation, such as the I-concept of Descartes' Cogito or the God of his ontological argument, can we derive a complete table of the categories. Of course, both must be rehabilitated, in light of Kant's devastating assault on rational psychology and theology.

The I-concept reemerges as Fichte's concept of "self-positing subjectivity," proposed by him as a basis for both formal logic and the categories. However, Hegel defends as superior Jacobi's God, a descendent of Kant's Spinozistic definition of God as the *omnitudo realitatis* from the Transcendental Ideal of the first critique.

In Chapters 3 and 4, I describe Hegel's relationship to precritical metaphysics and to Kant's critique of it. Unlike certain commentators, I distinguish very sharply between Hegel's critique of metaphysics and Kant's own. On my view, Hegel's has little to do with calling into question the conviction that empirically unaided thought can, all by itself, know the fundamental nature of reality. It is instead devoted to showing that the logic presupposed by precritical metaphysics, the logic of the Aristotelian tradition, led it into error.

Since Kant himself relied on this logic, even doing so in his critique of the tradition, Hegel tars him with the same brush. The Scholastic remainder in Kant's thought, especially his logic, compromises Kant's own critique of Scholastic metaphysics. The very same problems that compromise this tradition's approach to psychology, cosmology and theology compromise Kant's efforts to identify its shortcomings. In Chapter 3, I focus on the classically logical topics of judgment, syllogism, contradiction and identity. In Chapter 4, I focus on the ontological or transcendental logical topic of categories, treating Hegel's distinction between the finite categories, shared by Kant and the tradition alike, and the infinite ones Hegel himself prefers. I here devote special attention to Hegel's defense of rational theology against Kant's critique of it, focusing especially on Hegel's response of Kant's idea that "existence is not a real predicate."

In Chapter 5, Hegel's critique and reconstruction of "the former logic" on a metaphysical basis begins in earnest. I start with Hegel's treatment of the laws of logic, identity, noncontradiction and excluded middle. Some wrongly equate Hegel's critique of these traditional logical laws with Kant's critique of the categories, as if both were a matter of adopting into an idealist framework what was formerly regarded as part of general metaphysics. I deny this holds good, at least in the domain of general logic, where Hegel's complaint is if anything the reverse, a rejection of the approach shared by Kant and the tradition alike of tying logic too closely to faculty psychology. I also accept that Hegel is a critic of the law of noncontradiction, and, rather than regard his critique as an embarrassment, I attempt to present it in a more sympathetic light: considering more recent criticisms of classical logic by paraconsistent logicians. I claim that Hegel, like other intelligent critics of the law of noncontradiction, emphasizes paradoxes in his account of their nature and limits. However, Hegel discovers an original class of category-theoretic paradoxes, rather than relying on traditional ones: for example, the liar or the truth predicate. These paradoxes concern identity.

In Chapter 6, I turn to Hegel's account of the nature of concepts – or, better, of "*the* Concept," as well as his derivation of the forms of judgment and inference. Whereas in Kant, these topics belonged to general logic, preceding and making possible a derivation of the categories (and Ideas) of transcendental logic, Hegel inverts this approach. He, unlike Kant, derives the nature of the Concept, as well as its necessary judgmental and inferential forms by beginning from an ontological theory of the categories. This theory furnishes him with what I contend is the master argument of the logic and the one that makes possible Hegel's account of the nature and forms of concept, judgment and inference.

This argument, which spans the entirety of the first two divisions of the logic, shows, in a phrase, that "there is nothing purely immediate or mediated." However, I interpret this claim in a less familiar way. I construe this claim not as an epistemological one concerning the manner in which sensible intuitions are always informed by our concepts but, rather, as a metaphysical one concerning the ubiquity of a type of structure in the natural and social worlds. The argument makes possible a complete taxonomy of forms of judgment and inference – but only on the condition that they are construed in terms of an ontological theory of the categories based in a version of the ontological argument.

In Chapter 7, I conclude by discussing a well-known feature of Hegel's argument in the logic: its circular structure, often depicted in terms of the Jungian ouroboros archetype (a snake eating its tail). While the status of Hegel's system as circular in this way is well known, I claim it can be related directly to the logocentric predicament. Essentially, Hegel's criticism of the two prior forms of logic is that they are non-self-comprehending sciences. Neither the Aristotelian tradition nor Kant, neither general nor transcendental logic, avoids self-opacity. Each comprehends its subject matter but fails to self-comprehend – indeed, the success and failure are connected. I explain how Hegel's *Logic* avoids this problem by rendering traditional logic a subordinate and dependent part of his metaphysics. This means rendering the subject matter of epistemology, knowledge and the relationship between the knower and the known, part of the subject matter of metaphysics, the fundamental structure of reality. However, this must be qualified, inasmuch as the close of the logic affords a perspective on its beginning not available there.

Acknowledgments

This project began its life as a dissertation written at Columbia University in the philosophy department while I was a graduate student there from 2013 to 2019. I first submitted it to Cambridge in the fall of 2020, and then, after receiving two helpful readers' reports, submitted the final version in August 2021.

I am grateful to my editor, Hilary Gaskin, whose guidance, advice and patience with me at every stage of the process was invaluable. I am also very grateful to the two anonymous reviewers for Cambridge for their helpful suggestions.

In the course of completing the project, I accumulated many debts to friends, teachers and colleagues, some of whom I would like to acknowledge here.

My advisor, Fred Neuhouser, gave comments on multiple drafts over the years. I thank him for his teaching, mentorship and steadfast support. I also thank the other members of my committee, Wolfgang Mann and Axel Honneth, for their assistance. Some other Columbia faculty members with whom I was able to discuss the project extensively were Chris Peacocke, Lydia Goehr, Pat Kitcher and Achille Varzi. A course co-taught by Peacocke and Sebastian Rödl in the spring of 2018 was particularly influential on my thinking. In particular, Peacocke's "metaphysics first" view (and critique of "no-priority" views) is an important inspiration for the interpretation of Hegel I defend. Anja Jauernig of New York University (NYU) and Des Hogan of Princeton University served as my external examiners and provided especially useful feedback on the Kant components.

When I took up my first position as a postdoctoral researcher at NYU, I had the benefit of being able to discuss Kant, Hegel, Freud (and much else besides) with the incomparable Béatrice Longuenesse. Her two rounds of careful comments on a full draft of the manuscript undoubtedly made it better than it would have otherwise been.

During the pandemic, Mark Alznauer and some of his students at Northwestern University also read the manuscript in its entirety and discussed it with me, an experience for which I am grateful. I also had a valuable opportunity to present at Andrew Chignell's seminar in Princeton.

At different stages, portions of the manuscript were read and occasionally commented on by the following people: Brady Bowman, Ulrika Carlsson, Kevin Harrelson, Thimo Heisenberg, Eliza Starbuck Little, Karen Ng, Clinton Tolley, Robert M. Wallace, Leonard Weiss and Andrew Werner.

Corey Dyck was a helpful source of information about the Wolffian background to Kant's logical theory. In the month before it was finished, Clinton Tolley read the manuscript in its entirety and offered very useful feedback.

Huaping Lu-Adler and Robert Pippin both shared portions of what were, at the time, forthcoming books.

I presented portions of this material in the philosophy departments of NYU, Harvard, Princeton, University College London, Tübingen University, Johns Hopkins University, Birkbeck, University of London, and the University of Leipzig. I thank audiences at these institutions for their feedback. I am also thankful to members of the philosophy faculty at Leipzig who hosted me during 2019–2020, especially Sebastian Rödl, Andrea Kern and Humboldt Professor Jim Conant.

I have attempted to thoroughly record my debts to the literature on Hegel's *Logic* throughout this book. However, some commentators, especially influential for my reading, deserve a blanket acknowledgment at the outset: Brady Bowman, Paul Franks, Stephen Houlgate and A. F. Koch.

Unfortunately, I was unable to engage with Houlgate's long-awaited commentary on the Being logic, which I understand will expand on his previous work. This commentary appeared in print after I made the final substantive revisions to the manuscript.

Abbreviations

Throughout this work, both in the body and in the footnotes, I provide references to the German and English versions of primary texts by Kant, Fichte and Hegel. The following are the abbreviations that I use:

Hegel

There are two editions of Hegel's complete works in German, Suhrkamp and Meiner. My references refer to the Meiner edition (1968 – *Gesammelte Werke, Deutsche Forschungsgemeinschaft* [Hamburg: Meiner]), except where otherwise indicated. References to the English translations refer to titles from the series Cambridge Hegel Translations edited by Michael Bauer. I have occasionally referred to other translations of works by Hegel not yet available in this series.

The *Science of Logic* is cited by the volume and page number for the German and just the page number for the English. The *Encyclopedia* is cited by the section number (§) followed, where relevant, by an A for the *Anmerkungen* (remarks) and/or a Z for the *Zusätze* (additions from student lectures). The 1831 lectures on logic are cited by the page number in the English translation and the page number in the German from Meiner. The *Lectures in the History of Philosophy* are cited only by the English section name and subsection name, for example, "Aristotle: Logic."

EL   *Enzyklopädie der philosophischen Wissenschaften im Grundrisse Teil 1: Logik. Werke* vol. 13/*Encyclopedia of the Philosophical Sciences in Outline: Part 1, Science of Logic.* 2010. Edited and translated by Klaus Brinkmann and Daniel O. Dahlstrom. New York: Cambridge University Press.

VL/LL   *Vorlesungen über die Logik, Berlin 1831*. 2001.
             Transcribed by K. Hegel. Edited by U. Rameil and H.
             C. Lucas. Hamburg: Meiner/*Lectures on Logic, Berlin,
             1831*. 2008. Translated by C. Butler. Bloomington:
             Indiana University Press.
VGP/LHoP   *Vorlesungen über die Geschichte der Philosophy. Werke*
             vol. 30/*Lectures on the History of Philosophy*. 1995. 3 vols.
             Translated by E. S. Haldane and Frances H. Simson.
             Lincoln: University of Nebraska Press.
WdL/SoL   *Wissenschaft der Logik. Werke* vols. 21, 11, 12/*Hegel's
             Science of Logic*. 2010. Translated by G. di Giovanni.
             Cambridge: Cambridge University Press.

Kant

References to the German are all to the Akademie Ausgabe (*Immanuel
Kant: Gesammelte Schriften*. 1902–. 29 vols. Berlin: De Gruyter). I use the
English translations from the *Cambridge Edition of the Works of Immanuel
Kant*, except where otherwise noted. For the first critique, I use the stan-
dard A/B page references to refer to the first (1781) and second (1787)
editions of the work.

A/B   *Kritik der Reinen Vernunft*. Ak. vol. 3–4/Kant, I. *Critique of Pure
             Reason*. 1999. Edited and translated by P. Guyer and A. Wood.
             Cambridge: Cambridge University Press.
P   *Prolegomena zu einer jeden künftigen Metaphysik*. Ak. vol. 4/
             Kant, I. *Prolegomena to Any Future Metaphysics*. 2004. Edited
             and translated by G. Hatfield. Cambridge Texts in the History
             of Philosophy. New York: Cambridge University Press.
JL   "Jäsche Logik." Ak. vol. 9/Kant., I. "Jäsche Logic." In *Kant's
             Lectures on Logic*. 2004. Edited and translated by J. Michael
             Young. Cambridge: Cambridge University Press.

Fichte

German references are to the version of Fichte's complete works edited by
his son Immanuel Hermann Fichte: Fichte, I. H. (ed.) 1971. *Fichtes Werke*.
Berlin: Walter de Gruyter and Co. This is not the favored edition, but I
refer to it because many of the English translations have references to it in

the margins. English references are to what were, at the time of this writing, the most recent English translation.

References to the first *Wissenschaftslehre* are by volume and page number (German) or just page number (English).

WL/SoK   *Wissenschaftslehre*. 1794–1795. *Werke* vol. 1/Fichte, J. G.
               Science of Knowledge. Edited and translated by J. Heath
               and P. Lachs. Cambridge: Cambridge University Press.

Introduction
German Idealism and the Logocentric Predicament

0.1 Logic in Hegel's *Logic?*

In spite of its title, Hegel's *Logic* seems not to have anything to do with logic at all.[1] Clearly, its ambitions go well beyond those of formal logic, the area of philosophy concerned with the nature of valid argument. The controversial philosophical doctrines the *Logic* contains seem unrelated to the most elementary rules of thought. Understandably, the *Logic* is more commonly considered a work of metaphysics, though this designation is also not without its problems.

On a received view, the *Logic* is a work whose primary aim is to defend an account of the fundamental nature of reality ("the Absolute"), even of God. Seen in this light, logic in Hegel's sense of the term means something like "the logos" of Platonic-Aristotelian metaphysics. Certainly this interpretation is one that Hegel himself invites when he describes the work's subject matter as "the logos, the reason of that which is, [*der Logos, die Vernunft dessen, was ist*] the truth of what we call things; it is least of all the logos that should be kept outside the science of logic" (WdL 21: 17/ SoL 19).[2] Yet if that is so, then Hegel's own designation of his work as one in logic can seem misleading.

An alternative approach to clarifying the sense in which Hegel's *Logic* is a logic would be to treat Hegel's *Logic* as a successor to the enterprise of "transcendental logic" began in Kant's *Critique of Pure Reason* (A 131/B 170).[3] Clearly, both Hegel and Kant are concerned to offer theories of the categories or, as Hegel calls them, "thought determinations" (*Denkbestimmungen*) (WdL 21: 48/SoL 42; EL § 24 Z1, Z2). Categories

---

[1] Krohn (1972: 7).
[2] Hegel also invokes *Nous* a famous passage attributing to Anaxagoras logic's "intellectual view of the universe" (WdL 21:34/SoL 29).
[3] Hegel himself draws this parallel to Kant's "transcendental logic" (WdL 21: 47/SoL 40).

such as cause, substance, quantity and quality are among the most fundamental concepts we possess, the templates for all others. The categories are presupposed in all our thinking, and in scientific inquiry as well. Yet as Hume and others had shown, such concepts are incapable of being derived from sense experience: Causation, understood as "necessary connection" rather than "constant conjunction," is an "idea" with no corresponding "impression." Unlike ordinary empirical concepts, which can be derived from sense experience through Locke's "comparison, abstraction and reflection," a priori concepts such as these stand in need of a special type of justification. If they are to be legitimate, then they will need to be shown to have a different source than sense experience. What, then, might that source be?

In keeping with his Copernican revolution in philosophy and transcendental idealism, Kant offered a clear answer. For Kant, the categories are contributed by the knowing subject as "conditions on the possibility of experience" (B 160). Rather than have the categories derive from experience, as Hume would have done, Kant will have experience, meaning "empirical knowledge," derive from them. This is Kant's idealist strategy of defending our entitlement to the categories, but it has well-known costs. In particular, it requires that the use of the categories in theoretical knowledge be restricted to objects of possible experience or "appearances" (*Erscheinungen*). They cannot be used to know things as they are in themselves.

Hegel too is involved in the enterprise of giving a theory of the categories but departs from Kant in important ways. He certainly agrees with Kant that there are nonempirical concepts of this type, with a pervasive role in both scientific inquiry and everyday experience. He also agrees that they stand in need of a distinctive type of justification that ordinary empirical concepts do not require. However, he attempts to avoid the cost of Kant's transcendental idealist strategy for justifying our use of the categories, namely, their restriction to the realm of appearances.

Here, matters become controversial, though the difficulties are less important to my question than might at first be apparent. There is one obvious parallel between Kant's transcendental logic and Hegel's speculative variety. Neither is an aesthetic, an analysis of sensibility and its a priori forms if any there be. Each concerns itself with conceptual thought and the categories or "thought determinations" internal to it. So much is uncontroversial. Beyond this, however, it is difficult to say much about what would unite the two projects. All readers of Hegel would agree that he wants to avoid the "subjectivist" character of Kant's theory of the categories and embrace a more resolutely "objective" theory. How, exactly, he does so is unclear, and the recent literature offers a range of options.

Does Hegel, for example, reject Kant's idealist theory of the categories in favor of an alternative pre-Kantian or "realist" theory, an ontology such as those found in the Scholastic-Aristotelian tradition? Does he instead adopt Kant's theory but amend it in such a way that we are no longer left disconnected from things-in-themselves? Or is this, perhaps, a false choice from Hegel's point of view? Might his position be some type of hybrid of these approaches? And, if so, how, exactly would the synthesis be achieved? Which element, if any, would predominate? The jury, it seems, is out.

Yet this is of little use in the present context. Whatever the precise nature of Hegel's theory of the categories, it will not help us understand whether, and in what sense, Hegel's *Logic* is a logic. Even granting that Hegel's logic is some type of descendent of Kant's transcendental logic, this would simply relocate rather than resolve the issue. As Kant himself was well aware, transcendental logic is not logic in any ordinary sense either: "general logic." Hegel registers this too when, in a remark concerning transcendental logic, he says that the latter differs from ordinary logic or what has usually gone by the name "logic":

> *Recently Kant has opposed to what has usually been called "logic" another, namely a transcendental logic* ... Kant distinguishes it from what he calls general logic because it deals with concepts that refer to intended objects a priori, and hence does not abstract from all the content of objective cognition, or in that it contains the rules of the pure thinking of an intended object. (WdL 21: 47/SoL 40, italics mine)

At a first approximation, the difference between general and transcendental logic is this. In the former, we abstract from the object, considering only the internal consistency of our thinking. In the latter, we consider the object, albeit from a maximally abstract perspective. Of course, the question of the relationship between general and transcendental logic is controversial, but this much can safely be said. In concerning itself with such topics as causality, quality, quantity and so on, transcendental logic has a substantive content lacked by ordinary logic owing to its formality. Although not yet empirical science, transcendental logic operates at a slightly lower level of abstraction than formal logic.

Hegel's speculative logic departs from ordinary logic in this respect as well, perhaps even to a greater extent than Kant's transcendental logic. For Hegel, substantive notions such as cause, quality, quantity and so on are just the beginning when it comes to enriching logic with content. Yet Kant, at least, does his readers the courtesy of providing an account of the precise relationship of his innovative contentful form of logic and the traditional variety (A 50/B 74). Unfortunately, Hegel does not seem to do so, at least not in any comparably explicit way. We are therefore left with the impression that Hegel was oblivious to the existence of logic in the ordinary sense, though this impression turns out to be misleading.

Even a cursory glance through Hegel's *Logic* confirms that logic in the traditional sense is a frequent topic of discussion. Evidently, innovative varieties of logic from the German idealist period are by no means the only ones Hegel recognizes. Alongside discussions of speculative and transcendental logic, there are others focusing on what Hegel calls "ordinary logic" (*die gewöhnliche Logik*) (WdL 21: 35/SoL 30; WdL 12: 28/SoL 525). This is especially true in the so-called "Subjective Logic," which treats the trio of classically logical topics familiar from Kant and Wolff: concept, judgment and inference.[4] Yet there is also a discussion of the traditional laws of logic at the outset of the Doctrine of Essence in the "Objective Logic," such as the laws of identity, noncontradiction and excluded middle.

Evidently, logic in the ordinary sense is a concern of Hegel's *Logic*, but what exactly is common logic for Hegel? What would a reader of his time have understood by this phrase? One obvious approach to answering this question is historical, and it is Hegel's own conception of the history of logic that deserves to be heard first. Formulations such as "ordinary logic" "common logic" or even "the former logic" imply much more unanimity among Hegel's predecessors than actually seems to have existed. When we turn to Hegel's remarks on the history of logic, we find out why. As it turns out, Hegel has a fairly monolithic conception of the history of logic. To all appearances, Hegel shares Kant's assessment that there have been few developments of consequence in this science since the days of its founding by Aristotle.

> *Aristotle* is the founder of this science ... To this day, the logic of Aristotle represents the logical [sphere], which has merely been made more elaborate, primarily by the Scholastics of the Middle Ages. The Scholastics did not add to the material, but merely developed it further. The work of more recent times with respect to logic consists primarily in omitting many of the logical determinations spun out further by Aristotle and the Scholastics, on the one hand, and in superimposing a lot of psychological material [on the other]. (EL § 20Z)

---

[4] Krohn (1972: 7–8).

... we have still Aristotle's science of abstract thought, a Logic, to consider. For hundreds and thousands of years it was just as much honored as it is despised now. Aristotle has been regarded as the originator of Logic: his logical works are the source of, and authority for the logical treatises of all times; which last were, in great measure, only special developments or deductions, and must have been dull, insipid, imperfect, and purely formal. And even in quite recent times, Kant has said that since the age of Aristotle, logic like pure geometry since Euclid's day – has been a complete and perfect science which has kept its place even down to the present day, without attaining to any further scientific improvements or alteration [*die keine Verbesserung und kein Veränderung erhalten hat*] (VGP 2/LHoP 2 "Aristotle: 4. The Logic:)

From a certain perspective, Hegel's conception of the history of logic is disappointing. Can a catch-all term such as "the former logic" really do justice to the more than two millennia of reflection on this subject that includes Aristotle's logical writings, Stoic logic, Scholastic logic, Port-Royal logic, the logic of the Leibniz–Wolff school, and Kant's logic? Here, there is a strong temptation for the commentator to step in and add some much-needed nuance and complexity to Hegel's account of the history of logic. However, I will defer completely to Hegel's own account of the history of logic and argue later that a failure to do so has led to fundamental distortions of Hegel's thought on this topic.

Ultimately, then, Hegel and Kant are in broad agreement about the history of logic, though it would be a mistake to conclude from this that they agree about logic itself.

> Kant thought further of logic, that is, the aggregate of definitions and propositions that ordinarily passes for logic [*das im gewöhnlichen Sinne Logik heißt*], as fortunate because, as contrasted with other sciences, it was its lot to attain an early completion; since Aristotle, it has taken no backward step, but also none forward, the latter because to all appearances it seems to be finished and complete. If logic has not undergone change since Aristotle – and in fact, judging from the latest compendiums of logic, the usual changes mostly consist only of omissions – then surely the conclusion to be drawn is that it is all the more in need of a total reworking [*einer totalen Umarbeitung*]. (WdL 21: 35–36/SoL 31)

As we have seen, Hegel refers more than once and by and large approvingly to Kant's famous remark about the history of logic from the preface to the first critique. As Hegel reminds us, Kant said that logic had not needed to take a single step since its founding by Aristotle, in contrast to that endless battlefield of controversies, metaphysics (B viii). Yet Hegel here sounds a note of disagreement, remarking that if this is true then

Kant ought to have drawn the opposite conclusion. Rather than conclude that logic is complete, Kant ought to have concluded that a change is long overdue:[5]

To be clear, Hegel is not denying that the older logic was successful in the modest task it set itself. In spite of the sarcastic barb, he does share Kant's view that logic attained a certain form of completeness in Aristotle: in particular, observing and classifying "the phenomena of thought as they simply occur." Yet it is clear that Hegel regards this as insufficient:

> A logic that does not perform this task [the task of Hegelian logic – JM] can at most claim the value of a natural description of the phenomena of thought as they simply occur. It is an infinite merit of Aristotle, one that must fill us with the highest admiration for the power of his genius, that he was the first to undertake this description. But it is necessary to go further and determine both the systematic connection [*systematische Zusammenhang*] of these forms and their value. (WdL 12: 28/SoL 525)

Unfortunately, beyond the allusion to exploring the "systematic connection" between the forms of thought, Hegel does not specify what it would mean to "go further."

If we are to understand how Hegel aspires to surpass the tradition, we must better understand what he took the tradition to have already achieved in the logical domain. As we will see in more detail later, Hegel also inherits from Kant and the tradition the conviction that four topics are central to logic.[6] They are as follows:

  i.   The laws of thought, for example noncontradiction
 ii.   Concepts
iii.   (Forms of) judgments
 iv.   (Forms of) inferences (syllogism).

Broadly speaking, these topics are unified by a conception of logic as the authoritative source not only of the laws of good reasoning (i) but also of the basic materials or templates good reasoning uses (ii–iv). So we have four areas distributed among two main desiderata. Unclarity about either laws or materials could lead to different types of error. These four topics are discussed in passing in Kant's first critique, and more extensively in his logical writings. All are discussed in Hegel's *Logic* as well.

---

[5] See also Bowman (2013: Introduction: "A Totally Transformed View of Logic": 0.1 Hegel's Metaphysical Project).

[6] Dyck (2016).

To be clear, the four topics do not form a natural set in Hegel's *Logic* in the way that they did in more traditional works such as Kant's and also those of logicians before him.[7] Treating them as if they did, however, can be useful. The aim of doing so would not be to falsely assimilate Hegel to the tradition. On the contrary, it would be to take the full measure of his divergence from the tradition by comparing his views on these typical topics to the views of his predecessors, including those of Kant himself. If Hegel is broadly in agreement with Kant about the history of logic, he is by no means in agreement with Kant about logic itself.

As we have already said, Hegel's treatment of logic's laws and materials is part of a broader philosophical enterprise and encompasses much that is patently extralogical on virtually any conception of formal logic: a purified reconstruction of the entire history of philosophy, a survey of definitions of the Absolute, reflections on the nature of God, comparisons of different world religions (Christianity, Buddhism, Islam), then recent innovations in sciences such as chemistry, biology and physics. The logic not only treats much that we would expect empirical sciences of nature to treat but also, it seems, much that is supernatural – Hegel's antipathy to otherworldly forms of religion and metaphysics notwithstanding. If that is so, then we are confronted with a question one commentator, Paul Redding, has put with admirable clarity: What is the place of "logic commonly so called" in Hegel's *Science of Logic*?[8]

Admittedly, there are good reasons to doubt an investigation of Hegel's views on more conventional logical topics would be fruitful. In addition to being few and far between, these discussions are somewhat incongruous with their surroundings, where topics that are anything but abstract and formal are discussed (life, freedom, chemistry and so on). Even considered on their own, Hegel's more classically logical discussions are by no means the most promising or influential part of his legacy. Notoriously, Hegel, at one point, appears to deny the law of noncontradiction, providing

---

[7] In my view, Hegel includes both the Aristotelian-Scholastic tradition *and* Kant under the heading "the common logic." I here follow Hanna (1986: 305), who emphasizes that Kantian general logic is traditional, at least from a Hegelian point of view. Pippin (2018: Ch. 1) holds a different view, presenting Kant as a revolutionary figure in logic whose lead Hegel followed.

Whether or not Hegel held it, the view that Kant's logic is continuous with the Scholastic variety may have independent merit. See Dyck (2016) and also Tolley (2017).

Though he acknowledges differences between Wolff and Kant, Dyck is interested in Kant's remarks from the 1770s onward to the effect that Wolff's general logic is "die beste," "die beste die man Hat," "die beste die man antrifft." Dyck makes a compelling case that this is no mere backhanded compliment (2).

[8] Redding (2014).

fodder for some his critics in the Anglophone or "analytic" tradition who view him as an opponent of exact thinking.[9] More recently, Hegel's fortunes have improved considerably with the massive revival of interest in nonclassical logics among Anglophone philosophers. Today certain logicians, for example Priest, are far more approving of this particular part of his thought than even a great many Hegel scholars.[10] Still, this remains a minority view, and it is noteworthy that those hoping to gain a hearing for Hegel's thought in analytic philosophy have, by and large, denied that he is a critic of the law of noncontradiction.

An additional reason for concern has less to do with Hegel's own unorthodox views in logic than with the broader tradition of logic in which he worked. Figures in this tradition have always seemed to their analytic critics to be much too interested in the (subject–predicate) judgment as well as the syllogism. These were topics central to Aristotelian logic but marginal (at best) in the new and more powerful mathematical variety invented by Frege. Syllogisms can be reduced to special cases of a more general theory, a project announced in the introduction of Frege's *Begriffschrift*. More fundamentally, the central place items such as judgment had in the older logic was thought to be a symptom of that logic's impurity. In particular, judgment was thought of as being of merely grammatical or psychological significance.

Hegel may have aspired to transcend the tradition, but he can seem overly indebted to it just the same. As if to confirm his critics' worst fears about the impurity of traditional logic, Hegel tells us that his *Logic* is a work in which logic and metaphysics coincide.[11] Hence, its focus on judgment could now be redescribed in even less flattering terms: as an artefact of Aristotelian substance–accident ontology. Yet much recent scholarship shows that Hegel considered the "logic-and-metaphysics coincide" idea to be his work's chief innovation.[12] Before turning to the topic of the relationship between logic and metaphysics in Hegel's own work, it is worth reflecting on why the two areas of philosophy would have seemed distinct to readers from his time, and often still do to us today.

---

[9] For an alternative perspective, see the section concerning "the myth that Hegel denied the law of non-contradiction" in Stewart's (1996) anthology *The Hegel Myths and Legends* (Chs. 16–17).

[10] See Priest (1989: 388–415, 1995, 2006), as well as Bordignon (2017), Ficara (2020a: Ch. 16 "Hegelian Paraconsistentism") and Moss (2020: Ch. 5 "Absolute Empiricism and the Problem of the Missing Difference") for discussions of the parallels.

[11] "Logic thus coincides [*fällt daher … zusammen*] with metaphysics" (EL § 24).

[12] Pippin (2017, 2018) and Pinkard (2017).

One reason concerns the differing roles they have traditionally had in philosophy. Logic may be necessary to help us avoid certain gross errors in reasoning, such as embracing a contradiction or drawing an invalid inference. However, it does not suffice for metaphysical truth. If principles as elementary and widely known as those of logic could resolve the persistent controversies of metaphysics, then one imagines they would have been resolved long ago. This is not to deny the obvious fact that logic is a field of sophisticated inquiry in its own right. It is merely to remind us that it is somewhat rare for its more technical findings to bear on fraught metaphysical questions, especially of the traditional variety.[13]

To be sure, logic is authoritative in a way vaguely comparable to metaphysics ("first philosophy"). It lays down rules for our thinking in all other areas of philosophy and the sciences. However, logic is also typically neutral, incapable of being invoked on behalf of any especially controversial philosophical position, metaphysical or otherwise.

Finally, logic has occasionally been said to be completely empty of content, lacking any subject matter at all.[14] This is a view sometimes attributed to Kant, in his general logic. It is also sometimes attributed to the early Wittgenstein, who thought this was an implication of logic's status as metalinguistic rather than a science of such abstract objects as "Concept" and "Object." Yet regardless of whether we hold that logic is *completely* empty or not, it should be clear that it lacks the type of content traditionally attributed to metaphysics: For example, we could recall here the three objects of special metaphysics in Kant's time (God, the world, the soul). First-order logic, it is sometimes said, presupposes a nonempty world, a world with at least one object over which we can quantify. Yet this has no serious bearing on metaphysics, beyond ruling out such extreme views as that nothing exists.

While these philosophical intuitions concerning logic are deeply entrenched, they also suggest an intriguing possibility for any philosopher willing to challenge logic's traditional role. I mean, quite simply, the possibility that logic, whose status was traditionally to be a point of unquestioned common ground for proponents of rival philosophical points of

---

[13] Dummett (1991) sought a "logical basis for metaphysics." Yet even he would have acknowledged that this involved a conception of metaphysics that is quite deflationary. For this and other criticisms of Dummett's proposal see Peacocke (2019).

[14] See Conant (1991: esp. 133, 138) for whom this view is characteristic of Kant and the early Wittgenstein, though not of Frege. For Frege, logic has a subject matter, though one more abstract than those of other sciences. Logic studies the laws governing concept and object, just as physics studies the laws governing matter in motion.

view, might nevertheless be invoked on behalf of a particular one. In this case, the position that a reformed logic would be marshaled to support will be Hegel's own: more specifically, his metaphysics. Hegel may well be one of the only figures in the history of philosophy to claim that his preferred metaphysics can be read off of logic – or, at least, the correct logic.

0.2   What Justifies a Law of Logic? A Dilemma

In this study, I argue that Hegel's thought contains a response to a very old problem from the history and philosophy of logic. This is a problem going back to Aristotle, though one I hope to show took on a new and unexpected significance in the wake of Kant's critical philosophy. Just to give the problem that interests me a name, I will call it "the logocentric predicament."[15] The name suggests a parallel with "the egocentric predicament" from early modern philosophy. Very roughly, this is the problem of how one can be in a position to verify one's perceptions if there is no getting outside "the veil of perceptions." The logocentric predicament is also a bootstrapping problem, though arguably an even more fundamental one. It concerns the justification of logic's most fundamental laws and materials. We rely on these principles in all our ordinary efforts to justify ourselves through rational argument. How, then, can they themselves be justified without already relying on them? In asking for such justification, we need not suppose that logic's principles are further premises in the arguments we make. Carroll's regress, from the parable of Achilles and the Tortoise, is commonly taken to show that this cannot be the case.[16] Yet logic's laws are undoubtedly underwriting our inferences somehow, even if they do not serve as premises. This makes urgent the question of these principles' justification, the source of their legitimacy.

---

[15] I here follow Ricketts' (1985: 3) discussion of the logocentric predicament. I believe I am the first to relate German idealism to the logocentric predicament, though others have sought solutions to problems with which it is easily confused.

In my view, the logocentric predicament is different from, and arguably more fundamental than, the Agrippan Trilemma that Franks (2005) relates to German idealism via the PSR from early modern rationalism. The logocentric predicament challenges our ability to express anything truth-apt at all, and not just to achieve ultimate justification in epistemology, metaphysics or natural science.

In this regard, the problem I emphasize might seem to more closely resemble the one that exercises Pippin and Pinkard's Hegel: making sense of making sense, the sense-making of all possible sense-makings (Pinkard 2017; Pippin 2017). But, once again, the problem that interests me is more specific, since formal logic – logic in the traditional and narrower sense – represents only one form of sense-making, alongside aesthetic judgment, normative evaluation and so on.

[16] Carroll (1895: 691–693).

The stakes are high. At issue is the justification of justification itself via the logical principles on which it depends. If we cannot answer it, then not only logic or philosophy but all our efforts at rational argument in all areas of human knowledge might conceivably be thrown into doubt. Here, the analogy is once more useful. An extreme manifestation of the egocentric predicament is skepticism about other minds and the external world. A comparably extreme manifestation of the logocentric predicament would be skepticism about logic, perhaps not *all* logics but at least *classical* logic. Yet in attempting to answer the question of what justifies a law of logic, we confront a dilemma.

At first, it may seem that our entitlement to these principles is some type of brute fact, one for which no reason can be given. They are, perhaps, self-evident to anyone who reflects on them (whether for psychological, semantic or even perhaps pragmatic reasons). They could also be said to be foundational in a formal system where they are the unproven basis on which everything else is proved. Or maybe they are unchallengeable for some other more exotic reason. "Justifications come to an end somewhere." At a certain point, "my spade is turned." Nor does this stopping point seem arbitrary, in the way regress-stoppers are sometimes said to be.[17] In this case, there is a principled reason for why we cannot expect to go deeper in our efforts to justify ourselves.

However, this approach soon proves inadequate. Today, as ever, there are figures who do not find such principles self-evident in any of these senses. As is well known, there are (alleged) counterexamples to them: for example, dialetheias, apparent cases of true contradiction, many of which are millennia old.[18] The liar from the well-known paradox is the primary one. His claim about what he says is both true and false, true if it is false and false if it is true. Even today, however, it is not the only such example.

Zeno's account of motion in the arrow paradox is a classic example, not unknown to Hegel. It was later emphasized by Engels and other dialectical materialists.[19] On this account, motion cannot simply involve being at one place at one time and another place at another, later time. That would be consistent with being at rest all throughout – popping out of existence at one moment, only to emerge in a different place at another. Instead,

---

[17] Franks (2005: 8).
[18] Other examples include: truth value gaps and gluts; vague predicates; certain legal situations; and, most obviously, paradoxes of self-reference (the liar). See, once again, Priest (1985, 2006).
[19] See Engels (1947).

motion appears to involve a type of "blurring" in which a thing is in two slightly different positions at one and the same time.

To be clear, we may not be entirely persuaded by such counterexamples. However, the mere fact that anyone should regard these cases as potential counterexamples is unsettling enough on its own. After all, it was claimed that those laws are self-evident to anyone who reflects them. Prima facie, this is not so, regardless of whether we ourselves share the dissenting perspective. We can deny that our interlocutor denies what they claim to deny, but this seems ad hoc. In the face of this type of skeptical challenge, appeals to brute fact can seem complacent.

A second possibility is that we respond to this request for a justification of the laws of logic in the way we would in any other area of philosophy, attempting to give some type of rational argument in the way we so often do as philosophers. However, this approach soon confronts a significant obstacle as well. In the first place, it is unclear what could possibly be more fundamental than the laws of logic (psychology? language? natural science? something else?). How would we express the propositions of this base level and their interconnections without relying on logic's laws and materials? However, we can grant for the sake of argument that something more fundamental can be identified.

The deeper problem is that the logical principles in question are so elementary, so fundamental, that any argument we might be able to give for such principles would, it seems, already presupposition them. In a way, this is unsurprising, since the nonoptionality of such laws for rational discourse is their whole point. Our argument would need to invoke them in order to take even a single step from premise to conclusion. No sooner has an inferential step been taken than a law of logic has been invoked. If the preceding approach seemed complacent, then this one seems far worse. It helps itself to the very principles whose credentials are in question. It is circular. It could be argued that this is virtuous, rather than vicious, circularity. Yet this seems arbitrary. Relying prematurely on principles one hoped to justify at a later stage seems as objectionable here as in any other area.

Worse still, the problem quickly generalizes, and in a way that should become evident when we recall that logic not only concerns laws of thinking (well) but also the basic set of materials thinking presupposes. This bootstrapping problem does not simply arise when we attempt to argue for a law of logic and find we must rely on it in doing so. It also does so when we attempt to justify the use of certain basic materials employed in reasoning: for example, the predicate or negation.

At issue is less compliance with a logical law than the legitimation of some logical tool but the problem has the same abstract form. Here too these materials are so fundamental that any attempt to legitimate them would seem to already rely on them. The issue is not so much that of relying on principles one has not proven to hold true but the more basic one of even invoking notions one has not legitimated. Why these notions, rather than others? Why any?

In some version or other, this problem is very old, going back to Aristotle's *Prior Analytics*. There, Aristotle proposes the disturbing possibility that there can be no demonstration of the principles on which all demonstration depends. These principles would seem to be either brute or justified circularly.

In vol. 2 of his *Logical Investigations* Husserl also raises a version of this problem for the nascent program of "psychologism."[20] In this program, logic is said to derive from an empirical science: psychology. However, a science is a body of empirical propositions, standing in particular logical (deductive) relations to one another. If that is so, then the attempt to derive logic from psychology will be circular, relying on the very laws it seeks to derive.

Frege encounters a version of this problem, closer to the second "materials"-based version we considered than the first "law"-based one.[21] This he does when he is forced to deny that the language of the *Begriffschrift* can be used to talk about that language. We are, apparently, forbidden from making even the most basic statements about this language. Notoriously, there is no way to utter the apparent truism "The concept horse is a concept," in Frege's system.[22] This statement treats a concept as an object, thus violating Frege's famous rule from the *Foundations of Arithmetic* that the two ("concept" and "object," *Begriff* and *Gegenstand*) cannot exchange their functions.[23] Yet such statements as these are necessary if we are to induct others into our way of speaking. If the form of this problem reminds one of Wittgenstein's idea of a ladder one must climb and then cast away, then this is no coincidence. Similar problems are broached in the *Tractatus*.[24] There, the propositions of logic, those on which all our sayings depend, cannot themselves be said, only shown.[25]

---

[20] Husserl (2013: § 19: 43–44).
[21] Frege (1991: esp. 140) and Ricketts (1985).
[22] Frege (1892).
[23] Frege (1980).
[24] Wittgenstein (2005: 6.54).
[25] Wittgenstein (2005: 4.121).

Finally, a version of this problem has been raised in the recent literature on inference by authors such as Boghossian and others. Boghossian helpfully describes it as the problem of rule-circularity, relying on the very rule one is attempting to prove. Here he is explaining how it would arise if one tried to construct an inferentially based justification for the rule of inference known as *modus ponens* (MPP):

> This brings us, then, to the inferential path. Here there are a number of distinct possibilities, but they would all seem to suffer from the same master difficulty: in being inferential, they would have to be *rule-circular*. If MPP is the only underived rule of inference, then any inferential argument for MPP would either have to use MPP or use some other rule whose justification depends on MPP. And many philosophers have maintained that a rule-circular justification of a rule of inference is no justification at all. (Boghossian 2000: 231)

The solutions preferred in this more recent literature are closer to the first family of responses, even if they do not all fit perfectly there. Appeals to "default justification," pragmatic entitlement and virtuous circularity are by no means all best characterized as appeals to brute fact, let alone crude ones. However, they are alternatives to inferential justification of rules of inference.

As we will soon see, the idealists' favored solutions differ, belonging to this second family of inference-based solutions. They are therefore in a certain sense more ambitious – but also perhaps less likely to succeed.

0.3 Jäsche on the Role of Logic in Kant and Post-Kantian German Idealism

Is there any reason to think this age-old problem in the history and philosophy of logic, present in Aristotle and also in recent philosophy, might have been important to German idealism? After all, German idealism is a movement more commonly thought of as preoccupied with questions in metaphysics, epistemology, ethics, politics, "life," the philosophy of history, aesthetics – but almost never logic, at least if that term is understood in its usual sense. None of its major protagonists is considered an important contributor to logic, and this received view is one I would not contest.

Yet German idealism is above all a post-Kantian movement, a response to Kant's critical project that revolutionized philosophical reflection on all of these topics. Moreover, logic had a new and unprecedented role in Kant's project. If that is so, then it would not be at all surprising if logic were important to the idealist reception of his thought. In any case, it is from this post-Kantian perspective that I will approach the idealists' interest in the topic. As I hope to show, there was one question – less a question within logic than one about logic – that was important to the idealist reception of Kant. So far as I know, this question has been absent from treatments of German idealism in recent years. Integrating it into discussions of this movement could therefore allow us to see the movement in a new light.

Here, it may be valuable to consult an observation on the philosophical scene in Germany *c.* 1800 by Benjamin Jäsche, a student of Kant best known for compiling his lectures on logic for publication. As Jäsche observes in the preface to the first edition of these lectures from 1800, a rift appeared to have opened between Kant and his immediate followers in their attitude toward the laws of logic, such as the laws of identity and noncontradiction. Kant's idealist followers found themselves confronted with the dilemma just considered, which arises when we consider the question of what justifies a law of logic. When we do find we must either treat such laws as brute or else as justified in a way that seems destined to be circular.

> [T]here is no doubt about Kant's judgment on this point. He frequently explained, determinately and expressly, that logic is to be regarded as a separate science, existing for itself and grounded in itself [*für sich bestehende, und in sich selbst Gegründete Wissenschaft*], and hence that from its origin and first development with Aristotle, right down to our times, it could not really gain anything in scientific grounding. In conformity with this claim, Kant did not think either about grounding the logical principles of identity and contradiction on a higher principle, or about deducing the logical forms of judgment. He recognized and treated the principle of contradiction as a proposition that has its evidence in itself and requires no derivation from a higher principle. But now whether the logical principle of identity and of contradiction is really incapable of or does not need any further deduction, in itself and without qualification, that is of course a different question, which leads to the highly significant question of whether there is in general an absolutely first principle of all cognition and science, whether such a thing is possible and can be found. [Fichte's] doctrine of science believes that it has discovered such a principle in the pure, absolute I, and hence that it has grounded all philosophical knowledge perfectly, not merely as to form but also as to content. And having presupposed the possibility and the apodictic validity of this absolutely one and unconditioned principle, it then proceeds completely consistently when it does not allow the logical principles of identity and of contradiction, the propositions A=A and -A =-A, to hold unconditionally, but instead declares them to be subaltern principles, which can and must be established and determined only through it and its highest proposition: I am. (JL 523–524/7–8)

Once more, we run across Kant's (in)famous remark that logic had attained early completion and had not had to take a single step since Aristotle. Yet what is more interesting than the remark itself are the implications Jäsche and other idealists drew from it. Usually the passage is cited to as evidence of Kant's backwardness in the area of logic.[26] Here, however, it serves a different, more constructive role.

In particular, it is meant to be a clue to understanding the role of logic in the first critique. At least according to Jäsche, Kant's conviction that logic is fundamentally in order informs Kant's decision not to present any type of rational argument for logic's basic laws and principles, such as the laws of identity and noncontradiction. Certainly, Kant had not sought anything as ambitious as a noncircular argument, one that would show that these logical laws could be derived from some more fundamental principle that did not already rely upon them.

As Jäsche indicates, this had become especially clear in Kant's Metaphysical Deduction of the categories. There, logic's table of forms of judgment is appealed to for the very important purpose of identifying the categories. Yet very little explicit indication as to how this table might itself be argued for was given.

By contrast, Kant's immediate followers were dissatisfied with his attitude toward logic, which they thought of as complacent.[27] As Jäsche explains, they took the opposing view that logic's laws and materials would have to be derived from a more fundamental principle. Here, Jäsche alludes to Fichte's own first principle, a version of the Cogito: "I am." Yet there is an obstacle standing in the way of any such attempt. Would not the argument that takes us from philosophy's first principle to a law of logic have to rely on that very law?

Fichte himself had taken up this question in the opening argument of his *Science of Knowledge* (*Wissenschaftslehre*), the argument Jäsche alludes to when he mentions the Fichtean principle I=I.

> The laws of (common) logic … have not yet been proved valid, but are tacitly assumed to be familiar and established. Only at a later point will they be derived from that proposition whose assertion is warranted only if they are also. This is a circle though an unavoidable one. (WL 92, SoK 93–94)

---

[26] Russell (2015: 463).
[27] S. Maimon is among the most important early idealist critics of Kant's logic. See Beiser (1987: 309) as well as (Wolff 2013): 98 n. 18).

Here, Fichte alludes to the striking idea of a proof for the laws of logic. However, he also brings up the problem of circularity that we have seen dogs any attempt to argue for the laws of logic. There is precedent for the project of proving logic even earlier in Fichte's career. Fichte first voices the idea of a noncircular argument for the laws and materials of logic in the programmatic text "Über den Begriff der Wissenschaftslehre" ("On the Concept of the Science of Knowledge") (1794/98). Here Fichte could not be less ambiguous in his insistence that it is his philosophy that will ground logic, and not the reverse: "[L]ogic borrows its validity [*entlehnt ... ihre Gültigkeit*] from the Science of Knowledge, but the Science of Knowledge does not borrow its own from logic" (SW 1 67). Even a principle as fundamental as the law of noncontradiction will not be presupposed by his philosophy but, rather, deduced from it (SW 1 67)[28]

My basic proposal in response to Jäsche's observation is that the rift that had opened up between Kant and his idealist followers can be seen as a version of the very dilemma in the history and philosophy of logic we have been discussing. In Jäsche's portrayal, the idealists choose the way of rational argument with its attendant risk of circularity, Kant the way of self-evidence with its risk of complacency.

Yet if this is so, it raises a difficult historical question. Why would the German idealists, who proclaimed themselves Kant's followers, depart from him on such a fundamental question? The answer, I think, can only be that they believed the fate of the critical philosophy itself depended on a fundamentally revised view of the role of logic in philosophy.

0.4   Marburg Neo-Kantianism versus German Idealism

Although somewhat arcane, the question of the role of logic in the first critique nearly always emerges as important for figures seeking to understand that work's argumentative structure.[29] Yet the specific way in which it became important for Kant's idealist followers is unique. I hope to illustrate its uniqueness through a comparison of the idealists' Kant interpretation with that of another school, arguably much more influential in the reception of Kant: the Marburg Neo-Kantians.[30]

Here, I will focus on the specific issue of the relationship between general and transcendental logic. For the Marburgers, it was wholly

[28] Martin (2003) provides an excellent account of the circularity problem in Fichte.
[29] Reich (1992: 2).
[30] Here, I draw on Edgar (2010) and Heis (2018).

unacceptable that Kant's table of categories should have been derived from the table of forms of judgment given in the logic of the day. They understood the fundamental premise of Kant's system to be "the fact of science," that is, the truth of Newtonian natural science. Hence, they saw the twelve categories of transcendental logic as "abstractions" from a more fundamental set of twelve principles more immediately relevant to Newtonian natural science (Kant's "system of principles" from the Analytic). They then saw the twelve forms of judgment from general logic as still further "abstractions."[31]

In other words, pure general logic was not fundamental but in an important sense derivative. Indeed, it was at a twofold remove from what was genuinely fundamental in Kant's thought, the principles from his theoretical philosophy that formed the basis for natural science. Although Cohen is a famous exponent of this approach, a more accessible example of such a reading can be found in Cassirer.

A notable advantage of the Marburg interpretation is the anti-psychologistic interpretation of Kant it makes possible. The ultimate foundation of Kant's claims is not faculty psychology but scientific knowledge "printed in books," as Cohen is fond of saying.

Yet the interpretation also has a serious flaw. It ignores Kant's fairly clear insistence that relying on "the fact of science" is merely an expedient for use in the more popular presentation of his views given in the *Prolegomena* (P 4:274–275/25–26). The Critique itself does not rely on this presupposition, even if the *Prolegomena* does. Guarding against this error is the point of Kant's distinction between the "analytic/regressive" and "synthetic/progressive" methods of these two different works. Yet this is a distinction the Marburgers appear to elide. Some are even led to claim (implausibly) that it is the *Prolegomena* rather than the first critique that provides the more accurate representation of Kant's considered view.

Given the problem with the Marburg approach, there is reason to consider an alternative. More specifically, there is reason to consider an alternative account of the role of logic in the critical philosophy. Here, the German idealists provide a contrasting perspective. For the Marburgers, as we have seen, the problem posed by logic for the critical philosophy is one of overconfidence: more specifically, the overconfidence it seems to reflect on Kant's part in philosophy and what it can achieve vis-à-vis

---

[31] For Cassirer, the categories, as concepts of objects in general, are prior to the logical forms of judgment: "[W]hen expressed in exact logical notation, the types and forms of synthetic unity [the Categories – JM] are precisely what yield the forms of judgment" (Cassirer 1981: 172).

natural science. For the German idealists, the problem is, if anything, the opposite, one of underconfidence.

As I read them, the German idealists, such as the Marburgers, are preoccupied with Kant's decision to derive the laws and materials of transcendental logic (categories, ideas) from those of ordinary or general logic (forms of judgment, forms of inference, laws of thought). In a way, it is unsurprising that they too would have been led to this topic. The German idealists were doubtful that the order of exposition in the first critique reflected the order of the argument. They sought to discover in it a fundamental "first principle" from which the whole of Kant's critical philosophy could be derived. This project, which may have begun as a merely reconstructive one, quickly took on a revisionary aspect. Particularly vulnerable to criticism were those doctrines Kant had laid down as self-evident but apparently not argued for in any sustained way: for example, the distinction or dualism between the knowing subjects and the object of knowledge, the sensibility–understanding distinction, the finitude of our knowledge as contrasted with that of an infinite knower (God) and so on.

Although not itself one of the *most* prominent examples of a possible point of vulnerability in the critical system, Kant's commitment to the logic of the day quickly attracted a similar sort of scrutiny. Here too this scrutiny is based on the suspicion that logic was both fundamental to the argument and insufficiently well-defended. The idealists argued that closer attention to this logic would reveal that it could not bear the weight Kant placed upon it in his critical system. For example, it was important to Kant to demonstrate that his table of the categories was complete. Yet Kant was less explicit than he might have been about *why* it was so important to him to achieve this goal.

Given the paucity of explanation Kant provides, some readers doubt that it can have been central to his project as he suggests. Yet, as I hope to show, the German idealists did not share this view. I will later attempt to provide an explanation that does justice to the idealists' conviction that the fate of the critical philosophy itself turns on this issue. As is well known, the idealists regard Kant's attempt to prove completeness as a failure. In their view, it fails because of the role of the logic of the day in it. In my retelling, this will be the most important place that logic enters into the dispute between Kant and his idealist followers.

To the idealists, this failure was symptomatic of a deeper problem in the critical philosophy: Kant's uncritical attitude toward the logic of the day. Kant had declared that all sciences must justify themselves at the bar of the critical philosophy, but apparently made an exception of logic. It was, after all, complete and had been for millennia. Yet despite drawing on logic's findings at crucial junctures in his own argument, he had comparatively little to say about the reasons for its success. Certainly, Kant had not done for logic what he had done for mathematical, natural-scientific and metaphysical knowledge: At least in the first critique itself, he had not provided the same type of probing account of the nature and sources of the knowledge claims made in logic as he had for these other fields. Kant asks, in each chapter of his *Prolegomena*, "how is pure mathematics possible?" "how is natural science possible?" "is metaphysics possible?" Yet despite relying on logic throughout his attempt to answer these questions, he never poses the corresponding "how possible?" question for it.[32]

In fairness to Kant, logic seemed to him to be much less mysterious in this regard, and he had good reasons for thinking it unproblematic. Yet as we will soon see, this was thought by the idealists to be incompatible with the spirit of his philosophical project. Was this uncharacteristically complacent attitude toward logic not a betrayal of the critical philosophy's basic aspiration to subject all knowledge claims to critical scrutiny? Did this lapse in critical scrutiny not also constitute a lapse in self-scrutiny, inasmuch as the logic of the day formed an important presupposition of the critical philosophy itself?

Although this criticism has been made many times since, and in many different traditions, there is no more influential proponent of it than Hegel. Yet it is seldom asked in the recent literature what influence this may have had on the shape of Hegel's own mature system and the relationship between speculative logic and ordinary logic in it. In many prominent recent studies, it goes almost completely unmentioned. Sometimes its importance is explicitly minimized. In the interpretation defended here, Hegel's objection to Kant's reliance on logic will be treated as central. What is more, I will argue that this objection is fundamentally anti-Kantian, rather than superficially so.

0.5   A Heideggerian Hegel? Logic and "the Question of Being"

As I hope to show, Hegel's solution to this problem ("the logocentric predicament") invokes ontology, and in a way that prefigures the approach to logic taken by a subsequent German philosopher: Heidegger. I therefore

---

[32] Kant's failure to provide a critique of logic is an important theme in Lu-Adler's recent study of his logical writings (Lu-Adler 2018: Ch. 5 "Logic and the Demands of Kantian Science").

want to embark on one more historical digression before introducing Hegel's resolution of the dilemma.[33]

In a lecture course from the 1930s on logic, Heidegger poses for his students a simple but disarming question: What does logic have to do with philosophy?[34] After considering and discarding various influential answers, Heidegger introduces his own. Logic, he tells us, is inseparable from "the question of being." Heidegger anticipates that this will sound surprising but claims that this is only because the connection has been occluded in modern mathematical logic. This is a technical discipline that has lost touch with the traditional concerns of metaphysics, chief among them the question of being. Yet Heidegger also insists that the connection between logic and being is one that modern logicians have never been able to completely sever, even in modern logic.

In another such course, Heidegger defends this provocative claim by examining the Platonic metaphysics that the new crop of mathematical logicians were led to invoke in the nineteenth century in their struggle against psychologism.

> Therefore we could say that although this critique of psychologism is from the outset utterly clear on the guiding distinction between empirical and ideal being ... These are questions that did not surface first of all in the nineteenth or twentieth centuries, but that already engaged Greek philosophy, especially Plato. This distinction is the same as the Platonic one between sensible being ... and the being that is accessible through reason. (Heidegger 2010: 44)

Resisting the reduction of logic to empirical psychology would require placing logic's laws and materials in a realm not unlike Plato's intelligible world. In outlining his aims for the course, Heidegger proposes to uncover the traditional historical association between logic and what he maintains is the central question of metaphysics, the question of being.

As a clue to the discovery of this connection Heidegger cites the logical copula "is" without which judgment would be impossible.[35] Here in the logical form of judgment itself, we find ourselves confronted with the

---

[33] I here, once again, follow Hanna (1986): 310), who draws a similar parallel between Hegel and Heidegger. Both regard logic as, in Hanna's terms, "founded" rather than "founding."

[34] Heidegger (1984: 18). "But what does logic have to with all this? What does logic have to do with the freedom of existence? How does the basic question of being enter here? Logic does not treat being directly, but deals with thinking."

[35] "And finally, determinative thinking, as thinking about beings, brings, in its own way, the being of beings to expression. The simple statement 'A is B' shows this in the most rudimentary way" (Heidegger 1984: 20).

notion of being. This is to say that we find ourselves confronted with the question of what this little word, pervasive in our language, could mean. What is it for anything, a number, a planet, a person, a state, to be at all? What definition could we possibly give of something so ordinary and pervasive? In the ensuing lectures, Heidegger endeavors to show that previous figures always bore the connection between logic and metaphysics in mind. Leibniz is his main example.

Elsewhere Heidegger makes clear that his preferred way of relating logic to the question of being is somewhat different from that of the tradition. It is less to relate logic to metaphysics as the tradition knew it than to what Heidegger calls fundamental ontology/the existential analytic of Dasein. Swiftly and crudely summarized, this means situating the subject matter of logic in structural features of ordinary, lived experience (specifically, the most fundamental forms of behavioral and linguistic comportment toward the world and toward others).

Whatever the merits of this approach, and it certainly resonates with Hegel's project on certain broadly Kantian-idealist interpretation, I find myself drawn to another – though also one suggested by Heidegger's writings. This approach would take its bearings from Heidegger's insistence that the project of Being and time was always, in a sense, provisional. In particular, there was to be a third division in which Heidegger would overturn the "subjectivism" and idealism inherent in the idea of an existential analytic: more specifically, the idea that the question of Being could be pursued only in relation to Dasein, that being whose being is at issue for it. It is precisely this overcoming of subjectivism that Heidegger aims to achieve in his later work, though here too the question of why he made the "Kehre" (turn) is controversial. The vicissitudes of Heidegger's relationship to metaphysics notwithstanding, this nonsubjectivist approach to grounding logic in the question of being would seem to be the one Heidegger finds in the tradition. Hence, it is this latter approach I want to take to Hegel's way of relating logic and metaphysics.

0.6 Logic and Metaphysics (General and Special)

The main claim I will defend concerning the metaphysical foundations of logic in Hegel's thought requires that we recall the dilemma from earlier. In the face of a challenge to justify logic, we find ourselves confronted by a choice between an appeal to brute fact, on the one hand, and to viciously circular argument, on the other. Hegel, I think, chooses the way of rational argument, rather than that of the appeal to brute fact that he associates

with the tradition. With the possible exception of his idealist predecessor, Fichte, Hegel may be the only figure to ever do so. There is scarcely
anybody in the history of philosophy or today of whom I aware who is so
bold as to attempt an argument for the principles on which all rational
argument defends. By far, the dominant approach has been to treat these
principles as, in some sense, brute. Hence, the interest, I think, of Hegel's
project as I interpret it here.

Yet if Hegel is to argue for the principles on which all rational argument depends, he must avoid vicious circularity. Doing so would seem
to require two things. The first is a set of resources that do not already
presuppose laws and materials of ordinary logic, even such elementary
logical laws as noncontradiction. The second is a method of argument
that is not that of ordinary logic, for example syllogistic argument,
or arguments in premise–conclusion form. If Hegel can satisfy these
requirements, he will have done something that has likely never been
accomplished. So far as I know, it has never even been attempted. I
mean the task of discovering a form of discourse that is both rational and
argument-driven while at the same time unregimented by formal logic.
The benefit of this form of discourse is that it would furnish an external
perspective on formal logic, one from which the latter could be critically
appraised and revitalized.

Beginning with the starting point, I want to explore the possibility that,
for Hegel, the laws of formal logic derive from general metaphysics or
ontology.[36] As with traditional logic, traditional metaphysics – in particular, general metaphysics or ontology – has itself become a proper part of
Hegel's *Logic*. Just as he did with logic, Hegel tells us that the subject matter of metaphysics, in a narrower and more traditional sense of that term,
corresponds to a particular part of his logic.

> The objective logic thus takes the place rather of the former metaphysics
> which was supposed to be the scientific edifice of the world as constructed
> by thoughts alone. – If we look at the final shape in the elaboration of this
> science, then it is ontology which objective logic most directly replaces in
> the first instance. (WdL 21: 48/ SoL 42)

Objective Logic, which corresponds to ontology, precedes Subjective
Logic. Hegel tells us elsewhere that the latter corresponds to traditional

---

[36] Many have argued that Hegel's *Logic* is best approached as ontology, but the interpretations most
important for my own are two very well-known instances of treating Hegel's *Logic* as ontology,
Houlgate (2006: 116) and Doz (1987: 22–23). I am also indebted to the more recent *Ontologie des
Selbstbestimmung* of Martin (2012).

logic. Correspondence, in this context, refers to an overlap in subject matter. Objective Logic treats the subject matter of traditional ontology, the categories. Subjective Logic treats the subject matter of traditional logic, the forms of judgment and inference. (Some of this subject matter can be found earlier, but I set this aside for now.)

What, then, is the relationship between Hegel's reconstituted version of ontology and his reconstituted version of logic? While the two are undeniably interdependent, I want for the purposes of addressing the "logocentric predicament" to focus on the dependence of Subjective Logic upon Objective. It is this part that is relevant to my project of recovering a Hegelian solution to the logocentric predicament. However, I will return to the issue of dependence in the reverse direction at the end.

The question of how, exactly, logic and metaphysics relate in Hegel is much discussed in recent scholarship. However, the face of the question I am interested in here differs from the one that dominates present discussions. Since Hegel tells us that logic and metaphysics coincide, it is often thought that he is telling us something about the entire logic. Swiftly and crudely summarized, his point would be that it is consistently logical and metaphysical throughout, a study of the categories of thought and those of what is. The categories and forms of judgment or inference are one and all "objective thoughts." They are simultaneously forms of thinking and of being, though there are subtle issues about how best to understand this claim.

By contrast, the question that interests me concerns the relationship between two parts of the logic, whatever may be said about the whole. What is more, my question is more directly concerned with logic and metaphysics in the pre-Hegelian senses of those terms. What becomes of formal logic and precritical metaphysics when they reemerge in Hegel's system? More specifically, what becomes of the subject matter of these two sciences? The answer I give concerns the dependence of the former on the latter, not their thoroughgoing identity with one another. While I will not address interpretive questions concerning Hegel's slogan here, I do want to note that there are other ways for things to coincide beyond simply being identical.

In claiming Hegel's *Logic*, or at least the first part of it, can be approached as ontology, I build on and develop the work of a number of commentators. By far the most important for my project is Houlgate, whose interpretation of the logic as a presuppositionless derivation of the categories of ontology is seconded throughout this study. However, the proposal that Hegel's logic is an ontology, not original in itself, takes on a unique significance in the context of my project's guiding philosophical problem: the logocentric predicament. In terms of the dilemma posed above, there is one simple reason why the strategy of deriving (formal) logical principles from general metaphysical or ontological ones is promising. It is that, at least in its distinctive Hegelian guise, *ontology is pre–formal logical.* That is not of course to say that it stands outside "speculative logic," since, for Hegel, scarcely anything does. It is rather to say that the ontology of the first part of the *Logic* is innocent of any formal logical principles: the laws of identity and noncontradiction, the forms of judgment and valid inference, even, I will suggest, concepts (if these are defined in any theoretically sophisticated way). It is, we might say, primordial ontology, giving the point a Heideggerian spin. Interpretive issues aside, I think that there is independent philosophical interest to the idea of a form of thought, outside of the ambit of formal logic but nevertheless rational.

As I will explain later, there is a *formal* reason for the primordiality of ontology, at least as put forward in the Doctrine of Being. All of the ontological principles Hegel considers have a much more primitive structure than the ordinary logical ones. In Hegel's idiom, this is a matter of the "immediacy" of the former and the "reflected" or "mediated" nature of the latter. The former do not even have the structure of a "proposition" (*Satz*), let alone "judgment" (*Urteil*), whereas the latter do. As I will put it later, Hegel's ontology is prepredicative and noninferential – but pursues a form of rational argument nonetheless. Just what such a form of argument might be is too difficult a question to answer at this early stage.

Having a non(-formal)-logical basis from which to proceed is not enough, however. We also need a non(-formal) logical method of argument to get from these simpler principles to their more complex descendants. I believe we find this in the dialectic, which, I argue, does not use the laws and materials of logic. Using its twin strategies of immanent critique and determinate negation, the dialectical method operates on individual concepts. It therefore completely dispenses with the logical apparatus of claim and argument that are the philosopher's usual stock in trade. In short, it too operates at a logically simpler level, pre–formal logical but not for that reason nonrational. Though this only scratches the surface of its unusual method of proceeding, we can say that, in Hegel's logic, unit of analysis is the concept. I deny that the logic is made of judgments or inferences of any kind: even perhaps the "speculative judgments" of which his logic is sometimes said to consist (erroneously in my view).

It would be understandable to worry that Hegel, as I interpret him, is a Romantic irrationalist, rejecting formal logic and therefore reason itself.

This may be the position of Jacobi or Schelling in one or another of their phases, but not Hegel. The later Heidegger, an inspiration for my interpretation, often finds himself accused of the same. In my view, Hegel's uniqueness lies in his aspiration to find a *via media* between traditional, formal logic and the forms of mysticism or esotericism characteristic of the Romantics.

An important outcome of this investigation will be greater insight into why Hegel accords categories such a preeminent status in his speculative logic. This is something many of Hegel's readers take for granted as unproblematic. Perhaps this is because Hegel is a follower of Kant's critical philosophy, who had given categories a central place in his transcendental logic. Perhaps it is because Hegel is fundamentally Aristotelian metaphysician, a figure for whom logic just is metaphysics. If that were so, then it would be unsurprising that Hegel regards categories as important to logic, since they are the part of general metaphysics or ontology. Or perhaps Hegel's position is some hybrid of Kantian-idealist and Aristotelian-metaphysical ones – so that his interest in categories is overdetermined. However, I believe there is more of a mystery about why Hegel is interested in categories than either reading alone, or any combination of them, can accommodate. Such readings obscure one of Hegel's more important innovations over both Kant and the tradition. Unsurprisingly, I understand this innovation in terms of the history and philosophy of (formal) logic: more specifically, the logocentric predicament.

Today, the theory of the categories is not considered part of logic, as topics such as substance, quantity and quality are concrete in a way the concerns of formal logic are not. Even traditionally, however, the theory of the categories had what was at best an ambiguous status between logic and metaphysics. It was considered both a study of the fundamental types of predicate and of the fundamental forms of being. Through its treatment in the *Categories*, it was considered part of the *organon* containing Aristotle's logical writings. Yet it was clearly also a topic in the central books his *Metaphysics*, where the material from the *Categories* resurfaces. In this new context, the categories are said to describe properties of every being or entity considered as such, that is being-qua-being.

What is more, category theory was not only ambiguous but also marginal in both of the fields to which it was thought to belong. It was upstaged by special metaphysics (theology, psychology and cosmology), on the one hand, and syllogistic, on the other. How, then, did Hegel come to accord the theory of the categories such an important role?

As I hope to show, Hegel's approach differs from that of Kant, who sought to claim category theory for a new transcendental logic. Kant's new transcendental logic was to be distinct from the earlier general logic but also compatible with it. Indeed, the former would rely on the latter in numerous respects. By contrast, Hegel will incorporate category theory into his *Logic* in a way that leaves no room for this type of rapprochement.

Hegel will first resolve the ambiguity concerning category theory as either a metaphysical or a logical discipline. He will do so decisively in favor of metaphysics: more specifically, general metaphysics (ontology). Then he will argue for the unorthodox thesis that all of logic's other traditional branches (the laws of logic, concept, judgment and syllogism) have their foundation in his ontological theory of the categories.[37] On this basis, then, Hegel will justify subsuming the whole of logic under a traditional type of metaphysics, as well as reforming that logic in whatever way this change requires. Far from deriving the categories from logic, as Kant had done, Hegel will derive logic from them. Seen in relation to the traditional logic, then, Hegel's approach to category theory is both more radical and less Kantian in its aims than it has often seemed. It is also something not often attempted in the Aristotelian tradition, or ever so far as I am aware.

As we saw earlier, Hegel rejects this prioritization, but only now do we see that he proposes to completely invert it. A well-known Marxist trope applies here. Having found Kant standing on his head, Hegel turns him right side up, arriving at a radically non-Kantian form of metaphysics. The alternative Hegel will defend draws on an ontological or general metaphysical theory of the categories, developed on a logic-independent basis (though, of course, not independent of *speculative* logic). This then forms the foundation for a new logic of concept, judgment and syllogism, contentful in a way the older variety is not.

However, this is only half the story when it comes to the metaphysics Hegel uses to criticize "the former logic." While all I have said so far would suggest that the foundation Hegel lays for the principles of ordinary logic is one that overlaps with "general metaphysics" (ontology), it overlaps with "special metaphysics" as well.

---

[37] Varzi (2009 defends a similar view of logic. More broadly I am informed by Peacocke's (2014, 2019) "metaphysics-first" view. The view is that in any given domain of philosophy, the metaphysics of the entities in that domain is prior to the theory of meaning or intentional content for that domain.

> But objective logic comprises within itself also the rest of metaphysics, the
> metaphysics which sought to comprehend with the pure forms of thought
> such particular substrata, originally drawn from the imagination, as the
> soul, the world, and God, and in this type of consideration the determina-
> tions of thought constituted the essential factor. (WdL 21: 49/SoL 42)

Some interpreters are wary of going this far, preferring a Hegel whose metaphysics is confined to some more austere enterprise: a table of the categories
or a case for generalized hylomorphism. Here too the suggestion that Hegel
pursues not only general but also special metaphysics is not uncommon,
but it assumes a special importance in the context of my project.

Hegel's antipathy to "special metaphysics" in its traditional form reflects
a wariness of the "representations" or "picture-thoughts" of God, the soul
and the world found in Christianity. More broadly, Hegel is no orthodox
Christian and was throughout his life hostile to otherworldly and dualistic forms of religion (though also sensitive to the esoteric, this-worldly
teaching of Christianity reflected in the doctrine of the incarnation). Still
it is the residues of these crudely dualistic forms of religion in Kant's
doctrine of the postulates that Hegel objects to in his great predecessor's thought most of all. One theme of my discussion is that, perhaps
counterintuitively, the more one attends to Hegel's hostility toward traditional religious teachings, the greater his debt to at least certain forms
of precritical metaphysics becomes. The example of Spinoza proves that
these two stances are by no means incompatible but can, in rare cases,
be mutually supporting. Yet, as with Spinoza, it would be going too far
to conclude that Hegel is an atheist. Hegel nevertheless insists that the
first part of his logic overlaps with "special metaphysics" and insists that
each definition of the Absolute can be treated as an account of God. God
may be a metaphor with questionable uses, but that does not mean Hegel
regarded it as completely dispensable either. Not every metaphor is a *mere*
metaphor.

In addition to textual reasons, there are strategic ones pertinent to
present debates. Kantian-idealist interpreters of Hegel have assimilated
forms of Aristotelian general metaphysics previously invoked against their
readings: for example, an ontology of substantial form, once said to be
incompatible with Hegel's idealism on a broadly Kantian interpretation.
Successful or not, the assimilation suggests that future iterations of this
debate, which appears not to have been concluded to many people's sat-
isfaction, will take place on a different terrain. Regardless, I will give a
central place to one particular instance of overlap between Hegel's logic
and special metaphysics or theology: his ontological argument.

One way to motivate this idea is to recall a criticism of Hegel's project from the direction of Kant's critical philosophy. Even granting that Hegel successfully derives the traditional subject matter of logic from a set of ontological categories, what would prevent this from being a scheme of abstract concepts with no concrete, existential import? What would make it anything more than a mere game thought plays with itself, without ever making contact with reality? Thoughts without content are empty, after all. Fichte, whose early system appeared while Kant was still alive, received this criticism from Kant himself.[38] Obviously, Hegel did not, but his *Logic* continues to be met by versions of it.

While Hegel's followers have many answers to this type of charge, recent treatments have turned to one area of Hegel's thought in particular: his rethinking of the division of labor in our knowledge between concept and intuition, understanding and sensibility, category and form of intuition. Another related response concerns Hegel's "identity theory of truth," summed up in Wittgenstein's famous phrase that, when we think or say something, we and our thinking or saying "do not stop anywhere short of the fact."[39] Both lines of response have resonances with recent Anglophone philosophy, especially in the writings of Quine, Sellars, Davidson and McDowell.

While I will not contest these answers to the Kantian allegation directly, I will focus on an answer that has not so far as I know been heard in the recent literature.[40] Essentially, it is that Hegel's categories avoid a merely subjective status because they are concepts of God: more specifically, the God of the ontological argument. It is part of their essence or nature to exist, so that if their existence is even so much as possible, it is necessary. As I hope to show, Hegel's ontology, and especially the first (Being), incorporates a Hegelian version of the ontological argument for the existence of God, well-known from Anselm, Spinoza and Descartes.

Like "that being than which no greater can be conceived," Spinoza's substance that is *causa sui* or Descartes' God whose essence is to exist, Hegel's categories are concepts that raise a claim to necessary instantiation. They are ones whose noninstantiation or emptiness is meant not to be even

---

[38] Martin (2003: 33).
[39] Wittgenstein (2009: 49).
[40] In this, I am hearkening back to Henrich's first book on the ontological proof (1960), though he is there somewhat unsympathetic to Hegel's ontological argument. The more sympathetic treatments of Hegel's ontological argument from which I have benefited more directly are Harrelson (2006), Williams (2017) and Melichar (2020). I follow Harrelson in locating an ontological argument much earlier in the logic than is often supposed.

so much as possible, conceptually speaking. As we will see, Hegel concedes Kant's point that most concepts without intuitions are empty – but Hegel thinks it is going too far to claim that all are. If the claim of Being to necessary instantiation is upheld, then it will transmit necessary instantiation to all its successors. This protects the entire chain from remaining wholly out of touch with reality. It is for this reason, I think, that the ontological argument crops up again and again throughout the logical progression. The advent of a new category very often means a new version of the ontological proof.[41]

As we will see, Hegel's version of the proof is closest to Anselm's or Spinoza's in that it leverages a concept of God as maximally comprehensive. Such a being would have to exist, not least because there is no room for anything else to do so independently of it. (Obviously, this oversimplifies. It is not space per se that concerns us but logical or conceptual space that does so.)

Once we see that is so, we are in a position to further question the conception of a category Hegel is said to have inherited from Kant and Aristotle by prevailing readings. Whether general metaphysical (ontological) or transcendental logical, whether a "predicate" of any (full-fledged) being simply insofar as it is a being or a "concept of an object in general," the categories of Aristotle and Kant share an important feature: Each is one over many. After all, there are a plurality of *onta* falling under Aristotle's categories, and of appearances or "objects of possible experience" falling under Kant's as well. Interpretive debates rage over whose categories, exactly, Hegel's more closely resemble, usually with a view to settling the larger issue of the nature of Hegel's metaphysics and whether it can be rendered compatible to Kant's critical or transcendental philosophy. Yet once we bear in mind Hegel's interest, not only in a successor to ontology or transcendental logic but also to theology and the ontological proof, the picture becomes more complex. Hegel's categories, it now seems, are less "one over many" than "one over one," at least until we enter the *Realphilosophie*.[42]

---

[41] So, for example, Hegel discusses the ontological argument in connection between Being (*Sein*) (WdL 21: 76–77/SoL 65–66), Reality (*Realität*) (WdL 21: 99/SoL 86), Concrete Existence (*Existenz*) (WdL 11: 325, 420), Disjunctive Syllogism (WdL 12: 127/SoL 625).

[42] Bowman (2013: 166), following Fulda, holds that Hegel's Concept is a *singulare tantum*. I prefer Henrich's (2001) *Hen-Kai-Pan*. This adds the further thought that the Concept, in addition to being one, is all. This issue aside, I want to ask how the other logical categories appear, when seen in light of the Concept as a *singulare tantum*. My proposal is that they can be seen as candidates for this status. *Substance*, for example, the Concept's immediate predecessor is meant to bear this status, as is Parmenidean Being and the Absolute Idea. Indeed, there is reason to think it is true of all Hegel's categories. This would follow, essentially, from two facets of Hegel's method:

Both Aristotle's categories and Kant's are finite, from Hegel's perspective, and his categories more closely resemble the master concept of a philosopher who rejected category theory in any form: Spinoza. Notwithstanding Hegel's very real reservations about the anti-idealist monism of these figures, Spinoza's substance and Parmenides' One are better templates for Hegel's categories than any found in Aristotle and Kant.

Another way to put the point would be to say that Hegel is appropriating for his theory of the categories aspects of the broader philosophical systems of Aristotle and Kant that transcend their respective theories of the categories.[43] Hegel's Absolute Idea famously resembles Aristotle's thought-thinking-itself, which, as Michael Frede points out, belongs to his theology and not to his ontology.[44] Frede ascribes to Aristotle a view I believe Hegel also held. Roughly, this is the view that ontology and theology both constitute parts of metaphysics because they concern the question of being and that of the highest being: the question of what it is to be *tout court* and the question of which being best exemplifies this. I am skeptical of any attempt to integrate Aristotle's ideas into an interpretation of Hegel that omits this latter, theological component and focuses instead on category theory or the theory of substantial forms.

I follow Kreines in being similarly skeptical of any account of Hegel's relationship to Kant that includes only the Analytic and not the Dialectic. Perhaps such an account would treat Hegel as pursuing a general metaphysics or theory of the categories but be uninterested in his special metaphysics of the unconditioned or Idea. Indeed, I attempt to go beyond Kreines, integrating the Dialectic in its entirety, and not just the Antinomies. In this connection, I further argue that the paradigmatic Idea for Hegel is neither the soul nor the world-whole from the paralogisms or Antinomies but, rather, the *omnitudo realitatis/ ens realissimum* from the final section Transcendental Ideal of the first critique.

Going further, I challenge the common idea that it is above all "categories" that Hegel's Logic concerns. I contend that Hegel's categories more

---

1. that a category is always criticized in and through its metaphysical use rather than antecedent to its metaphysical use ("learning to swim without getting wet") and
2. that it is always criticized on its own terms and therefore in isolation from others and from experience ("immanent critique").

What *use* does one make of a category *in isolation*? The only possible answer seems to me to be that it is the monist use of a category, made by figures such as Parmenides, Spinoza, and others.

[43] Cf. Lau (2008).

[44] Frede (1987: 81–99). See also Düsing (2009: esp. 7–8). Düsing offers an interpretation of Hegel whose point of departure is the ambiguity between ontology and theology in the traditional Aristotelian definition of metaphysics.

closely resemble Kant's Ideas of the unconditioned than his categories, "concepts of an object in general." So lofty are Hegel's ambitions that even Kant's Ideas of reason are insufficient from a Hegelian perspective. However, they at least improve upon Kant's categories, or pure concepts of the understanding.

My proposal is that Hegel has not simply changed the subject from category to Idea but announced a break with his predecessors. This break consists in Hegel's conviction that it is something more closely resembling an Idea, rather than a category, which will be the default in a theory of the fundamental constituents of thought. For Kant, the use of Ideas by metaphysicians intent on gaining knowledge of the unconditioned is, in effect, the misuses of categories whose home is natural science, perception and common science. Hegel effectively inverts this picture, so that the metaphysical use of an Idea is the default case and that of a category in an ordinary or natural-scientific context its misuse. Ideas are not overambitious categories that need humbling. Categories, Kantian Aristotelian or otherwise, are overly modest Ideas – ones that need emboldening.

As I have said, the main obstacle to this project is the fallacy of explaining the less obscure by the more. Yet Hegel's contention is that these ontological and theological principles are in no way obscure, at least when they are approached in the right way. Part of Hegel's achievement is to have recast ontology and theology as thought's default-justified employment rather than its most extravagant excess. What is more, if successful, he will not only have challenged but inverted a received view. That is, he will have shown that it is the categories and formal logical laws and materials, assumed as unproblematic by ordinary thought, natural science and transcendental philosophy, that stand in need of a more ambitious justification than they have received thus far.

0.7   Pippin's Hegel

In this book, my principal aim is to address a question in the philosophy of logic from a Hegelian perspective. It is not to defend, in detail, a controversial interpretation of Hegel's metaphysics. However, I do rely throughout on an account of Hegel's metaphysics as fundamentally un-Kantian. In my retelling, Kant is indeed a "subjectivist," Hegel a figure who allows us to recapture a form of "objectivity" missing from earlier idealisms. However, everything turns on what, exactly, it means for Hegel to overcome Kant's subjectivism. It is possible to go awry by ignoring the ways in which Kant is himself already overcoming subjectivism: for example, by rejecting Berkeleyan–Cartesian idealism; preserving the possibility of thinking things in themselves by means of the categories, even if this does not yield theoretical (scientific) cognition; and so on.[45] However, the symmetrical version of this error would be that of being overly impressed by Kant's own efforts in an anti-psychologistic, anti-empiricist, anti-Cartesian direction, so much so that one is convinced that the essentials of Hegel's position are already in place.

While this is a broader issue than I can discuss here, I do want to address just one "logical" face of it. In a recent book, Robert Pippin offers an account of Hegel's relationship to Kant's logic that differs from the one I will present here. For Hegel, as Pippin presents him, Kant's subjectivism would seem to be limited to his contention that the forms of sensible intuition are species specific. There is nothing objectionably subjectivist about Kant's (pure) general logic, which is why Hegel can draw on it to construct a metaphysics. Of course, Kant did not himself regard (pure) general logic as having serious metaphysical potential. Yet Hegel shows it can realize this potential once we resolve the problem posed by the forms of sensible intuition, namely, their "parochialism."

For Pippin, one of Hegel's main sources of inspiration in Kant is the metaphysical deduction of the categories, an argument I think of Hegel as repudiating.[46] Pippin is doubtless aware of Hegel's well-known criticisms of this argument, so the question becomes that of just how anti-Kantian these criticisms truly are. The project of the metaphysical deduction is to derive the categories of transcendental logic from the forms of judgment in (pure) general logic: for example, the category cause–effect from the judgment form ground–consequent ("if ... than"). According to Pippin, Hegel sees that this derivation would constitute a metaphysics once it is freed from its association with certain residually empiricist elements of Kant's thought: for example, Kant's "subjectivist" account of the forms of intuition.[47] Perhaps Hegel objects to Kant's use of resources from the logic of the day as lazy and unoriginal. However, this does not undermine the idea that Hegel is deeply indebted to the general idea of deriving the categories from the forms of judgment.

In order to understand what could be wrong with the metaphysical deduction from a Hegelian perspective, we must dwell a bit longer on the

---

[45] These are some of the considerations raised by Ameriks (1985, 2000) and Guyer (1993) in defense of Kant, and responded to by the Hegelian Bristow (2007).

[46] Pippin (2018: 64).

[47] Pippin (2018: 74 ff.).

meaning of the term "subjectivism." By subjectivism, I understand the general Hegelian allegation, made across a range of areas of philosophy, that Kant gives undue weight to the standpoint of the knowing (and acting) subject. Pippin, in my view, possesses an overly narrow understanding of subjectivism as "parochialism." He argues that its main source in Kant could be his conception of the forms of intuition: more specifically, his tendency to regard them as "species specific." This leads him to conclude that once the problem posed by the forms of intuition is solved the threat of subjectivism is mitigated. Accordingly, Hegel is free to adopt Kant's findings concerning that other stem of our cognitive power, the understanding and its concepts. Since it is here that the project of the metaphysical deduction takes place, there is no risk of subjectivism. As far as Pippin's Hegel is concerned, the rot of subjectivism does not spread beyond Kant's first stem.

In disagreeing, I would like to adapt a point made in the criticism of this type of Hegel interpretation by Tolley,[48] who observes that logic, for Kant, is subjective in a perfectly straightforward sense. Logic studies the knowing subject: more specifically, its faculties of understanding and reason. Logic's laws, as Kant conceives them, just are principles internal to these faculties. They are principles presupposed in any possible exercise of them. They describe what it is in the nature of these faculties to do. They are, in short, constitutive norms of those faculties. Logic, as Kant defines it, is the "science of the correct use of the understanding and of reason in general" (JL, 530–531/16). On this conception, logic is not empirical psychology, so there is no risk of what Frege called "psychologism," that is, reducing the normative laws of logic to descriptive generalizations. For empirical psychology, sensible intuition would be required. Yet logic is still founded in a type of teleological faculty psychology nonetheless.

While this is a well-known feature of Kant's position, Pippin does not in my view respect it sufficiently. For Pippin, as I read him, Kant anticipates Frege in being a fundamentally anti-psychologistic thinker. Pippin is careful to note certain discrepancies: Kant espouses a logic of judgments and act types, while the latter espouses one of propositions.[49] I certainly have no quarrel whatsoever with anti-psychologistic interpretations of Kant,

---

[48] Tolley (2019a: III. Human Understanding. Kant on the Subjective Universality of Logic). While I agree with Tolley that logic, for Kant, remains subjective, I would not go so far as to claim that logic, for Kant, concerns a merely human faculty ("for Kant logic seems instead to be first and foremost precisely the science of finite, especially human, discursive intelligibility").

[49] Pippin (2018: 70–71).

which have well-known advantages. Among other things, they explain the difference between transcendental psychology and both the empirical and rational (metaphysical) varieties. Yet, in my view, any interpretation that omits the irreducibly psychological dimension of Kant's logical theory is simply implausible.[50]

If one is an analytic neo-Kantian, then there is less of a need for faculty psychology. A "conceptual scheme" or "space of reasons," the analytic stand-ins for Kant's categories, does not necessarily presuppose a teleological faculty psychology. Perhaps this is because of the linguistic turn many analytic neo-Kantians implicitly give Kant's thought. Presumably, if one were to regard Kant's logical forms as (meta)linguistic, then there would be no need to ground them in a faculty. This approach would also, implicitly, socialize and historicize the categories, and in a way anticipating Hegel. The focus would shift from the norms self-imposed by the individual reasoner to the patterns of use in a linguistic community. However, Kant's logical theory does, I think, center capacities, and to pretend otherwise would be anachronistic. It is, as one recent commentator puts it, a "capacities-first" approach to philosophy. Yet I deny that Hegel is an adherent of the "capacities-first" approach, even of a version that avoids the common skeptical pitfalls.

To be clear, I am not alleging that Pippin is tacitly relying on these claims from analytic neo-Kantianism. However, this makes it more mysterious, not less, why Pippin would pass over the subjectivism inherent in Kant's logic. By effacing this dimension of Kant's logic, Pippin is able to claim, wrongly in my view, that Hegel overcomes the subjectivism of Kant's critical philosophy by fleeing one part of it for another – aesthetic for logic – whereas I will argue that Hegel is fully able to do so only when he avails himself of resources that exceed the critical philosophy.

What, then, is the nature of this break? Kant's subjectivism is not, I think, limited to his belief that the forms of intuition are "species specific." It refers more broadly to his relentless (in my view, oppressive), insistence that reflection on any conceivable philosophical topic begins from a reflection on the relevant capacity: mathematics and natural science referring to the faculty of reason; art and biology to the faculty of judgment; morality and politics and world history to the faculty of practical reason and so on. It is precisely this anthropocentric – or, better,

---

[50] In presenting Kant's logical theory Pippin (2018: 61) speaks often of "distinctions and relations," "conditions," "sense-making" and so on. This shifts the emphasis off of psychological faculties, mental capacities and cognitive powers.

logocentric – outlook that Hegel is urging us to transcend (though I have not yet said anything about the specific problems Hegel identifies with it). Some commentators prefer to have Hegel adopt such an approach but avoid its unwelcome consequences. They set to work explaining away all the unwelcome associations that the notion of a faculty may have. I choose a different route, preferring to emphasize Hegel's affinities with figures, traditions, and ideas that are simply illegible from a Kantian point of view.

Significantly, Pippin denies the accuracy of Hegel's own description of his project as a departure from Fichte's earlier, "subjective," idealism, but I will advocate that we take Hegel's self-presentation seriously. Unlike Hegel's absolute idealism, *Fichte*'s "subjective idealism" is everywhere permeated by the anxiety that reason will be compromised through any departure from its closed circle. Hence, Fichte simply rejects any role in his system mind-independent world of the substance-monist, the (Romantic) philosopher of nature, and of traditional Scholastic-Aristotelian ontology. The "self-positing" subject or "I" and its acts of "counter-positing" a world are all that will concern us in the *Wissenschaftslehre*. By contrast, the objective idealisms of Schelling and Hegel are free of this anxiety and confident that reason's self-alienation entails its self-recovery, and in a strengthened form. By losing itself in contemplation of nature, Substance, or Being, reason acquires a knowledge of the holistic character of reality that would elude it otherwise. By recovering itself subsequently, it is able to draw on this knowledge to achieve insight into itself as the one-and-all, a conclusion Fichte's dualistic approach can only approximate through a *progressus ad infinitum*. The objective idealist dynamic of self-alienation and self-recovery is often associated with the relationship between the realms of nature and spirit, but I believe it unfolds in the course of the logic as well. How else would the *Logic* provide a template for what is to come in the system? The idea that any such approach would have to be reductively naturalistic reflects a form of Fichtean paranoia completely alien to Hegel.

As I have indicated, Hegel's renunciation at the logic's outset of a logocentric outlook may only be provisional. For Hegel is ultimately a profoundly logocentric thinker. Indeed, this temporary renunciation of logocentrism may be for the sake of something more resolutely rationalistic than even Kant's Enlightenment creed: "reason in the world." However, it is important that we set aside the standpoint of thought thinking itself, so we do not beg the question against nonlogocentric positions, such as the Parmenidean one presented at the outset of the Doctrine of Being. It is generally accepted that in such writings as the *Phenomenology* Hegel begins with a position that is the polar opposite of his own, radical empiricism, only to show that it entails an absolute idealist alternative. My own view is that the *Logic* does something similar, though the opposed position is not an anti-idealist epistemology but an anti-idealist metaphysics: Parmenidean (Eleatic) monism, in a form Hegel associates closely with Jacobi and Spinoza. It would not quite be in character for Hegel to simply forbid the pursuit of rival philosophical approaches, perhaps in the way Kant or the logical positivists sometimes do. Hegel, I think, prefers to allow them to proceed, knowing all the while that they will undermine themselves (though not before making the unique contribution that it is each one's destiny to provide).

In proceeding on the basis of (pure) general logic, as Pippin's Hegel urges, we would, in effect, be treating something subjective as the basis of metaphysics. The laws and materials of logic are *not* subjective in the sense that the forms of intuition are: "species specific." According to Kant, they hold good for any possible thinker, and we can grant this provisionally for the sake of argument. They are objective in the sense that they are inter-subjectively valid, among finite subjects (and any others there may be). Yet it remains the case that the laws of logic, as Kant understands them, are "in" the subject. They are not "in" the subject in the way that conscious mental states inhere a mental substance for a Cartesian or early modern philosopher. No law of logic is a "quale," a "raw qualitative feel" or "what it's like" aspect, in modern terms. Yet they are, rather, "in" the subject in the way that the activity inherent to a thing's nature is in it, according to Aristotelians. Pippin's Hegel, in contesting Kant's claim that the forms of intuition are species specific, removes *one* impediment to treating logic as metaphysics. However, this is, in my view, insufficient for showing that a form of judgment is a form of being. The logocentric predicament is not the "egocentric predicament," but it can present a similar face. Both involve the threat of confinement within a restricted sphere, the ego or reason. I have urged that the threat is credible in both cases and that counteracting it in the former case is not sufficient to counteract it in the latter.

Hegel, as I interpret him, rejects Kant's logic and therefore the possibility of a project like the one Pippin describes – but this still leaves the question of Hegel's relationship to precritical metaphysics and Kant's critique of it. My aim in this study is to show how Hegel's metaphysics, on a traditional interpretation, resolves the logocentric predicament, and not necessarily to defend that interpretation as superior to more modern alternatives. I do agree that it would be folly to completely equate Hegel's position with those of the precritical, dogmatic metaphysicians of

the Leibniz–Wolff school. However, I seriously doubt the best versions of
the (neo)metaphysical reading genuinely risk this. I further am indebted
to those who have argued that Hegel's metaphysics follows those forms
of rationalism that employ rational argument, rather than a far-fetched
intellectual intuition of supersensible objects. My own minor contribution to this debate is just one historical point concerning the logocentric
predicament.

The project undertaken here gives us one novel reason to reject the common accusation that Hegel, interpreted in this way, turns out to be a precritical, "Wolffian" or rationalist thinker. No precritical thinker, so far as I
am aware, pursued ontology and theology in a pre– or non–formal logical
way. Nor, more importantly, did any do so with the aim of providing
a non–formal logical ground or basis for a radically reconstituted logic.
Certainly Hegel does not see this aspiration in the tradition, which he
views as complacent about logic.

Ultimately, though, I base my preference for this interpretation on philosophical, rather than interpretive, grounds. To me, the project of resolving the logocentric predicament in the way Hegel proposes is so novel,
ambitious and interesting for it to be blacklisted as "precritical metaphysics." To some extent, Hegel's idea of metaphysics as a non–formal logical
enterprise constitutes a novel defense of metaphysics, not encountered so
far as I know in the tradition. Seen as "primordial" in the way I advocate,
metaphysics no longer appears as thinking's greatest extravagance. It is,
instead, thought's most basic, default-justified employment.

"Irrational Cognition of the Rational"
Hegel's Critique of Aristotelian Logic

In this chapter, I consider Hegel's case against "the former logic," postponing for future chapters the question of what Hegel's alternative is meant to be. As I hope to show, that case takes the form of an immanent critique of traditional logic. In a phrase, Hegel's critique is that this logic allows us little more than an "irrational cognition of the rational" (WdL 12: 43/SoL 541; cf. Reich 1992: 2).

Hegel objects to the broadly psychological approach to logic taken in the tradition, though he is well aware it does not involve the reduction of logic to empirical psychology. However, Hegel's objection should not be confused with the accusation of "psychologism" Frege would later level at earlier logicians. In particular, Hegel's concerns have nothing to do with the reduction of the normative to the descriptive. A large part of the reason for this is that the tradition relies on a teleological faculty psychology, operating from within the first-person perspective. It does not rely on an empirical psychology in any modern sense, one that relies on the detached third-person perspective of natural science. This means Kant's position is better able to accommodate the normative character of logic than the later programs that Frege criticized as "psychologistic." Yet it does not mean that it evades the objections of subsequent idealists such as Hegel.

Instead, Hegel's objection is that this broadly psychological approach precludes the tradition from a satisfying response to the dilemma from philosophical logic considered earlier. In particular, this approach threatens to render the justification of logic brute in a way that is complacent. As I hope to show, Hegel considers this objection an immanent critique of formal logic. In his view, this logic is based on the supreme value of justifying ourselves through rational argument. It prescribes to other areas of philosophy and the sciences the norms must observe in order to construct rational arguments. However, it has no such argument for its own most basic principles, treating them instead as justified, as it were, by default. Indeed, it cannot do otherwise. These principles are so fundamental that any argument for them would likely already use them, and in so doing risk circularity. Even so, Hegel regards the traditional approach as betraying an aspiration basic to logic and philosophy themselves. Honoring this aspiration requires a rethinking of the role of logic in philosophy. Yet this will also demand a solution to the problem of circularity.

1.1   Presuppositionless Knowing: Natural Science, Mathematics, Formal Logic and Religion

In the very first line of the very first paragraph of his *Encyclopedia Logic*, Hegel declares that philosophy differs from all other sciences in two crucial respects. It cannot presuppose an object, nor can it presuppose a specific method of coming to understand that object.

> Philosophy lacks the advantage from which the other sciences benefit, namely the ability to presuppose [*voraussetzen zu können*] both its objects as immediately endorsed by representation of them and an acknowledged method of knowing, which would determine its starting-point and progression. (EL § 1)

For Hegel, each of the sciences is defined by the type of object that is its subject matter. Mathematics studies numbers; geometry, space; physics, material bodies; biology, living organisms and so on. If the sciences are to give us knowledge of the world around us, then presumably they are committed to the belief that objects of these types exist. What, though, is the status of that belief or claim?

In Hegel's view, its status is that it is taken for granted as unproblematic. This is not because the claim in question has *no justification*, as if it were little more than an arbitrary stipulation the relevant science required in order to proceed. It is because the claim, made at the outset of the science in question, has a fundamentally different and much simpler type of justification than the more rigorous kind the science will go on to provide for subsequent claims it makes. The justification for the initial assumption is characteristically direct, or, in Hegel's terms, "immediate." In other words, we are supposed to simply be presented with the relevant fact, if it is one, straightaway in a certain type of experience ("endorsed by representation").

Hegel calls such objects "presupposed objects" because, from the perspective of the sciences, it is a brute inexplicable fact of our experience that different types of objects exist. The task of science is to construct a body of knowledge about a given type of object, on the natural assumption that this type of object exists. It is not to address skeptical anxieties about whether objects of that type do, in fact, exist. The mathematician tells us about numbers, the chemist about chemical elements, the biologist about living things. Yet none has much to say to the skeptic who denies the existence of any such subject matter (Thompson 2008: 34).

According to Hegel, philosophy does not have a "presupposed object" in the way the sciences do. It does not regard as settled the question of whether some type of object exists or not. Certainly, it does not regard experience as the final word on this issue. This is not necessarily to say that philosophy rejects the presuppositions of the sciences, as if its only possible role were to undercut assumptions on which our knowledge depends. Philosophy *can* adopt that role, which is why skepticism is a permanent possibility for it. However, it need not do so. This is not just because philosophy may concur with the presuppositions of the sciences but for a more fundamental reason. Even where philosophy does concur it will characteristically attempt to go beyond the type of justification experience provides.

Instead of the "immediate" or direct justification experience provides, philosophy seeks a "mediated" or indirect one. Instead of an experience that presents us with the object, philosophy offers us an argument proceeding through a series of steps to the conclusion that there is such a thing as an object of this kind. Why proceed by this more indirect route? It certainly seems much more demanding, so much so that one could be forgiven for wondering if it is worth the trouble. The answer, I think, is that the latter approach allows us to achieve a new type of insight into the same fact. The type of "immediate" experiential justification that we rely upon in the sciences and ordinary life can only tell us *that* something is the case. It simply presents us with the relevant fact. Yet a type of "mediated" justification through argument we construct in philosophy will tell us *why* it is the case. Here, the same fact will appear in a new guise as a consequence of some further fact or set of facts.

We now come to the second part of Hegel's claim. This part concerns not "the presupposed object" but rather "the presupposed method." Hegel also denies that philosophy may presuppose a method in the way the sciences do. Once a science has its subject matter, it must then decide how to proceed in studying it. In claiming that the method of a science gives us a "starting point," Hegel may be thinking of methods of proof that have us begin from a set of axioms about the subject matter we are studying. This is the method followed in geometry, where we start with definitions, axioms and postulates, all concerning space and all meant to be intuitively obvious from our perceptual experience. We then proceed to prove all propositions in the system on the basis of them.

Even in the sciences, this method is not yet sufficient. It only tells us about the "starting point" rather than the "progression." Even given the truth of the axioms, definitions and postulates, how is it that the proof of the propositions that make up the science will proceed? One natural answer is that it will do so through a type of rational inference in which the propositions making up the science are inferred from these axioms, postulates and definitions. For this reason, then, one particular science would become important to all the others, provided they were interested in proving their claims true: formal logic. As the source of the forms of valid inference, logic was presupposed by all other sciences, and, in par-ticular, the proofs they contained. Of course, it was not itself sufficient for the construction of any scientific proof, but it was necessary.

Yet Hegel also rejects reliance on a presupposed method. Part of the reason concerns the broadly Euclidean strategy of appealing to axioms, definitions and postulates at the outset as the unproven basis on which everything else in the system will be proven. For Hegel, philosophy can-not rest content with the stipulation that certain axioms, postulates, and definitions are true. If they cannot be proven to be so through rational argument, then they are nothing to the philosopher. Nor even will a jus-tification based on experience suffice, since this will land us in the same problem as before.

Once we move beyond axioms, definitions and postulates to the propo-sitions of the science itself and their logical interrelations, further prob-lems arise. Here, the interrelations are meant to be (at least partly) spelled out by formal logic. Yet for Hegel, philosophy cannot simply defer to formal logic, as if it were not just as appropriate an object of criticism as any other science. Here too, then, philosophy is entitled to ask after the justification of this science's foundational presuppositions. However, the stakes are even higher than before. After all, logic is fundamental in a way the other sciences are not. All other sciences have turned out to justify themselves not only on the basis of their choice of object taken from the sphere of "representation" but also on the basis of a method provided by this science, logic.

If we ask for logic's justification, both in terms of its object and method, then we are asking for a type of justification on which all other sciences indirectly depend. If the stakes are higher, the challenge is also greater. After all, logic will not be able to justify its method of argument in the way the other sciences had. It cannot claim that method is vindicated by logic, on pain of vicious circularity. Yet if it cannot do so it is unclear how it might defend itself.

Hegel's presuppositionless approach, which relies neither on a presupposed object nor on a presupposed method, informs his views on the relationship of philosophy to religion. Because philosophy and religion concern the same subject matter, namely God, we are likely to come to philosophy with a received set of views about the topic:

> It is true that philosophy initially shares its objects with religion. Both have the *truth* for their object, and more precisely the truth in the highest sense, in the sense that *God* and God *alone* is the truth. Moreover, both treat the sphere of finite things, the sphere of *nature* and the *human spirit*, their relation to each other and to God as their truth. (EL § 1)

In fact, it is inevitable that we will come to philosophy with preconceptions. That is because the "representations" we acquire from experience are always prior to the type of contemplative thinking that we engage in when we do philosophy. Here, Hegel is doubtless thinking of "representations" such as the metaphorical ones of God found in religious stories, works of art, songs and so on. If that is so, then it is very likely impossible to begin doing philosophy without preconceptions drawn from experience:

> Philosophy thus may definitely presuppose a *familiarity* with its objects indeed it must do so as well as an interest in them from the outset, if only because chronologically speaking consciousness produces for itself *representations* of objects prior to generating *concepts* of them. What is more, only by passing *through* the process of representing and by turning *towards* it, does *thinking* spirit progress to knowing by way of thinking [*denkendes Erkennen*] and to comprehending [*Begreifen*]. (EL § 1)

In spite of this, philosophical thinking does demand that we not simply rely on these presuppositions in establishing the truth of the claims we wish to defend. Instead, we must present a type of argument. This is an alternative to the type of appeal to experience. Why prefer the former to the latter? The answer, Hegel tell us, concerns "necessity."

> While engaged in thoughtful contemplation, however, it soon becomes apparent that such activity includes the requirement to *demonstrate the necessity of its content, and to prove not only its being but, even more so, the determinations of its objects.* The aforementioned familiarity with this content thus turns out to be insufficient, and to make or accept presuppositions or assurances regarding it appears illegitimate: of making a beginning, however, arises at once, since a beginning is something immediate and as such makes a presupposition, or rather it is itself just that. (EL § 1, italics mine)

An argument characteristically tells us *why* a certain claim is true. It does so by showing that the claim follows "necessarily" from some other claim. By contrast, the appeal to experience merely tells us *that* it is true. Even when experience is trustworthy as to whether a truth holds good it tells us little about why.

Hence, Hegel concludes that we must aspire to more than the "immediate" justification that experience affords and consider a "mediated" one. Yet, if we are to construct this type of argument, we must not treat the presuppositions we have made as premises in it. Otherwise, the argument would be viciously circular. This is the entire point of a presuppositionless approach. By avoiding merely *presupposing* that something is true, we put ourselves in a position to *prove* (noncircularly) that it is.

1.2   Hegel and the Logic of the Aristotelian Tradition

In this section, I consider Hegel's account of the logic of his day, the logic of the Aristotelian tradition. Crucially, this account is informed throughout by Hegel's ideal of philosophy as a form of presuppositionless knowing. As we will see later, Hegel reproaches the logic of his day for failing to live up to this ideal. Indeed, as he tells us here, this logic defined itself in terms of a presupposed object, on the one hand, and a presupposed method, on the other. This suggests Hegel regards it as insufficiently presuppositionless to qualify as true philosophy and on two separate counts (object and method). The discussion I focus on can be found in the following addition:

> When we speak of thinking, it appears initially to be a subjective activity, one of several faculties possessed by us, such as memory, representation, volition, and the like. If thinking were a merely subjective activity and as such the object of logic, this science like any other would have its specific object. It could then appear to be arbitrary to make thinking and not also the will, imagination and so forth the object of a particular science. That thinking should receive this honour may well be due to the fact that we grant it a certain authority and that we regard it as what is truly human, distinguishing humans from animals. To become familiar with thinking even as a merely subjective activity is not without interest. Its more specific determinations would be the rules and laws with which one becomes acquainted through experience. Thinking viewed in this way as determined by laws makes up what usually otherwise constituted the content of logic. *Aristotle* is the founder of this science. He possessed the strength to assign to thinking what belongs to it *per se*. Our thinking is very concrete, but with respect to its manifold content we need to sort out what belongs to thinking or the abstract form of the activity. The activity of thinking, acting as

a subtle spiritual bond, connects all this content. It is this bond, this form itself, which Aristotle highlighted and defined. To this day, the logic of Aristotle represents the logical [sphere], which has merely been made more elaborate, primarily by the Scholastics of the Middle Ages. The Scholastics did not add to the material, but merely developed it further. The work of more recent times with respect to logic consists primarily in omitting many of the logical determinations spun out further by Aristotle and the Scholastics, on the one hand, and in superimposing a lot of psychological material [on the other]. The interest in this science lies with becoming acquainted with the procedures of finite thinking, and the science is correct when it corresponds to its presupposed object. (EL § 20 Z)

Hegel initially describes the former logic as a science defined by its "presupposed object." This object was a certain mental activity, thinking. What is more, thinking in this sense was defined as the activity of a certain psychological faculty we possess, the faculty of thought. Here, Hegel uses the term "thought" in a narrower sense than is common, either in ordinary usage or in the rest of his Absolute Idealist philosophy. "Thought" here means employing concepts, making judgments, drawing inferences and so on. Understood in this narrow sense, thought is to be distinguished from other mental activities such as sense perception, desire, imagination, memory and will. For Hegel, thought is abstract in a way these other activities, which he calls concrete, are not. Unlike thought, all of the others have an inherent connection to sensible representations, on the one hand, and inclinations or desires, on the other. Moreover, thought is formal in the sense that it applies itself to the material these other activities present to it. We judge and infer about what we sense, imagine, wish, will and so on. For Hegel, this science (logic) presupposes as self-evident the fact that we think, understood in this narrower and more technical sense of the term. Hegel does not deny the plausibility of this claim. Clearly, we do engage in this type of intellectual activity, often without engaging in any of the others. If this activity is to originate somewhere, then presumably it does so in a faculty distinct from that responsible for the others.

Here, Hegel notes that this common-sense belief hardly justifies giving thinking the importance we give it in logic. If thinking genuinely were just one mental activity alongside others, it would be arbitrary to base our science on it. Psychology does so, but philosophy requires a deeper justification for its choice of topic. Hegel alludes in passing to a traditional justification. This is the fact, if it is one, that we alone among the animals can think, and that thinking is presided over by a faculty of thought. Yet, as Hegel adds, this is another "presupposition." Significantly, Hegel describes this assumption as merely probable. This is not evidence that Hegel took seriously the proposal that animals think. Rather, it is a strong indication that he did not consider the fact that they do not have a secure enough starting point for logic. Evidently, the justification for basing our science on thinking will need to come from somewhere else.

Moreover, as Hegel explains, this logic also had a presupposed method of discovering the laws or rules of thinking: abstraction. In attending to the acts of thinking performed by the faculty of thought, it would abstract from all of the concrete material contributed by the other faculties, especially sensibility. In this way, it would discover the formal rules this faculty necessarily obeys, at least when other faculties do not interfere. An example is the law of noncontradiction, thought by many in this tradition to be impossible to deny under conditions of reflective clarity. This is not to deny that we can affirm a contradiction but merely to offer a distinctive explanation of what has happened when we do. The explanation is that another faculty has interfered, a faculty such as the will, desire or imagination. Yet the laws something obeys when nothing else interferes have a special significance for this tradition. They articulate the *nature* of that type of entity. As a result, these laws represent an especially deep form of insight into thinking, articulating what thinking as such is. For this reason, these laws were meant to apply to any thinker as such, even a divine one. However, the laws discovered also have an additional normative significance for beings such as ourselves. They also explain what *good* thinking is.[1]

Why, though, should understanding what thinking is help explain what it is to think well? The answer, I think, reflects the "constitutivism" of the Aristotelian tradition. In the background is the assumption that many norms, perhaps all norms, are constitutive norms: For a thing (state, process) to be good is for it to be a good instance of its kind. The laws of logic are therefore of greater relevance to our ordinary lives than they might have at first seemed. They not only explain how we do think when no other faculty interferes but also how we *ought* to think even under conditions when interference can happen. These laws therefore place us under a certain type of obligation to think well and to avoid having our thinking interfered with in this way. This is a presupposed method because it (more or less) follows directly from the presupposed object. If there is such a thing as thinking in this sense, one activity or faculty

---

[1] For a different account of the role in Hegel's *Logic* project of this constitutivist idea see Pippin (2018: 76). However, Pippin associates it with Hegel's own logic, whereas I think of it as part of the Aristotelian–Kantian tradition in logic that Hegel meant his logic to displace.

among others, then "abstraction" from the contribution of the others is the obvious way to study its laws.

This puts us in a position to understand why thinkers in the Aristotelian tradition understood logic to have considerable authority over the other sciences. Logic's formal principles belong to the form of thinking as such. Logic is not just about what it is to think well, but what it is to think at all. Hence, we can be confident that its rules apply to our thinking in any area. The form of our thinking may apply itself to any number of different types of matter furnished by our other faculties such as sensibility. However, the form remains invariant in all these cases. This means that logic is foundational for the other sciences. Logic's laws are presupposed by all of them. After all, the mere fact that thinking is applying itself to one broad type of object rather than another is of little consequence to logic. It does not fundamentally change what it means to think (well).

This is not to say that the laws of logic are the only laws that there are, since there will be laws of the special sciences as well. In addition to the laws of thinking well, there may be laws concerning how to think well about some particular type of object or other. Nor is it even to say that the laws of logic are sufficient to yield the laws of any given special science. The laws of thinking well can never by themselves tell us what it is to think well about any given object type. However, it is to insist that logic's laws will be presupposed by all the laws of the other sciences. A principle of our thinking as fundamental as the law of noncontradiction will never be overturned by one that merely concerns the way planets in our solar system orbit the sun. Still, logic does have a somewhat ambivalent status. It is both prior to all other sciences and radically insufficient in comparison to them. This is perhaps reflected in the name given to the section of Aristotle's corpus containing his logic: the "organon" (tool or instrument). Logic is an "organon" because it is a tool or instrument necessary to construct bodies of scientific knowledge. Yet it is not a "canon," not a body of scientific knowledge itself.

Before proceeding, Hegel must address a point of obscurity in his account of the older logic. Hegel describes this logic as grounding itself in experience, but if any science were nonempirical then logic would seem to be. However, Hegel's characterization is apt. Unlike the other sciences, logic does not appeal to *sense* experience, the type of experience we have when the world affects our sense organs. Precisely not.[2] As we have seen,

---

[2] I here follow Houlgate (2006: 14–16), though he is discussing the Hegel–Kant relation in logic, not the Hegel–Aristotle one. Later, I argue that these come to the same thing.

knowledge of logic is acquired only when we abstract from the concrete content thinking acquires through sense experience. In spite of this, logic relies on a type of *intellectual* experience. The justification for logic's claims rests on a type of experience we have of finding them incontrovertible. Again, this is an experience we have when we focus exclusively on thinking's abstract form and leave aside its sensibly given matter.

This is why Hegel frequently describes logic as proceeding empirically, even though he nowhere maintains the absurd view that it relies on sense experience. Moreover, it also explains why Hegel frequently compares Aristotle's approach to logic with his empirical approach to the study of nature:

> Aristotle proceeded from observation, summoning forth the entire universe in a parade before his mind. He went through the general principles [of nature]. He gave the physiology of the animals – regarding their walking, their waking, their sleeping – as well as the human mind and spirit-regarding sensation, seeing, hearing, memory, fantasy, the nature of the state and of the will: in all this he went observingly to work, speculatively treating everything he observed. *He laid down experience as the foundation, and then passed over from it to the thinking concept. He observed and classified the forms of thought in the same manner as he classified the species forms of nature.* (VL 3, italics mine)

Different as they are from one another, both logic and natural science, for example biology, involve observing and classifying what is discovered in the course of experience. The sense in which logic is empirical is subtle. Certainly, its content of logic is not anything that can be gleaned from sense experience. Yet the form in which that content is apprehended is sensible, as if the syllogistic figures were so many species of animal laid out alongside one another in a classificatory scheme.

Like other critics of the received logic, Hegel complains that not all its topics were in any obvious way relevant to logic per se as opposed to rhetoric, oratory or even a certain type of intellectual self-discipline or hygiene. As he writes, "[t]he additions of psychological, pedagogical, and even physiological material which logic was at one time given, have later been almost universally recognized as disfigurations" (WdL 21: 36/SoL 31). What, then, belongs in logic, and what does not?

Hegel is less explicit on this point than he might be, but the answer implicit in his account seems to be the following. He describes the Aristotelian logic's rules as of three basic types: concept, judgment and syllogism, all terms of later coinage. He also describes a fourth area, concerned with an even more general set of rules that apply in the other three: "laws of thought."

1. The forms of inference/syllogism
2. The forms of judgment
3. The forms of concept/category
4. The laws of thought

I have said that logic was traditionally a source of rules for arguing validly. However, logic also sought to identify the more basic types of materials from which valid arguments could be constructed. These included the forms of judgment, the most basic types of statements that could legitimately figure in the premises and conclusions of valid arguments.

More controversially, the categories were also sometimes considered to be among these building blocks. Categories can be understood here as the most basic types of concept that could legitimately figure as the predicate in different forms of judgment. As we will see, however, they had an ambiguous status, having been considered part of both logic and metaphysics. Hegel is well aware of this, and notes it explicitly in a lecture.

> The Logic of Aristotle is contained in five books, which are collected together under the name Organon. The Categories … of which the first work treats, are the universal determinations, that which is predicated of existent things …: as well that which we call conceptions of the understanding, as the simple realities of things. This may be called an ontology, as pertaining to metaphysics; hence these determinations also appear in Aristotle's *Metaphysics*. (VGP/LHoP v. 2 "Aristotle: Logic")

The ambiguous place of Aristotelian category theory between the logic of the organon and the central books of the *Metaphysics* is one Hegel will have to address.

Finally, logic sought to identify certain more general rules: for example, the laws of noncontradiction, identity and excluded middle. These were the laws one would potentially violate by not judging or inferring in accordance with the forms identified. It is an interesting question whether one would commit a similar violation by misusing the categories: for example, claiming whiteness is Socratic, rather than that Socrates is white. Perhaps this is an error, but is it a *logical* one? The answer, I think, is no – and this only further underscores category theory's ambiguous status.[3]

---

[3] It would be better thought of as a "category mistake."

1.3   Two Forms of Finitude: Extra- and Intraconceptual

In consequence of its approach, traditional logic can offer us an account of only a certain specific type of thinking: "finite thinking." "Finite" is a well-known term of art in Hegel, even occasionally a term of abuse. However, it soon becomes clear that Hegel understands logic to be finite in a very specific sense, one which is not necessarily pejorative. Indeed, and as I hope to explain, a proponent of this logic would not likely deny the accusation of finitude. This means there is a bit of a mystery about why Hegel regards the finitude of the former logic as a problem. However, a clue is provided by a passage in which Hegel explains what it means for a thought determination to be finite.

For Hegel, a form of thinking is "finite" (literally: limited) because its principles are "finite" in two respects:

> [T]he finitude of the thought-determinations is to be construed in this double sense: the one, that they are merely subjective and are in permanent opposition to the objective; the other, that due to their limited content generally they persist in opposition to each other and even more so to the absolute. (EL § 25)

The first sense in which these principles are limited is that they are "subjective" rather than "objective." As is well known, Hegel distinguishes between numerous different senses of these terms (EL § 41 Z2). Here, however, Hegel's meaning seems to be relatively straightforward. These laws are present and operative "in" the subject, rather than "in" the world of objects. As Hegel will sometimes put it, logic presupposes "the standpoint of consciousness," a standpoint defined by a type of dichotomy between the thinking subject and the object of her knowledge. After all, we only discover these principles by abstracting from all that we experience of the objects through the senses. For this reason, we understand these laws to articulate the form of thought. Indeed, the laws we discover are internal to a psychological faculty we subjects possess. How, then, could they be anything but subjective? They are not just *in* us. They *are* us. To be sure, the principles of logic are "objective," rather than "subjective," in one important sense. They are universally and necessarily valid, meaning that they apply to any thinker as such, rather than just to me. Yet that is compatible with their being subjective in the sense that interests Hegel.

In many contexts, Hegel claims to be siding with common sense when he rejects the "subjectivism" of his Kantian opponent: For example, Hegel will ridicule the Kantian suggestion that space, time and causality are due to us. Yet there is little in common sense that speaks in favor of regarding a logical form, such as a form of syllogistic inference, as present in the world. To be sure, such a form of inference can be used to reason about states of affairs in the world, but that does not mean it is present there. The inference "All men are mortal, Socrates is a man ..." is not in the world in the way that the men, the mortals and Socrates are.

Moreover, there are good philosophical reasons for holding the view that logic is subjective. The fact that there are men, mortals and so on may be an empirical fact about objects in the world, learned when those very objects affect my sense organs in a certain way. By contrast, the fact that a given form of inference is valid is known a priori, simply through thinking.

To be sure, there are comparably abstract principles to those of logic that are regarded as present in the "objective world." For example, laws of nature earn this status, even though they too require us to go beyond much that has been directly observed. Yet these laws have a different significance entirely. They are posited to explain the behavior of objects in the world. They are said to be present and operative in a type of (necessary) connection among those objects. But, at least in the tradition as Hegel represents it, the laws of logic were never supposed to do anything other than be present and operative in our thinking, insofar as we think correctly.

Moreover, this logic is a science in which the principles employed are "finite" or limited, not only when considered in relation to the objective world but also when considered in relation to one another. Here, the literal rather than evaluative meaning of finite (limited) becomes particularly important. Hegel's meaning is simply that each such principle runs up against a limit in another treated as separate from it. But separate how?[4]

Although these principles are themselves logical, a certain type of logical relationship between them is absent – more specifically, a *deductive* relationship, such that each derives its justification from the others. The complaint is extremely common in Hegel's writings. We will consider a more famous instance of it presently, but the following one is representative:

> Such a logic considers it its vocation to talk about the necessity of deducing concepts and truths from principles; however, of what they call method, there is not the shadow of a deduction. (WdL 33: 29/SoL 24)

---

[4] A representative passage: "We must all familiarize ourselves with such forms of the understanding as Aristotle brings forth-they are forms of thinking, abstract forms and one-sided laws. Yet if they are to be of service to true thinking, we must not interpret them so separately from one another, [as Aristotle does,] since they would then be only forms of untruth, finite forms" (VL/LL 4).

This is a somewhat odd complaint, inasmuch as we are used to thinking of a deductive order obtaining within an argument between its premises and its conclusion. We rarely imagine that it must obtain between the forms of valid argument themselves. Deduction we expect, but not this type of (meta)deduction, a deduction of the principles deduction presupposes. Even so, Hegel regards the omission of this type of (meta)deduction as a form of hypocrisy on logic's part.

Another way to approach the issue Hegel raises of an absence of deductive order in traditional logic is by contrasting deduction in Hegel's strong sense with the type of empirical procedure this logic uses. The principles of logic, or at least the most fundamental ones, derive their justification from experience. They are arrived at through the method of abstraction. This means we have simply found them to be true. We have done so when we reflected from a specific instance in which they were operative. The point here is that the method of abstraction is an alternative to that of deduction. Deriving these principles from experience means not deriving them from one another.[5]

Hegel concedes this logic did draw certain types of connections between its principles but holds that these connections do not merit being called deductive. He compares logic's activity of drawing such connections to a children's game:

> Since in judgments and syllogisms the operations are mostly reduced to, and founded upon, the quantitative aspect of the determinations, everything rests on external differentiation, on mere comparison, and becomes a completely analytical procedure and a calculus void of concept. The deduction of the so-called rules and laws, of inference especially, is no better than the manipulation of rods of unequal lengths for sorting them out in groups according to size – than a children's game of fitting together the pieces of a colored picture puzzle [*als die spielende Beschäftigung der Kinder, von mannigfaltig zerschnittenen Gemälden die passenden Stücke zusammenzusuchen.*] Not incorrectly, therefore, has this thinking been equated with reckoning, and reckoning again with this thinking. (WdL 21: 36–37/SoL 32)

Hegel's meaning here is difficult to make out precisely, but it seems to be that such proofs do not so much eliminate the need for the appeal to experience as postpone it.

Consider a proof by contradiction that a given form of inference is valid. This would be a proof that proceeds by assuming the relevant form

---

[5] Houlgate (2006: 22–23) also draws this connection between the "finding" of the forms of judgment and their "finitude" vis-à-vis one another, though he is once again discussing the Hegel–Kant relation.

is invalid and showing that this would yield a contradiction. To be sure, the proof shows that one rule holds by appealing to another its rejection would violate, the law of noncontradiction. In the example, the form of valid inference may have been proven, rather than arrived at through the method of abstraction. Eventually, though, we reach a principle that will have been arrived at through an appeal to experience.

It may seem that this objection is little more than a technicality, but I believe it reflects a reaction we can often have to proofs in logic and mathematics. Especially in the case of the most fundamental principles, the proofs do not actually seem to convince us of anything we could not already have known intuitively. Does it actually help in justifying the form of inference from our example to know that refusing to conclude "Caius is mortal" would be to contradict oneself, as if the absurdity of refusing to do so were not already evident without being identified as a violation of some logical law? Of course, this leaves completely mysterious what an alternative type of proof might be.

There may be a certain type of logical relation between the principles of formal logic, but it is not deductive in Hegel's strong sense. It still leaves it a brute fact that we are justified in using these forms of concept, judgment and inference, these laws and no others. It is a brute fact about thinking, or about us and our cognitive faculties.

What is more, there are not only no true deductive relationships between the specific elements but also none between the broader element types. It is just a brute fact that we are justified in recognizing three types of element (concept, judgment, syllogism) and no others, a brute fact about our thinking. We could always conceive of elements or element types being added or taken away. Hegel will conclude that Aristotle's formal logic is an aggregate rather than a system. This is something Hegel finds intolerable, as we will soon see. We should be able to expect systematic rigor and deductive interconnection from logic if we can expect it anywhere. Yet this expectation is disappointed.

1.4   Hegel's Immanent Critique of Aristotelian Logic ("Irrational Cognition of the Rational")

Hegel accuses the formal logic of his day of a type of inconsistency that fatally undermines it. He argues that this logic cannot meet the very type of demand for justification that it makes of all other areas of philosophy and the sciences. As we have seen, logic justifies its principles empirically, but in so doing it exempts its own principles from the very type of justification through rational argument it rightly insists is necessary in other areas of philosophy and the sciences. Hegel expresses this objection in the following passage where he proposes a new logic in which

> the usual subject matter, the kinds of concepts, judgments, and syllogisms, would no longer simply be taken up from observation and thus gathered up merely empirically, but … derived from thinking itself. If thinking is to be capable of proving anything, if logic must demand that proof be given, and if it wants to teach how to give proofs, then it should be capable above all of proving the content most proper to it and seeing its necessity [*so muß sie … ihren eigentümlichsten Inhalt zu beweisen, dessen Notwendigkeit einzusehen, fähig sein*]. (EL § 42)

Hegel's claim is not that the empirical approach is illegitimate per se. It is simply that logic is committed to regarding rational argument as superior. He has a point; it is not unreasonable to think that so-called "inductive inference" is logically invalid. At a broader level, however, logic is part of philosophy, and as Hegel has already said, philosophy itself shares this view. In philosophy, we are interested to know not just that a fact obtains but why. The special sciences place limits on how far this "why?" question can be pressed. Yet philosophy recognizes no such limits.

Hegel extends this criticism beyond logic's treatment of particular principles to its treatment of the general classes of principles. He argues that traditional logic has no deductive argument not only for the principles that make up this science but also for the types of principles that form the different divisions of the science's subfields: concept, judgment, syllogism, law. In other words, it has no rigorous justification for why these topics belong within its purview and also why these and only these do so. For Hegel, this is a distinctly logical form of hypocrisy in the treatment of logic's principles and the broader divisions into which they can be classified. It is, as he memorably puts it, "irrational cognition of the rational."

> In the customary treatment of logic, a variety of classifications and species of concepts are adduced. It immediately strikes one as inconsequential that the species are introduced in this way: "There are, as regards quality, quantity, etc., the following concepts." The "there are" conveys no other justification than that we find the named species and that they show up in experience. What we have in this manner is an empirical logic – an odd science indeed, an irrational cognition of the rational [*eine irrationelle Erkenntnis des Rationellen*]. In this the logic sets a very bad precedent for compliance to its own teaching; it allows itself to do the opposite of what it prescribes as a rule, namely, that concepts should be derived, and scientific propositions (therefore also the proposition: "There are such and such species of concepts") demonstrated. (WdL 12: 43/SoL 541; Reich 1992: 2)

In spite of this, the prospect of deriving the laws and materials of logic by arguing for them, rather than treating them as brute, confronts a significant obstacle: vicious circularity. Put in the most general way, the problem is that it seems impossible to justify these laws and materials without already relying on them.

Hegel only describes how this obstacle would work in the case of the first and most basic of logic's formal principles: concepts. However, the argument easily generalizes to other cases: judgment, inference and law. Here is Hegel in this section:

> What the nature of the concept is cannot be given right away, not any more than can the concept of any other subject matter. It might perhaps seem that, in order to state the concept of a subject matter, *the logical element* can be presupposed, and that this element would not therefore be preceded by anything else, or be something deduced. (WdL 12: 11/SoL 508, italics mine)

Admittedly, we are not often tempted to think of an account of concepts as laying down a normative standard of thought. Yet this was true in the older logic, and for a fairly straightforward reason. This logic regarded other sciences as beholden to its account of concepts because of the importance of definition in these sciences. These sciences had to rely on logic's account of concepts both when they defined the subject matter that made them the sciences they were and when they defined the more specific phenomena within their purview. After all, a definition given in these sciences could be correct only if it respected logic's account of a concept: for example, as a principle citing a characteristic all things falling under it share in common. This is not sufficient for scientific truth, since a logically well-formed definition could be incorrect. Yet it is necessary, in that any correct definition must at least be logically well-formed.

The problem that interests Hegel arises when we are no longer satisfied to simply ask what ultimately legitimates a special science's concepts and be told that logic's concept of a concept does so. We now ask what ultimately legitimates logic's concept of a concept itself and encounter a unique difficulty. Unfortunately, the mode of justification just used will not suffice in this one special case. After all, logic cannot define its own subject matter in this way. Indeed, it seems that doing so would be circular. To do so would be to appeal to the very concept of a concept whose credentials are in question. Accordingly, it must treat such a definition as a brute fact.

There may be a number of different ways to invoke what I have called bruteness, but as we have seen Hegel thinks the logic of his day did so in a specific way. It argued that the nature and role of concepts are brute facts of our experience. More specifically, they are facts arrived at by abstracting from the empirical content of our thought and language and discovering therein certain formal principles (concepts). As we have repeatedly seen, Hegel regards this appeal to brute fact as hypocrisy, at least when it comes from logic. However, this approach is understandable in light of the difficulty confronting any alternative. How are we supposed to argue for a certain law of thought, or legitimate a certain set of materials that thinking requires, without already assuming what we want to prove?

Once again, the problem generalizes. It is not just the problem of legitimating concepts without relying on concepts but also that of legitimating judgment without relying on judgment, inference without inference, laws without relying on those very laws. Given the plurality of principles, and types of principle, it is perhaps possible that each could do the other's washing in some complicated way. Yet this would only postpone rather than eliminate circularity. Sooner or later the circle has to close, and we are back where we started with the problem of relying on the very principles whose credentials are in question. If Hegel is to advocate an alternative approach to defining concepts, he will need to overcome the problem of circularity.

1.5   From Formal to Speculative Logic

Ultimately, then, Hegel's objection to traditional logic is that this science, like so many others, is non-presuppositionless, meaning it presupposes both an object and a method. Its object is the faculty of thought, and its method abstraction from everything sensible. Yet this catches it in an inconsistency, whereby it is forced to simultaneously advocate for "mediated" forms of justification and yet rely on one that is "immediate."

In order to avoid the inconsistency in which he maintains traditional Scholastic-Aristotelian logic found itself caught, Hegel proposes a new approach to logic in which neither an object nor a method is presupposed.

> As far as the *beginning* that philosophy has to make is concerned, in general it seems to start like the other sciences with a subjective presupposition, namely a particular object, such as space, number, etc., except that here *thinking* would have to be made the object of thinking. And yet, it is thinking's free act of placing itself at that standpoint where it is for itself and thus *generates and provides its own object for itself* [*wo es für sich selber ist und sich hiermit seinen Gegenstand selbst erzeugt und gibt*]. Furthermore, this standpoint, which thus appears to be an *immediate* one, must transform itself into a *result* within the science itself, and indeed into its final result

in which the science recaptures its beginning and returns to itself. In this way, philosophy shows itself to be a sphere that circles back into itself and has no beginning in the sense that other sciences do. Hence, its beginning has a relationship merely to the subject who resolves to philosophize, but not to the science as such. Or, which comes to the same thing, the concept of the science and hence its first concept – which because it is the first contains the separation whereby thinking is the object for a seemingly external, philosophizing subject – must be grasped by the science itself. (EL § 17, italics mine)

This logic will not define itself as a science that studies a certain "presupposed object," thinking. In other words, Hegel's logic will not presuppose that thinking exists and has the characteristics it seems to us to have. In particular, it will not presuppose that this is one mental activity among others or that the mind has distinct capacities for (conceptual) thought and for sensibility, imagination, will and so on. Nor will it be able to presuppose that there is a legitimate area of philosophical or scientific inquiry that studies thinking. As Hegel tells us, this is the main difference between his own philosophy and the special science of psychology. Both centrally concern thinking, but only the latter "presupposes" thinking as its "object."

Admittedly, certain claims about the mind must hold true if we are to have the capacity to read and understand the *Logic*. Yet this is just to say that we must be equipped with a certain psychological capacity if we are to understand the *Logic*'s arguments. It is not to say that these arguments themselves rely on the premise that we are so equipped. As Hegel puts it, the fact that human beings have such a capacity matters for the philosopher who embarks upon the logic project but not to the logic itself: "[It] has a relationship merely to the subject who resolves to philosophize, but not to the science as such" (EL § 17).

As numerous proponents of a reading of Hegel's logic as presuppositionless have long argued, not everything on which the logic relies is a *presupposition*: a type of premise we must accept as true if the argument for a philosopher's conclusion is to succeed. A *presupposition* is not the same as any fact that must obtain if some type of causal prerequisite for reading or writing philosophy is to be fulfilled. As I interpret him, Hegel is denying that thinking is a presupposition but conceding it may be required in some other sense.

Why, though, would Hegel want to avoid presupposing all of these claims? What could possibly be the harm in doing so? What is gained when we avoid presupposing the truth of such claims about the mind?

Hegel avoids *presupposing* the truth of such claims concerning thinking and its necessary "determinations" so that he will be in a position to *prove* them in a more satisfying way and on an independent basis.[6] As he writes, in the passage just considered, "this standpoint, which thus appears to be an *immediate* one, must transform itself into a *result* within the science itself." Hegel explains that these claims are to be found not just in the course of his philosophy but at its very conclusion: "… and indeed into its final result."

Importantly, this recursion will take place not just in Hegel's system as a whole (logic, nature and spirit), though it will also occur there. As it happens, the philosophy of spirit does make good on the philosophical psychology that the *Logic* presupposes. However, this will also occur in the *Logic* itself, which ends with an account of theoretical cognition, including the form of it achieved in the *Logic*. As Hegel says, this circular self-comprehending structure is found not only in the system as a whole but also in each of the system's three subdivisions. That is why the system is "a circle of circles" as opposed to just "a circle" (EL § 15). In this way, philosophy shows itself to be "the science [that] recaptures its beginning and returns to itself." This is a familiar claim about Hegel's *Logic*, but we are here in a position to see it in an unfamiliar light. It is an outcome of his confrontation with traditional logic.

At the close of the *Logic*, we will be in a position to obtain a superior type of justification for these claims than we would if we had treated them as first premises of the argument. Instead, we draw the relevant conclusions about the mind from a different set of premises that do not directly concern the mind. This is true of the claim that there is such a thing as conceptual thought, distinct from sensible representation. By not presupposing that there is a faculty of thinking, we will be in a position to (noncircularly) prove it. Yet because we are ourselves thinkers, the knowledge we acquire is a type of self-knowledge. This is what Hegel means when, in the passage cited earlier, he speaks of "thinking's free act of placing itself at that standpoint where it is for itself and thus *generates* and *provides its own object for itself*."

Similarly, we have not presupposed that there is a *science* of thinking because this gives us the opportunity to prove that there is. We do not do this by being told what such a science would be and how it would proceed. Rather we arrive at this conclusion by realizing that such a science is none

---

[6] Here, I acknowledge a debt to Nuzzo (2016), who also argues that Hegel's logic presupposes no thinker at the outset – perhaps so that it can prove the existence of one at its close.

other than the one in which we have already been engaged, and which is now coming to a close. Hegel explains this as equivalent to the thought that the science "recaptures its beginning."

In my view, the logic presupposes neither that there is such a thing as thinking as distinct from sensing, imagining, willing and so on nor that thinking has a set of laws and rules, nor further that there is a science whose task is to study them. However, the truth of all of these claims is a precondition of following the course of the logic. The claims in question must be true if we are to embark on the path of such a science, even if the science itself need not treat them as such. If that is so, then we can finally understand why Hegel does not want his science to begin in the way others do. It is so that it can end in the way no other ever has: by comprehending itself. The self-comprehension of Hegel's *Science of Logic* will be the topic of my conclusion (Chapter 7).

Because of this aspiration to achieve a self-comprehending science, Hegel's many well-known claims to the effect that his *Logic* is the science of "pure thinking" or of "thought determinations" cannot be taken completely at face value. Indeed, I would recommend that they be seen in the same light as claims such as the following: The logic is "the Idea in the element of pure thinking," "the Concept giving itself its own determinations" and so on. It is always possible to offer an account of the opening of the logic project in terms that will only become available later. In just the same way that this account of the logic framed in terms of the Absolute Idea would be question-begging, so too would any account framed in terms of thought and its determinations.

This is not to deny Hegel's description of his project as an investigation of thinking, and its laws and determinations, but to attribute to this self-designation a different status. As Hegel makes clear, these claims rely on a merely provisional justification that is less rigorous than the one he ultimately hopes to provide.

> The determinations offered here and in the following sections are not to be taken as assertions and as my opinions about thinking. Since, however, in this preliminary exposition no derivation or proof can be given [*keine Ableitung oder Beweis stattfinden kann*], they may be regarded as facts such that in the consciousness of anyone who has and contemplates thoughts it is found empirically to be the case that the character of universality and likewise the subsequent determinations are on hand in them. To be sure, for the observation of the facts of one's consciousness and representations, it is prerequisite that one be already educated in the tasks of paying attention and engaging in abstraction. (EL § 20A)

In the relevant section, Hegel introduces the philosophical psychology that undergirds his logic, a psychology that distinguishes between "representation" (*Vorstellung*) and "thinking" (*Denken*). It is by reference to this psychology that Hegel is able to introduce the idea of a science of thinking and its constitutive determinations. However, the psychology is itself provisional and can only be fully justified subsequently. At this early stage, it is only supported by "facts of consciousness," not empirical facts of sense experience to be sure but of intellectual self-reflection. Yet the psychology that undergirds Hegel's idea of a science of thinking and its determinations will later be upheld by a "proof" or "derivation." In the lectures, Hegel does not hesitate to include even the I or apperception and thinking themselves in the category of things assumed only provisionally as "facts of consciousness" but later proven: "From where we now stand [before the onset of the science of logic], the claim that I and thinking are completely identical can only be based on an appeal to representation. Logic is the science of truth" (LL 8/10–12). Just what kind of proof or derivation will replace the early appeal to representation remains to be seen. Subsequently, I will contend that it is at precisely this point that the psychological approach of Kant and the tradition gives way to Hegel's ontological alternative.

1.6 Conclusion: Kant as "Minor Post-Aristotelian"?

In this chapter, I have reconstructed Hegel's critique of the formal logic of his day.[7] This logic's psychological approach threatens to render the laws of logic brute in a way Hegel claims is objectionable. Given that Aristotelian logic is now widely considered obsolete, the interest of this critique may seem limited. However, it is clear from Hegel's characterization of this logic that his critique of it can serve another function. It can double as a critique of Kant's (pure) general logic.

As I have said, I am opposed to importing into my discussion of Hegel a conception of the history of logic occasionally favored by Kantian-idealist interpreters. This is one on which Kant's great innovation over a tradition of thinking about logic going back to Aristotle is to have distinguished more sharply between logic and ontology than was done in philosophy before him, especially in the Leibniz–Wolff school. Given Kant's persistent criticisms of figures in this tradition for trying to obtain metaphysical

---

[7] The allusion in the heading is to a famous remark of Paul Samuelson's deriding Marx as a "minor post-Ricardian."

knowledge through mere conceptual analysis, this conception of his role in the history of philosophy is understandable. This aspect of Kant's thought is on full display in sections such as the Amphiboly, where he unmasks metaphysical principles such as the principle of identity of indiscernibles as, in effect, abuses of more modest logical ones.

Yet there is another tendency in Kant's thinking about logic that this received view does not accommodate well. This is his belief that logic is fundamentally in order, and has been for more than two millennia since its founding by Aristotle. This is also reflected in Kant's allegiance to a form of logic centered around the judgment and the syllogism, and believed to be derived from Aristotle's logical writings. It is also, perhaps a bit more controversially, reflected in Kant's appeal to a teleological form of faculty psychology in which logical laws are constitutive norms, those it is in the nature of the faculty to obey (Dyck 2016).[8]

As Hegel tells us, this was common in the tradition, particularly among the Scholastics, but if that is so we face a quandary. Is Kant breaking with an ontological approach to logic (category theory)? Or continuing the broadly psychological one of the Scholastic-Aristotelian tradition? Pippin's "anti-psychologistic" answer is, I think, neither – and this certainly makes for some extremely interesting neo-Hegelian philosophy. However, I myself suspect Hegel's answer would have been the latter option.

As I have said, the conception of logic's history that Hegel himself endorses is one on which there is fundamental continuity between Kant and the Aristotelian tradition. Again, this is a conception of the history of logic suggested to Hegel and other German idealists by Kant's remark that logic had been complete since Aristotle. They infer from this remark that "(pure) general logic" is not an area of his own critical philosophy at all but rather a separate science. It is less the province of any distinctly Kantian doctrines than it is of "the logicians." It is less a part of the critical philosophy itself than it is a separate body of knowledge, drawn on at various points in the argument but independent. It is less a part of the revolution in philosophy Kant hoped to effect with his Copernican turn than it is of philosophy's heritage going back two millennia.

For this reason, Hegel seldom, if ever, so far as I am aware, speaks of Kant as having his own (pure) general logic: more specifically, his own tables of the forms of judgment and inference. Instead, he often, nearly

---

[8] These are, once more, among the parallels Dyck draws between Kant's "general logic" and that of Wolff.

always, speaks of Kant as having "borrowed" these resources from the tradition:

> In this context, the Kantian philosophy incurs a further inconsequence by borrowing the categories for the transcendental logic [*sie entlehnt für die transzendentale Logik die Kategorien*], as so-called root concepts, from the subjective logic where they were assumed empirically. (WdL 12: 44/SoL 541)

Of course, it could be maintained that Hegel regards Kant as having gone beyond the tradition in one respect. This he would do in his ideas concerning the nature status of logic's principles than in his conception of what, exactly, those principles include. Seen in this light, Kant would be an innovator in the philosophy of logic rather than in logic itself.

However, this does not seem to be born out either. As we have seen throughout this chapter, Hegel regards the former logic as empirical in character, and he here simply reprises this claim in his critique of Kant. Here, Hegel argues that the critical philosophy's reliance on the logic of the day introduced an empirical component into its foundation. As Hegel remarks somewhat acidly, Kant might have saved himself time and trouble by simply consulting experience directly rather than relying on an empirical form of logic.

Why, though, would general logic of this type be an insecure foundation on which to erect the edifice of transcendental logic? To make this more precise, we should recall the tables of forms of judgment and inference from which Kant's tables of categories in the Analytic and of Ideas in the Dialectic are drawn. Accordingly, the basic principles of general logic are those from which the basic principles of transcendental logic derive, in some way that is difficult to specify. Why, though, should principles derived in this way be suspect? It is to this question that we now turn, moving from Hegel's critique of the traditional Aristotelian logic, assumed by Kant, to his critique of a form of idealist logic that is Kant's own innovation: transcendental logic.

CHAPTER 2

The Ontological Proof as "the True Critique of the Categories and of Reason"

Hegel on Kant's Transcendental Logic

I now turn to Hegel's critique of Kant's transcendental logic, which both parallels and incorporates his earlier critique of formal logic. Here, Hegel pursues a similar strategy, mounting an immanent critique of Kant's transcendental logic: specifically, accusing it of failing to noncircularly self-justify. In Kant's transcendental philosophy, a knowledge claim is legitimate only if it can be shown to be consistent with the nature and limits of our faculty of knowledge. However, the knowledge claims Kant himself makes in offering his account of the nature and limits of this faculty cannot be proven to be legitimate in this way, since this would be question-begging.

This does not necessarily mean that the critical philosophy's claims to knowledge are false, but it does mean that they are vulnerable. To defend them, Kant must appeal to some more ultimate source of justification. In key instances, such as the derivation of transcendental philosophy's categories and ideas from the tables of forms of judgment and inference, this more ultimate source is the logic of the day. Here, Hegel's discussion of this logic from Chapter 1 becomes important in clarifying why Hegel thinks Kant's appeals to this logic do not succeed. Essentially, these appeals covertly introduce an empirical body of knowledge into the very foundations of the critical philosophy.

Hegel considers the attempts by Reinhold and Fichte to offer a reconstituted version of Kant's critical philosophy that will surmount this objection. However, he finds these attempts wanting. In particular, he rejects Fichte's attempt to derive the categories of transcendental logic and the laws and materials of general logic from an indubitably certain first principle, a post-Kantian version of Descartes' Cogito: specifically, one distinct from rational psychology and its metaphysics of soul substance. Hegel concedes that this starting point is certain but denies it is conceptually primitive.

In place of Fichte's approach, Hegel proposes a derivation of the categories from a type of monist principle that is genuinely primitive: Being.

Oddly enough, Hegel takes this derivation to be equivalent to a rehabilitated, post-Kantian version of Spinoza's ontological argument. The reasons
become clearer against the backdrop of Hegel's critical engagement with
Jacobi and the effort to rescue the ontological argument from its misap-
propriation by Romanticism. Ultimately, Hegel's provocative claim is that
the critical philosophy's foundational project of deriving the categories can
only be carried out on the basis of an argument that Kant rejected as the
epitome of dogmatic, precritical metaphysics: the ontological argument.

2.1   Kant's Analytic: Marburg Neo-Kantian
versus German Idealist Readings

I begin with a broad overview of Kant's project in the first critique, an
overview by no means intended to be the authoritative. Rather, it is the
account I believe is most helpful for understanding post-Kantian idealism.
On the proto-German-idealist interpretation of Kant that I will defend
here, his first critique aspires to a form of systematic rigor highly valued
by subsequent figures such as Fichte and Hegel. Kant's insistence that
his critical philosophy constitutes a system reflects more than an aspiration to be thorough and treat each topic in its proper place. Systematicity
means a form of unity that can only truly be achieved if we exhibit all of
human knowledge as following with fairly strict necessity from a securely
grounded first principle. Kant's idealist followers do not think he achieves
this form of systematicity satisfactorily, but they do believe elements of it
are present in his thought: in particular, the idea of a first principle for all
our knowledge. The unshakable first principle from which Kant proceeds
concerns the nature of the mind. Yet, as we will see, there is some difficulty
in determining which of Kant's claims it is meant to be. The most obvious
choice was thought to be Kant's transcendental unity of apperception ("I
think"), though even this principle could be understood in different ways.

On this interpretation, Kant means to present a continuous anti-
skeptical argument, rather than simply side-step skeptical challenges from
Humean or Cartesian opponents. Indeed, reading Kant this way becomes
urgent once we take account of the more radical forms of neo-Humean or
Cartesian skepticism that arose in the wake of his first critique, ones which
make it unacceptable to begin from the putatively uncontroversial starting
point that we possess "experience," or empirical knowledge (if this was
ever Kant's aspiration).

Moreover, this interpretation has Kant reject methodological naturalism,
the claim that philosophy should presuppose the truth or well-foundedness

of natural-scientific and mathematical knowledge. This is, of course, consistent with the possibility that Kant ultimately seeks to uphold the claims to knowledge made in these fields. On this view, transcendental philosophy is a strongly foundationalist project, if not in exactly the sense that the Cartesian one is. The point is that transcendental philosophy, though unprecedented in the history of philosophy, shares a common philosophical aspiration to supremacy. It is not one on a par with other intellectual enterprises but prior to them. As I will explain, this reading is almost the exact inverse of the one advanced by another better-known school, many of whose adherents regarded the German idealist appropriation of Kant as one of the greatest travesties in modern philosophy: the Marburg neo-Kantians. Their interpretation is therefore a useful foil for the protoidealist one I develop here.

Kant's broad aim in the first critique is to explain how a certain distinctive type of knowledge is possible, "synthetic a priori knowledge" (A 9/B 13). Swiftly and crudely summarized, this is a type of knowledge that is both nontrivial and universally and necessarily valid. Kant takes himself to have learned from Hume that sense experience alone is incapable of providing us with the justification for this type of knowledge. It only ever tells us that things are thus-and-so, not that they must be. However, Kant claims that this type of knowledge can be justified if we break with the received realist view of knowledge, a view on which subjects know objects that exist and have the character that they do independently of our knowing them. Kant effects a Copernican revolution in philosophy with his claim that it is not our knowledge that must conform to the objects but the objects that must conform to our knowledge (B xvi). Essentially, the proposal is that our faculty of knowledge might itself be the source of certain "conditions" objects must meet in order to be cognized by us. If that were so, then we could be assured these conditions would always apply to the objects of our knowledge. What, though, can Kant mean by "conditions" on the objects?

The answer lies in Kant's notion of form and his related claim that his is a "formal idealism."[1] For Kant, we are by no means wholly responsible for the existence of the objects we experience. That would perhaps be true of God, an infinite knower, but we are not knowers of this type. Instead, we are dependent on independently existing objects that must affect us if we are to have knowledge of them. We are, in this regard, finite knowers who do not wholly create the objects we know. As Kant concedes to the

---

[1] See P (4:337), where Kant contrasts "formal idealism" with Cartesian and Berkeley idealism.

empiricist tradition, objects must affect our faculty of sensibility and provide us with sensible representations.[2] Hence, objects furnish the "matter" of all knowledge.

However, Kant holds that there is one respect in which we might be productive of the objects: It is possible that we should contribute their form. This would be the form that all matter provided by sensible intuition would necessarily have to bear. If this were so, then synthetic a priori knowledge would be possible. We would be able to know in advance of experience that all its objects must be subject to the conditions that our faculty of knowledge imposes on them, that all must bear reason's "form."

However, this strategy, even if successful, would be subject to a certain limitation or restriction, which is the other main component of Kant's transcendental idealism. We would be able to have only synthetic a priori knowledge of what Kant calls appearances or objects of possible experience, those which are subject to the conditions our faculty of knowledge imposes on them. We could not have such knowledge of what Kant calls "things-in-themselves," objects considered apart from the conditions under which beings like ourselves can know them.

This much is uncontroversial, but we now come upon a more contested issue. If we are to understand how Kant proceeds in the *Critique of Pure Reason* itself, as opposed to its preface, we must briefly rehearse his strategy of argument. Kant is clear that in the preface he has merely proceeded "hypothetically," whereas in the *Critique* itself he will proceed "apodictically."

> In this Preface I propose the transformation in our way of thinking presented in criticism merely as a hypothesis, analogous to that other hypothesis, only in order to draw our notice to the first attempts at such a transformation, which are always hypothetical, even though in the treatise itself it will be proved not hypothetically but rather apodictically [*nicht hypothetisch, sondern apodiktisch bewiesen wird*] from the constitution of our representations of space and from the elementary concepts of the understanding. (B xxii)

Here, I attempt to explain the distinction Kant draws. In the preface, Kant defends a merely hypothetical claim that runs as follows. *If transcendental idealism were true, then synthetic a priori knowledge would be possible.* Equivalently, Kant will say he is proposing a type of (thought) experiment. We are invited to consider the possibility that transcendental idealism is true and then reflect on the way in which this would help explain the possibility of synthetic a priori knowledge.

---

[2] Locke, rather than Berkeley or Hume, would likely be the relevant empiricist.

However, Kant will pursue a different method of argument in the body of the *Critique* itself. His motivation for doing so is that the argument of the preface has, in fact, accomplished very little. At most, this argument shows that transcendental idealism, if it were true, would explain much. Yet, it does not follow from this that transcendental idealism actually is true or that it has explained anything yet. In my view, it would be a mistake to assume that Kant already regards the issue as settled at this early stage. Transcendental idealism and the Copernican revolution may hold out the promise of explaining the possibility of synthetic a priori knowledge. Still, more is required if we are to prove that these doctrines are true. Hence, Kant's arguments in the *Critique* itself will proceed not hypothetically but apodictically. They will seek to demonstrate for certain that transcendental idealism and the associated Copernican view of our relation to objects are true.

Many of Kant's successors, such as the Marburg neo-Kantians, embraced a different reading of the argument structure of Kant's critical philosophy, a reading based on the following considerations.[3] For Kant, synthetic a priori knowledge is not just possible for us. He is convinced that we do, in fact, have this type of knowledge. Moreover, Kant did not just accept this fact himself, as an avid observer of the (then) recent successes of the sciences. He made it the first premise in the *Critique*'s argument. According to these readers, then, Kant's theoretical philosophy in the first critique starts from the "fact of science" just as his practical philosophy in the second starts from the "fact of reason." Yet if that is so, then Kant cannot be agnostic about the truth of transcendental idealism when he moves beyond the preface to the body of the work. The preface has shown that we could only have natural-scientific knowledge if transcendental idealism were true and not otherwise. However, we do, in fact, have such knowledge. Therefore, transcendental idealism must be true. Of course, there is much more work for Kant to do going forward. He must determine how, exactly, our faculty of knowledge imposes conditions on the objects. He must explain in detail how this grounds the possibility of the scientific and mathematical knowledge we in fact possess. *That* idealism is true, however, cannot be in doubt, even if we are not yet sure *how* it can be.

Yet the Marburg interpretation faces a well-known obstacle: an important difference between the argument structure of the *Critique* and that of the *Prolegomena*, a difference that the Marburg neo-Kantians often elided. As Kant explains, these works adhere to two fundamentally different

---

[3] Cohen (1885: § 12) cited in Heis (2018), whose overview I draw on here.

methods in seeking an answer to the question "How is metaphysics possible?" The first is the "synthetic/progressive" method, and the second the "analytic/regressive" method. Kant writes:

> In the *Critique of Pure Reason* I worked on this question *synthetically*, namely by inquiring within pure reason itself, and seeking to determine within this source both the elements and the laws of its pure use, according to principles. This work is difficult and requires a resolute reader to think himself little by little into a system *that takes no foundation as given except reason itself, and that therefore tries to develop cognition [synthetic a priori knowledge within mathematics and the sciences – JM] out of its original seeds without relying on any fact whatever.*
>
> Prolegomena should by contrast be preparatory exercises; they ought more to indicate what needs to be done in order to bring a science into existence if possible, than to present the science itself. They must therefore rely on something already known to be dependable, from which we can go forward with confidence and ascend to the sources, which are not yet known, and whose discovery not only will explain what is known already, but will also exhibit an area with many cognitions that all arise from these same sources. The methodological procedure of prolegomena, and especially of those that are to prepare for a future metaphysics, will therefore be *analytic*.
>
> ... [In the *Prolegomena*] *we can confidently say that some pure synthetic cognition a priori is actual and given, namely, pure mathematics and pure natural science; for both contain propositions that are fully acknowledged* ... We have therefore some at least uncontested synthetic cognition a priori, and we do not need to ask whether it is possible (for it is actual), but only: how it is possible, in order to be able to derive, from the principle of the possibility of the given cognition, the possibility of all other synthetic cognition a priori. (*P* 4: 274–275/25–26, my emphasis)

In the *Prolegomena*, Kant pursues an Analytic or "regressive" method of argument. He begins from a "fact." This is the widely agreed upon premise that we do, in fact, have synthetic a priori knowledge in mathematics and the sciences. He then "regresses" to the conclusion that transcendental idealism and the Copernican view of the relationship between our faculties and the objects must be true. Only this conclusion could explain the possibility of the knowledge we do, in fact, have.

In this connection, it is worth noting a discrepancy between the chapters on mathematics and natural science and the final one on metaphysics. Kant will presuppose that we do, in fact, have synthetic a priori knowledge in mathematics and natural science, asking "*How* is mathematics possible?" "*How* is pure natural science possible?" (*P* 4: 280) (*P* 4: 294). However, he will not do so for metaphysics, asking only "*Is* metaphysics possible at all?" (*P* 4: 271). It still remains the case that the *Prolegomena* employs this regressive strategy of argument, at least in its first two sections. Why, though, did Kant employ this strategy of argument in only the shorter and more accessible version of his book, intended for a wider audience?

Kant himself is less explicit than he might be, but the reason must be that the analytic/regressive strategy of argument has significant limitations. Chief among them, I think, would be the way its starting point, the presupposition that we do in fact have synthetic a priori knowledge in natural science and mathematics, begs the question against an important opponent of Kant's critical project: the Humean skeptic. Here, we should recall that the main form synthetic a priori knowledge in natural science takes is knowledge of the causal laws of nature, which hold universally and necessarily. Yet this was precisely the type of knowledge whose possibility Hume called into question with his skeptical critique of received views of causation. Whether because the "idea" of necessary connection has no corresponding "impression" or because the validity of the inductive inference from "all instances observed so far" to "all instances" cannot be justified noncircularly, the presupposition that we have the type of knowledge Kant claims we do is by no means uncontroversial.

In the *Critique*, then, Kant pursues a "synthetic/progressive" method, arguing for transcendental idealism on independent grounds. In particular, Kant will begin by defending an idealist account of the relevant part of our faculty of knowledge and its relationship to the objects on which it imposes its form. He will then "progress" to the conclusion, if it is even available, that synthetic a priori knowledge of a certain broad type is possible for us. Admittedly, this means reading the critique as pursuing an anti-skeptical project, rather than some more modest nonskeptical one. Yet for our purposes the obstacles confronting such a reading are irrelevant. It is clear that it is the reading endorsed by Kant's idealist followers, many of whom were positively obsessed by the project of refuting the skeptic once and for all. Plausibly or not, they claimed to find the seeds for such a refutation in Kant.

If one is clear on the argumentative strategy of the *Critique*, then the challenge confronting it is obvious. What, exactly, justifies the account of the faculty of knowledge that provides the foundational first premise of the entire argument? This is the tough critical question nearly all of Kant's immediate followers in the idealist tradition would pose for him.[4] It is the question that I believe is the basis for Hegel's entire critique

---

[4] It is posed in a different way by Strawson (2007: 32) who calls the deduction "an essay in the imaginary subject of transcendental psychology."

of Kant. It is also one that I think is too often ignored in more recent discussions. We now turn to the question of how Kant proceeds to show that our faculty of knowledge imposes certain conditions on the objects of experience. Kant maintains that our faculty of knowledge has "two stems," sensibility and understanding, each of which employs two different types of representation, intuition and concept (A 15/B 29). As he later writes, "Objects are given to us by means of sensibility, and it alone yields us intuitions; they are thought through the understanding, and from the understanding arise concepts" (A 19/B 33). Hence, Kant will argue that the conditions our cognitive power imposes upon the objects would have to be of two fundamentally different kinds: sensible and intelligible (conceptual). He considers these two broad types of condition in the two broad divisions of the *Critique*, Transcendental Aesthetic and Transcendental Logic.

In his mature critique of Kant, at least, Hegel focuses predominantly on the Logic, not the Aesthetic. Clearly, he maintains that this is where the real interest of Kant's project lies, as well as some of its more problematic features. It would be interesting to ask why Hegel holds this view. The answer may reside in a belief about the Aesthetic, voiced much earlier in his career. In the early essay "Faith and Knowledge" (*Glauben und Wissen*), Hegel had argued, as would many after him, that the forms of sensible intuition identified in the Aesthetic (space and time) cannot be understood in isolation from the categories of the understanding described in the Logic.[5] In particular, they cannot have a nonderivative unity. Hegel claimed to be following Kant himself, who had indicated as much in a notorious footnote to the Deduction. In any case, it seems clear that the mature Hegel no longer devotes much attention to the Aesthetic at all, possibly because he is drawing on his earlier belief that it can effectively be collapsed into the Transcendental Logic. Whatever the reason, we will follow him in focusing primarily on the Logic.

In the Transcendental Logic's first division, Transcendental Analytic, Kant offers a "logic of truth" explaining how the type of synthetic a priori knowledge claimed by natural science is possible (A 62/B 87). Just as we might have been led to expect, Kant offers an idealist or Copernican explanation of its possibility. Natural-scientific knowledge is made possible by the intelligible (or conceptual) conditions that the understanding imposes on objects of experience. Kant defends this position of the Analytic in two large steps. In the Metaphysical Deduction, he takes the

5 Hegel (1988: 38–39).

preliminary step of identifying what the intelligible (conceptual) conditions our faculty of knowledge imposes on the objects of experience would have to be, assuming there even were any. In the Transcendental Deduction, he proceeds to show that the intelligible (conceptual) conditions he has just identified must, in fact, be imposed on the objects of experience by us.

In the Metaphysical Deduction, Kant attempts to identify what the intelligible (conceptual) conditions on objects would have to be. They could not be empirical concepts, derived from sense experience. If they were, then we could never know that all objects must necessarily conform to them. The most we could know, Hume showed, is that all objects observed so far have done so but not that all must. Hence, these concepts would have to be a priori, contributed by the understanding itself. Hume had further argued that the nonempirical concepts central to the sciences, such as cause, substance and so on, could not be derived from experience. However, Kant raises the "Copernican" possibility that experience, in a richer sense of the term, might derive from them (*P* 4: 313). In other words, these concepts might already be operative in the constitution of the objects of our experience or appearances. Kant therefore suggests the possibility that the a priori concepts he will identify could confer their form on the objects of our experience. More specifically, these concepts could serve as rules guiding the understanding in its activity of "synthesizing" or unifying the manifold that it is given in sensible intuition. If that were so, it would not be so much as possible for us to be presented with an object of experience that was not already subject to these concepts.[6] This would allow us to uphold the possibility of synthetic a priori knowledge of nature. How, though, can these a priori concepts or categories even be identified?

As Kant makes clear, there is an important condition of adequacy on any table of categories: "completeness" (A 81/B 106–107). We must be able to prove that the table contains all (and only) the categories that there are. One reason for this is that Kant maintains there are certain "usurpatory" concepts that must be excluded from the status of categories: for example, fate and fortune (B 116). Another becomes clear in the course of Kant's critique of Aristotle's theory of the categories. Kant says of his preferred alternative that

---

[6] It has seemed to some interpreters that Kant does allow for a type of experience in which the categories are not operative. See, for example, White Beck (1978), who calls this L-experience (Lockean experience).

It has not arisen rhapsodically [*rhapsodistisch*], as the result of a haphazard search after pure concepts, the complete enumeration of which, as based on induction only, could never be guaranteed. Nor could we, if this were our procedure, discover why just these concepts, and no others, have their seat in the pure understanding. It was an enterprise worthy of an acute thinker like Aristotle to make search for these fundamental concepts. But as he did so on no principle [*kein Principium hatte*], he merely picked them up as they came his way … his table still remained defective. (A 81/B 106–107)

Kant accuses Aristotle of failing to arrive at a complete table of categories. His table includes many empirical concepts, and not enough a priori ones. Kant maintains that Aristotle failed to achieve completeness because he relied on an inductive method. Aristotle took up the categories as he discovered them in his own thought and speech and those of his contemporaries. Notoriously, however, inductive methods cannot yield completeness. At best, they can tell us that these are the categories that have been discovered so far. They cannot tell us that they are all the categories that there are.

Why does the "completeness" or lack thereof of Kant's table matter? What, exactly, is at stake? The issue, I think, cannot be the incompleteness per se of Kant's table of the categories (the "horror scenario" is not that there might turn out to be a thirteenth or fourteenth category). Rather, the reason Kant wants to ward off "incompleteness" is that it is in fact a symptom of a deeper problem. This is the problem that if it were incomplete then Kant's category theory, his theory of the most basic concepts any knower can employ, would express a kind of truth that is insufficient for Kant's purposes. More specifically, it would express a merely contingent truth about us, rather than the type of necessary truth that the argument of the Analytic requires. This could be a psychological, anthropological, linguistic or sociohistorical truth about us – but the crucial point is that it would be, for all we know, contingent rather than necessary. If this threat seems exaggerated, we should recall that it is not enough for the table of categories to simply be complete (regardless of whether we are in a position to show this). It must be proven complete. The foundation of Kant's analytic is not just a necessary truth but one self-consciously affirmed as such. What is more, the synthetic/progressive method of the first critique, and by extension the deduction, raises the stakes. If the table of forms of categories reflects a contingent truth, then so too will the doctrines based on it.

In order to achieve completeness, Kant proposes an alternative deductive approach. This approach will begin from a principle. It will then proceed to deduce a complete table of categories used by the understanding.

Kant will derive his table of categories from the table of forms of judgment provided by the logic of the day. The categories synthesize the manifold of sensible intuition, so as to render it knowable. Knowing is a matter of forming judgments, however. Hence, the different types of category should correspond to the different forms of judgment recognized in (pure) general logic. Yet the deeper reason for the parallel between the two tables is that one and the same faculty underlies both: "The same function which gives unity to the various representations in a judgment also gives unity to the mere synthesis of various representations in an intuition" (A 79/B 104–105).

In any case, Kant believes that a deduction of the categories proceeding from this "principle" furnished by logic would be complete. As Kant famously declares in the preface, logic is itself complete and has not had to take a single step since Aristotle (B viii). However, it is only in this section of the Analytic (the Metaphysical Deduction) that we find out just how important this claim is to Kant's own project. Here, Kant tells us that logic's table of forms of judgment is compete. More fundamentally, his account of the understanding's judging activities that it represents is itself exhaustive and complete. Hence, Kant's own table of categories and his account of the understanding's synthesizing activities in it must be as well.

> In this manner there arise precisely the same number of pure concepts of the understanding which apply *a priori* to objects of intuition in general, as, in the preceding table, there have been found to be logical functions in all possible judgments. For these functions specify the understanding completely, and yield an exhaustive inventory of its powers. (A 79/B 105)

Ultimately, then, one can see why, for Kant, the completeness of transcendental logic could be vouchsafed by that of general (formal) logic.

Some readers of Kant have denied that his transcendental logic is based on general logic but maintained that the reverse is the case. Most famously, the Marburg neo-Kantians did so. One piece of evidence for this type of view is Kant's claim that there could be no analysis without a prior synthesis ("for where the understanding has not previously combined anything, neither can it dissolve anything") (B 130).[7] The claim is taken to mean that Kant thinks the analytical truths concerning what the contents of our concepts are presuppose synthetic a priori truths from transcendental logic, which invests those concepts with content in the first place.

---

[7] Cassirer, a typical neo-Kantian in this regard, refers to the "no analysis without prior synthesis" claim in his defense of Kant's MD (1981: 172).

Another piece of evidence, important to the Marburgers, lies in Kant's claim that the categories determine the manifold of sensibility in respect of the logical forms of judgment. For example, the category <substance-accident> determines which part of the intuitively given manifold can be judged of as the subject and which is the predicate. This is something logic alone cannot tell us, since <whiteness> is <Socratic> is as much a possibility, logically speaking, as <Socrates> is <white>.

> But first I shall introduce a word of explanation in regard to the categories. They are concepts of an object in general, by means of which the intuition of an object is regarded as determined in respect of one of the logical functions of judgment. Thus the function of the categorical judgment is that of the relation of subject to predicate; for example, "All bodies are divisible" … But when the concept of body is brought under the category of substance, it is thereby determined that its empirical intuition in experience must always be considered as subject and never as mere predicate. Similarly with all the other categories. (B 128)

However, it seems to me that neither of these claims undermines the priority of pure general logic over transcendental logic. They just remind us that general logic is in certain important respects deficient, because of its emptiness and formality.

Moreover, it is clear that the Marburgers' insistence on the priority of transcendental logic over general logic reflects their dubious interpretative assumption that Kant presupposes the "fact of science." In their view, Kant is proceeding analytically or "regressing" from the synthetic a priori principles of natural science to its conditions of possibility in transcendental logic. He then regresses further to transcendental logic's conditions of possibility in general logic. This is an interesting reading of Kant but it is not, I think, a reading the German idealists share.[8]

Although I limit myself to Hegel's critique of Kant's Metaphysical Deduction in what follows, I briefly summarize here Kant's Transcendental Deduction so that we have the conclusion of the Analytic's argument in view. Given the notorious difficulty of Kant's Transcendental Deduction, the idea that it can be briefly summarized will undoubtedly raise eyebrows. Yet at least for the purposes of reconstructing Hegel's critique of Kant, this approach is appropriate. Notoriously, Hegel himself holds that the Transcendental Deduction is simpler than it is often taken to be. In the

---

[8] Other Hegel interpreters and even some neo-Hegelians disagree. See Rödl (2012), who regards Kant's general logic as already informed by his transcendental logic, as well as by the role in the latter of sensibility and its a priori forms.

early text *Faith and Knowledge*, Hegel refers to the Deduction as "shallow."[9] This assessment seems to persist in the mature works:

> [T]he unity which constitutes the essence of the concept is recognized as the original synthetic unity of apperception, the unity of the "I think," or of self-consciousness. *This proposition is all that there is to the so-called transcendental deduction of the categories which, from the beginning, has however been regarded as the most difficult piece of Kantian philosophy.* (WdL 12: 17–18/ SoL 515)

The implication of this last sentence seems to be that the complexity of the Deduction is exaggerated. Though uncharitable as Kant interpretation, it may somewhat justify the cursory overview of the deduction I will give for the purpose of interpreting Hegel.

Having identified the categories in the Metaphysical Deduction, Kant then proceeds to show, in the Transcendental Deduction, that they must apply to all (possible) objects of experience.[10] Kant's fundamental premise in that argument is given in the following famous passage:

> The I think must be able to accompany all my representations; for otherwise something would be represented in me that could not be thought at all, which is as much as to say that the representation would either be impossible or else at least would be nothing for me. (B 131–132)

If some representations are to be mine, then I must (be able to) ascribe them to myself. Since that is just what it means for representations to be mine, this is an analytic truth. This is the so-called "analytic unity of apperception" (B 133–134). As Kant says, it is itself trivial like other analytic truths, but it has a further implication that is not so.

> Therefore it is only because I can combine a manifold of given representations in one consciousness that it is possible for me to represent the identity of the consciousness in these representations itself, i.e., the analytical unity of apperception is only possible under the presupposition of some synthetic one. (B 133–134)

As Kant explains, the "analytical unity" entails the "synthetic unity of apperception." If these representations are all to be mine, Kant argues, then it follows that they must all be brought together or combined with one another by me, "synthesized," as it were. The analytic unity of apperception implies its synthetic unity. Yet the different modes of combination can be none

---

[9] Hegel (1977: 69).
[10] Here I defer to Hegel's own understanding of the argument.

other than the twelve categories from Kant's table. Here Kant refers us back to a previous part of the argument. For, in the Metaphysical Deduction, it was shown that if the understanding did combine the sensible manifold, then it would do so in these twelve ways. Here, we learn that the understanding does, in fact, combine the manifold, simply in virtue of being self-conscious. Therefore, we can conclude on the basis of what we have now learned, together with the earlier premise from the Metaphysical Deduction, that it must do so in these twelve ways. Ultimately, I can be certain that the manifold of sensible intuition, just by virtue of being self-conscious, must stand under the categories. There is some reasonable controversy over whether the necessity of combination for knowledge is normative, constitutive or else some combination of the two. However, I leave this to one side.

The ultimate outcome of the Analytic is the realization that synthetic a priori knowledge of nature is possible because there are intelligible conditions to which any object of our experience must conform: the categories. The Analytic is by no means at an end, and there is much further work to be done. Summarizing crudely, the work of these sections is to explain in greater detail how it is that the categories apply to the sensibly given manifold for beings like ourselves. The second half of the deduction will do so for our forms of intuition, space and time and introduce a new psychological principle, the transcendental imagination.[11] The System of Principles will give "spatiotemporal definitions" of each of the categories.[12] However, these further sections are mostly irrelevant for our purposes, since they are mostly ignored by the mature Hegel.[13] It would be interesting to ask why Kant's idealist followers are often so uninterested in these further parts of the Analytic. It may reflect their commitment to a strong "conceptualist" interpretation of the Deduction. On this interpretation, the most important work of the Analytic is accomplished well before the forms of intuition are taken into account.

In any case, the most important takeaway for the idealists is that, even at this early stage, Kant has provided us with an assurance that the categories must apply to the given manifold of intuition. We have no comparable assurance that such knowledge is possible in the case of things-in-themselves,

---

[11] Henrich (1969).
[12] Watkins (2010).
[13] An exception is Hegel's early piece *Faith and Knowledge* (1986), which appeals to Kant's transcendental imagination. The latter is treated not so much as a psychological faculty but as the Absolute, a successor to Spinoza's substance, prior to subject and object (thought and extension). Indeed, Kant's error is mistaking the former for the latter.

however, since they are not necessarily subject to these conditions. Already in the Analytic, then, Kant's "logic of truth," we have a powerful reason for believing that we can know only appearances and not things-in-themselves.[14] Yet the most important part of Kant's case against transcendent metaphysics will come only in a subsequent division, the Dialectic, Kant's "logic of illusion." We will postpone a closer consideration of it for Chapters 3 and 4.

2.2   Hegel's Swimming Objection Reconsidered: Defending a Logical Interpretation

In the opening sections of his *Encyclopedia Logic*, Hegel presents his "swimming objection" to Kant's critical philosophy.

> It is one of the main viewpoints of the Critical philosophy that, prior to setting out to acquire knowledge of God, the essence of things, etc., the *faculty of knowing* itself would have to be examined first in order to see whether it is capable of achieving this [*das Erkenntnisvermögen selbst vorher zu untersuchen sei, ob es solches zu leisten fähig sei*]; that one must first come to know the *instrument*, before one undertakes the work that is to be produced by means of it. For should the instrument be insufficient, all the effort would then have been expended in vain. – This thought has seemed so plausible that it has elicited the greatest admiration and acclaim and drawn knowing away from its interest in the objects and work on them and drawn it back to itself, i.e. to the formal aspect. If, however, we do not delude ourselves with words, it is easy to see that other tools may very well be examined and evaluated in ways other than undertaking the actual work for which they are determined. But the examination of knowing cannot take place other than by way of knowing. With this so-called instrument, examining it means nothing other than acquiring knowledge of it. But to want to know before one knows is as incoherent as the Scholastic's wise resolution to learn to swim, before he ventured into the water. (EL § 10)

In approaching Hegel's "swimming argument," I will begin with a summary not intended to be in any way controversial. Only then will I be in a position to introduce what I consider to be a new interpretation of this well-known argument.

---

[14] If this argument from the Analytic exhausted Kant's critique of metaphysics, then he would be guilty of making a type of argument that Ameriks calls a "short argument" for idealism (2000: Ch. 3 "Kant, Fichte and Short Arguments for Idealism"). Yet it is, in my view, meant to be supplemented by the argument of the Dialectic, an independent justification for transcendental idealism. Still, it would be a mistake to conclude from this that the Analytic does not contain a distinct critique of metaphysics, even if this critique is inadequate on its own. For a similar view of the Analytic as serving a preliminarily anti-metaphysical purpose, see Hatfield (2003).

Kant's critical philosophy confronts the enterprise of traditional metaphysics with a challenge. Traditional metaphysics claims a certain distinctive type of knowledge: "knowledge of God, the essences of things etc." (EL § 10). Kant therefore confronts its proponents with the critical question of whether such knowledge is even possible for beings like ourselves, and, if so, how its possibility can be explained. The question, it seems, can only be answered through a preliminary examination of the faculty we employ to attain knowledge: "the faculty of knowledge." It is as if the faculty is a tool or instrument, and we must conduct a preliminary examination of it to determine what it can and cannot be used to do.

At this point, however, a serious problem arises for the critical philosophy, at least according to Hegel. The problem is that Kant himself confronts a version of the very same challenge with which his critical philosophy confronted metaphysics. No less than metaphysics, the critical philosophy also attempts to acquire a distinctive form of knowledge: in this case, knowledge of the faculty of knowledge itself. The critical philosophy can therefore also be confronted with the question of whether this type of knowledge is possible for us, and, if so, how its possibility can be explained. The question is no less apt here than in it is in the case of metaphysics.

According to Hegel, however, the critical philosophy is incapable of providing a satisfactory answer to the question. Kant cannot argue here as he ordinarily would on pain of vicious circularity. In other words, he cannot argue that knowledge of the faculty of knowledge is possible on the grounds that this is completely consistent with the critical philosophy's own account of the nature and limits of that faculty. To do so would be to invoke the very form of knowledge whose possibility is in question.

Hegel explains the problem by returning to his metaphor of the tool or instrument. If the critical philosophy is to examine the tool or instrument we use to attain knowledge, then it must use that very tool or instrument. However, this is to risk the very misuse we wanted to prevent by examining it in the first place. Hence, the critical philosophy reaches an impasse. If it is to offer an account of the faculty of knowledge, it must itself claim knowledge. Yet according to the critical philosophy, no such claim is legitimate until an account of the faculty has been given. Wanting to know before one can know is like wanting to swim before getting wet.

Here, it is important to note a limitation of the swimming objection that is not often appreciated in the literature. The limitation concerns its conclusion that the critical philosophy cannot demonstrate the legitimacy of its own claims to knowledge. This conclusion is completely consistent with the possibility that these claims' legitimacy can be demonstrated in some other way. In particular, it allows for the possibility that there is some more fundamental source of justification for the critical philosophy's account of the nature and limits of the faculty of knowledge. Moreover, it allows for the possibility of a source that might uphold the legitimacy of the type of claim to knowledge made here.

Even so, the objection, if successful, would displace the critical philosophy as the ultimate arbiter of which claims to knowledge are legitimate. Henceforth, the critical philosophy, if it is to be justified at all, would have to derive its legitimacy from that more ultimate source. However, this means that the critical philosophy is more vulnerable than it might have initially appeared, since its claims could either be upheld by that more ultimate source or not. Ultimately, then, Hegel's swimming objection is best posed in the form of a dilemma for the critical philosophy. It must either concede that its basic presuppositions are unjustified or else renounce its status as the ultimate arbiter of whether they are justified.

Although it is seldom realized in the literature, the swimming objection is primarily directed at a specific part of the critical philosophy.[15] As Hegel's subsequent remarks make clear, it is meant to apply to Kant's treatment of the categories in the Transcendental Analytic of the first critique. Here we should recall that Hegel cites this as the main instance in which Kant succumbed to the temptation to "know before we know," or swim before getting wet.

> No doubt a very important step was taken by subjecting the determinations of the old metaphysics to scrutiny. Naive thinking moved innocently among those determinations, which produced themselves straightaway and of their own accord. No thought was given to the question to what extent these determinations have value and validity for themselves. It has already been remarked earlier that free thinking is one that has no presuppositions. The thinking of the old metaphysics was not free, because it allowed its determinations to count without further ado as something pre-existing, as an a priori which reflection did not itself examine. By contrast, the Critical philosophy made it its task to investigate to what extent the forms of thinking were capable of being of assistance in knowing the truth at all. More specifically, the faculty of knowledge was now supposed to be investigated

---

[15] Most commentators do not relate Hegel's swimming objection to his objection to the role of logic in Kant's metaphysical deduction, despite the clear connection Hegel himself draws in the text. This is true of Habermas (1971: Ch. 1: 7–10), Ameriks (1985: 18), Bristow (2007: Ch. 2: 66, 95), Stern (2009: Introduction) and Kreines (2015: 141) from one direction and Horstmann (1995) and Houlgate (2006: 12–23) from the other.

> prior to knowing. In this there is contained the correct thought that the
> forms of thought themselves must indeed be made the object of know-
> ing. However, the misunderstanding of wanting already to know prior to
> knowing or of wanting not to set foot in the water before one has learned to
> swim, very quickly creeps into the process. To be sure, the forms of thought
> should not be employed unexamined, but examining them is already itself
> a process of knowing. (EL § 41 Z)

Kant asks whether the type of knowledge claimed in metaphysics is possible for us, and, if so, how. In answering this question, he claims that our
faculty of knowledge is the source of certain nonempirical concepts, or
categories, that he will ultimately show can only be used to know appearances but not things-in-themselves. Yet we can now turn this question on
Kant's own project. Is such knowledge possible for us, and, if so, can Kant
explain how it is possible?

Let us simply consider the first and most elementary step in Kant's argument. This is his claim that the intelligible (conceptual) conditions on
objects, if there even were any, would have to be (all and only) the twelve
categories in his table. It is a preliminary to Kant's subsequent claim that
there are, in fact, such conditions and that they must be imposed by our
faculty of knowledge on all objects of possible experience. How, then, can
Kant even make this preliminary claim to knowledge concerning the identity of the categories, if there be any? Ordinarily, Kant explains the possibility of a certain form of knowledge in the following way. He invokes
the claim that our faculty of knowledge is the source of a certain set of
(intelligible) conditions to which the objects must necessarily conform.
However, Kant cannot justify the claim(s) before us in this way, since
doing so would beg the question. After all, we do not even know yet what
these (intelligible) conditions would be, let alone that they are, in fact,
imposed on the objects by us. This claim is not yet available to be appealed
to in the argument, especially at this early stage. Kant wants to make a
claim to knowledge but is doing so before knowledge is possible. That is
like wanting to swim before getting wet.

As we have seen, however, the swimming objection is consistent with the
possibility that the critical philosophy's account of the nature and limits of
our faculty of knowledge has some more fundamental source of justification. As Hegel concedes, Kant himself appears to exploit this possibility.
After all, he does not claim that his transcendental logic alone can justify
the claim in question but, rather, appeals to general (formal) logic. Kant
bases his table of categories on logic's table of forms of judgment. This does
not necessarily mean that Kant's claim is false, but it does mean that it is

vulnerable. It is beholden for its justification to a source more fundamental than the critical philosophy: logic. This source might uphold its claims, but it might also reveal them to be baseless. However, Hegel gives us a powerful reason for doubting that Kant's attempt to derive a complete table of categories from the logic of the day can succeed. For Hegel, as we have seen, this logic is "empirical," though not in any straightforward sense.

> It is well known that the Kantian philosophy made it very easy for locate the categories. The unity of self-consciousness is quite abstract and entirely indeterminate. How is one then to arrive at the categories? Fortunately, the forms of judgment are already listed *empirically* in ordinary logic. Now to judge is to think a determinate object. The various forms of judgment that had already been enumerated thus provide the various determinations of thought. (EL § 42 A, italics mine)

What can Hegel possibly mean in describing this logic as empirical? If ever there were an area of philosophy or inquiry more generally whose principles were *not* empirical, logic would seem to be it. Guyer speaks for many in expressing his bewilderment at the suggestion:

> Hegel's charge that Kant's list of categories is merely empirically derived is also peculiar … To be sure, he may not have made the method of his logical derivation of the several aspects and forms of judgment terribly clear, but there can be no doubt that Kant intended his derivation of the categories to proceed by entirely a priori means from the underlying insight into the judgmental nature of knowledge or even consciousness itself. (1993: 187)

Yet if Guyer is here suggesting that the accusation of empiricism applies *directly* to Kant's table of categories then he is incorrect. It applies to the table of categories only *indirectly*, via the prior accusation that the table of logical forms of judgment is empirical.

Once we see that this is so, the table of the categories itself recedes, and the table of forms of judgment moves to the fore. Fundamentally at issue is a problem with the logic of the day from which Kant draws his table of judgments. Here, the account of Hegel's relation to traditional logic from the last chapter becomes important to understanding his critique of Kant.[16] As we saw in the last chapter, Hegel acknowledges that the traditional logic does not appeal to sense experience. However, he reminds us that it does appeal to a type of intellectual experience. This is the type of intellectual experience we have when we abstract from the sensibly given content of our thinking and focus only on the formal principles discovered

---

[16] See also Houlgate (2006:15).

therein. We then find they are incontrovertible for us. Here, it is important to ward off a potential misunderstanding. For this is not to say that we achieve intellectual intuition of an independently existing object. Rather we acquire self-knowledge of ourselves as subjects. The experience is meant to establish that these principles are constitutive norms of the faculty of thought. The purely intellectual knowledge achieved in logic is not rational psychology. The inconsistency with Kant's aspirations for his critical philosophy is much more subtle.

Unfortunately, this strategy does not completely solve the problem in Aristotle's original account that Kant is intent on overcoming. Even supposing we were in a position to distinguish knowledge in its purity from knowledge adulterated by the contributions of other faculties, there is a deeper issue. Knowledge from intellectual experience is no less vulnerable to the problem of induction than knowledge acquired from sense experience. Hence, the table of forms of judgment is incomplete. So too is the account of the understanding's activities it represents. Kant himself is aware of the centrality of the method of abstraction to logic, in general, and to its treatment of the forms of judgement, in particular. He cites the method of abstraction from sensible content as the source of the table of logical forms of judgment: "If we abstract from all content of a judgment, and consider only the mere form ... we find that the function of thought in judgment can be brought under four heads, each of which contains three moments" (A 70/B 95).[17] Yet from Hegel's perspective, Kant does not realize that this method is unable to yield completeness.

This idealist objection to Kant's table of categories has been seen by generations of interpreters as based on an uncharitable and oversimplified understanding of his project. Clearly there are more resources in Kant's text than the idealists appear to appreciate. The true principle from which both the forms of judgment and categories derive may be the understanding, or, more properly, the Idea, of this faculty. It may be the four headings of each table, themselves descriptive of the four activities constitutive of judgment. Perhaps it can be derived from judgment itself. Unsurprisingly, then, there is a long tradition of efforts to defend him from this idealist objection, including those of Klaus Reich, Michael Wolff and others.[18]

I here restrict myself to a brief remark in response. It seems to me that, in attempting to give Kant his due, this project misses the deeper import

---

[17] See also Cohen's defense of Kant against a similar accusation from Herbart. Their dispute centers around this passage (1885: § 7).
[18] Reich (1992) and Wolff (1995).

of the idealist objection to Kant's deduction of the categories. The deeper import of this objection becomes clear only when we realize that it is meant to work in concert with the swimming objection. Ultimately, the objection does not simply claim that *no* proof of completeness could be given. This would just be one horn of the dilemma. It also proposes that *any* such proof would have to rely on claims about our cognitive power in a way that is un-self-uncritical. This is the other horn. Far from refuting Hegel's objection, the success of these projects might conceivably confirm it. Nearly always, these authors are forced to seek a proof of completeness elsewhere than the Metaphysical Deduction, but this does not so much resolve as relocate the problem. Where if not from a claim about our cognitive power taken to be brute justified would a new basis for pure general logic be sought? The only solution to this problem, I think, can be to accept it as a risk but seek a more rigorous justification for this claim. That is what the German idealists are doing when they seek to identify a first principle from which all of Kant's philosophy, including general logic, can be derived.

2.3 Surmounting the Swimming Objection 1, toward a Post-Kantian Cogito: Reinhold, Fichte

Although the swimming objection is sometimes taken to show that Kant's critical project is untenable and metaphysics legitimate, it does not in and of itself establish any conclusion as dramatic as this one.[19] In a way this is unsurprising since, as Hegel himself reminds us, the objection originates with Reinhold, a figure who would never have embraced such a radically anti-Kantian conclusion. In this section, I will turn to Hegel's account of how Kant's immediate followers, especially Reinhold and Fichte, attempt to respond on his behalf to the swimming objection. They do so by attempting to reform the critical philosophy, rather than by rejecting it in favor of a more traditional form of metaphysics as Hegel will later do. I will then examine why Hegel does not find their proposals convincing.

Reinhold's proposal for how to avoid attempting to know before we can legitimately be said to know is his hypothetical method. In this method, the claim to knowledge with which one begins is proposed as a hypothesis or "problematic" claim.[20] In other words, we are endorsing it only

---

[19] Kreines (2015) and Stern (2009).
[20] See Habermas (1971: 7–8), who also discusses Reinhold's "problematic method" as well as its afterlife in Germany.

provisionally. Proceeding on the basis of this claim, we then arrive at a more fundamental ("primordial") truth. On the basis of this truth, we could then potentially vindicate the hypothesis with which we began. Provisional endorsement would then be converted into full or unqualified endorsement. There is a circle, then, but it is not vicious. It is, we might say, virtuous, to borrow a term from contemporary solutions to the logo-centric predicament that rely on so-called "virtuous circularity." Yet Hegel is unimpressed with Reinhold's proposal:

> *Reinhold* who recognized the confusion that prevails in beginning in this way, proposed as a remedy that one make a preliminary start with a *hypo-thetical* and *problematic* kind of philosophizing and continue in this vein Heaven knows how [*man weiss nicht wie*] – until somehow at some point along the line it would emerge that in this way one had arrived at the *pri-mordial truth*. Looked at more closely, this would come down to the usual procedure, namely analysis of an empirical foundation or a provisional assumption that has been put into a definition. (EL § 10A)

Hegel's objection to this approach is that it is self-defeating. He confronts it with a dilemma. Either the hypothetical claim with which we begin ("if x, then y") is a premise in the argument for the conclusion we want to reach or it is not. If it is a premise, then its hypothetical character will prevent us from reaching a conclusion that holds with necessity. If is not a prem-ise in the argument, however, then it is a mere heuristic device that can be dismissed. The real first premise in the argument is the first categorical statement made in our science. Yet this merely raises anew the problem of finding an adequate foundation for philosophy. Should it be some empiri-cal fact? A definition? Something else? We are back where we started. As we saw, Kant himself confronts a version of this problem when he proposes the Copernican revolution in the form of a hypothetical claim ("If it were true that the objects had to conform to our knowledge, then ..."). Yet unlike Reinhold, Kant correctly sees that if the hypothetical claim is meant to be the first premise, then anything it was used to establish would only have a conditional status. It is likely for this reason that Kant acknowledges the need to establish it apodictically in the Critique itself.

For Hegel, Fichte's approach is much more promising, and also more immediately relevant to the project of deriving the categories:

> The unity of self-consciousness, is quite abstract and entirely indetermi-nate. How is one then to arrive at the of the categories? ... It remains the *Fichtean* philosophy's profound contribution ... to have reminded us that the *thought-determinations* must be exhibited in their *necessity* and that it is essential that they be *derived*. (EL § 42A)

As with Reinhold, Fichte's approach has us begin with a putative claim to knowledge, rather than attempting to abstain from making any such claims until we are in a position to show they are consistent with the nature and limits of our knowledge. How, then, can we know whether the claim is legitimate or not? Is there not the risk that we will endorse a claim that will later turn out to be illegitimate? The answer is that we begin with a claim that is indubitably certain. There can be no question as to whether it is true or false, let alone whether it is a legitimate claim to knowledge or not. We then proceed to show that this indubitably certain principle entails others no less certain than it.

The indubitably certain principle with which Fichte begins is a version of Descartes' Cogito, "I am" or "I exist," adapted so as to respect Kant's critique of rational psychology. Fichte records the debt to Descartes himself, although it is clear that he understands it to extend more widely:

> That our proposition is the absolutely basic principle of all knowledge [*als absoluten Grundsatz alles Wissens*] was pointed out by Kant, in his deduction of the categories. But he did not lay it down as the basic principle. Descartes, before him, put forward a similar proposition: cogito, ergo sum – which need not have been merely the minor premise and conclusion of a syllogism. (WL 1: 98–99/SK 100)

For Descartes, it is impossible to doubt my existence as a thinker. Just in virtue of doubting it, I would be thinking. This thought, however, must come from a thinker, me. So far, so Cartesian. Here the parallels end, however. For Fichte, all that follows from the Cogito argument is that I, the thinker of this thought, am. However, I cannot know anything further about myself on this basis. Indeed, it does not even follow from the Cogito argument that the self whose existence I learn of existed before or will exist after. "What was I then before I came to self-consciousness? [*ehe ich zum Selbstbewusstseyn kam*] The natural reply is: I did not exist at all for I was not a self" (WL 1: 97/SoK 98). It follows from this that self-consciousness is not a matter of becoming conscious of a preexisting object. Rather, it is only in the act of being reflected upon that the self is first of all constituted as a self.[21] For Fichte, self-consciousness is self-constitution in a way that it was not for rational psychology. This makes the self different from any object, material, immaterial or otherwise. For an object to exist and to be reflected upon in an act of thinking are distinct. For example, a table can exist without being reflected upon by me. Yet in the case of subjects, these

---

[21] See McNulty (2016).

coincide: "To posit oneself and to be are, as applied to the self, perfectly Identical" (WL 1: 98/SoK 99). By treating the self as a distinctive type of object, the rationalist or Cartesian metaphysics of soul substance fails to respect this point. So too in a different way do empiricist bundle views of the self, materialist views of the mind as reducible to the brain and, indeed, a host of others. According to Fichte, all of these positions, different as they are from one another, share a common error. All illicitly assimilate consciousness of self to consciousness of objects. Yet, according to Fichte, Kant's "I think" gives us a way of thinking about the self that respects both the truth of the cogito argument and the limits of what it can establish.[22] We can know little more about the "I think" than that it is present in a certain act of accompanying my representations: "I think A, B, and C." It has no characteristics beyond its ability to do so.

Fichte claims to be following Kant's lead as well as departing from him in a fairly crucial respect (WL 1: 475ff./SK 48ff.). For Kant, the paradigmatic form of self-consciousness is the consciousness I have of my own representations ("The "I think" must be able to accompany my representations ..."). Fichte disagrees. Before I can become conscious of my representations as mine, he argues, there must be someone whose representations they are: me. This condition is fulfilled only in a distinct form of self-consciousness achieved in the Cogito. This is not consciousness of my representations but consciousness of me. Indeed, Fichte claims that the former presupposes the latter. To reverse them, Fichte maintains, would be to render the necessary unity of consciousness contingent: more specifically, contingent on given sensible representations.

> Why 'I' is being spoken of here? That, perchance, which the Kantians blithely piece together from a manifold of intuitions, in none of which it was contained individually though it is present in all together; so that the above cited words of Kant would mean this: I, who think D, am the same I who thought C and B and A, and through the thinking of my manifold thoughts I first become I for myself, namely that which is identical in the manifold? In that case Kant would be just such a miserable babbler as the said Kantians; for then, according to him, the possibility of all thinking would be conditioned. (SW 1: 475–476/WL 48–49)

Put another way, pure apperception, as Fichte understands it, would be adulterated or rendered impure by sensible representations, since which

---

[22] I here follow Longuenesse (2017), who argues that Kant accepts a version of the Cogito. On this view, Kant's alleged rejection of the Cogito in the paralogisms is merely a rejection of the idea that the Cogito argument by itself entails a rationalist metaphysics of soul substance.

ones a person has is contingent and varies across individuals. Admittedly, this worry can seem overblown from a Kantian perspective, since Kant famously claims in the Deduction that self-knowledge and knowledge of objects of experience are mutually dependent. Fichte denies this, insisting on a more primitive form of self-knowledge, prior to knowledge of objects (of experience). Fichte believes that Kant is wrong to resist the idea of a more primitive form of self-knowledge. What resistance there is to this idea in Kant is based on the mistaken belief that it is a form of rationalist metaphysics. Once we break that association, as Fichte does with his unique post-Kantian version of the Cogito argument, we are free to appeal to consciousness of self in a way that respects the critical philosophy.

However, Fichte is breaking with Kant in other more profound ways, as signaled in a remark from the introduction to the *Wissenschaftslehre*: "This intuiting of himself that is required of the philosopher in performing the act whereby the self arises for him I call intellectual intuition" (SW 1: 46). For Kant, concepts without intuitions are empty, intuitions without concepts blind (A 51/B 75). Yet Fichte is claiming that the I-concept is necessarily nonempty, or object-related all on its own. This is so even when no sensible representation is present. The Cogito is possible in a sensory deprivation tank, as Anscombe memorably claims in her essay on the first person.[23] For Fichte, this counterexample to Kant's "emptiness" thesis has more dramatic implications. One of Kant's most foundational commitments is that we human beings are finite knowers. We do not create the objects we know. They must exist independently of the act in which they are thought of using concepts. They must affect us in the relevant way and produce intuitions in us. Perhaps a divine knower would not operate under this constraint, but we are not such a knower. This divine knower would enjoy intellectual intuition, whereas our intuition is sensible (meaning our understanding is discursive).

Yet Fichte holds that we human knowers do partake of the intellectual intuition of a divine knower, albeit in a more modest way than Kant envisions. Indeed, we do so in the most ordinary act of thinking: the use of the I-concept. As soon as the I-concept is used by the subject, the particular object it describes is always already present: the subject herself. In this modest respect then, we finite human knowers are infinite knowers. In performing the "I think" we have a type of knowledge that is not dependent on any externally given object, a fortiori, any

---

[23] Anscombe (1975), but see also Peacocke (2014).

object of sensible intuition. Instead, we have an intellectual intuition of ourselves. Dramatic as these departures from Kant are, however, they are in the service of a recognizably Kantian aim. Although this is a larger topic than I can discuss here, Fichte believes his amendments are required to defend the freedom of the Kantian subject, even in its capacity as a theoretical knower.

For Fichte, the first and most important step philosophy must take after laying down its first principle, the I, is to deduce the not-I, a world independent from the I. Here, Fichte has a version of Descartes' problem. Descartes, once he was certain of his own existence, needed to prove that of the "external world." Fichte's not-I is not as determinate as the external world, but in both cases there is the need to take a step beyond the subject and into the world. Here, the Cartesian heritage gives Fichte a problem Kant does not have. That is because in Kant the self-consciousness of the subject and its consciousness of objects presuppose one another – indeed, they are co-constitutive. An abstract version of this point is made in Kant's Transcendental Deduction and a more concrete one later in the Refutation of Idealism.

Yet, as we have seen, Fichte has a different understanding of self-consciousness that blocks this type of move. For Fichte, self-consciousness is a prior phenomenon in which the subject is to itself an object. Hence, he must advance beyond this first stage to one in which the external world makes its presence known. For Fichte, however, the problem posed by the not-I differs from the type of global "external world" skepticism dramatized in Descartes. In Descartes, the problem is that the external world might differ radically from the way I perceive it to be, like in the evil demon or dreaming scenarios. In Fichte, by contrast, the problem is that there might be no mind-independent world at all, a problem prior to that of whether the external world is as I imagine it to be. Fichte's interest in addressing this problem may have been provoked by the early and influential criticisms of Kant's idealism as a form of Berkeleyan "subjective" idealism. It is likely that these discussions gave him an appreciation of the difference between Berkeleyan idealism and the distinct threat that Cartesian skeptical scenarios imply. In this way, the threat of a form of solipsism assumes priority over the threat of such scenarios as "the evil demon" or "the dreamer."

Yet there is an additional reason that advancing from the first to the second step is so important for Fichte. In attempting to deduce the not-I from the I, Fichte also means to refute the type of reductive materialism, at this time closely associated with Spinoza. The form of reductive materialism represents another path open to systematic philosophers of the period, though not to idealists. In taking this path, one begins with the not-I, a nonthinking substance. One then attempts to explain away the existence of self-consciousnesses on this basis. In other words, the project is not the idealist one of explaining the not-I by appealing to the I but the materialist one of explaining the I by appealing to the not-I. It would be legitimate to wonder if this position could fairly be attributed to Spinoza. After all, Spinoza himself treats thought as an attribute of substance, alongside extension. This means mind and body exhibit parallelism, with each mode of the attribute of thought having a counterpart body in the attribute of extension. However, this is not tantamount to a reduction of thought to extension so much as it is the subordination of both to the substance of which there are so many attributes. As we will soon see, German idealist followers would soon move beyond this one-sided portrayal of Spinoza, coming to see the latter as a kind of ally rather than a foe. Indeed, a more charitable attitude toward his views on precisely this issue, that is. the issue of mind and body, is an important part of the transition from the subjective idealisms of Kant and Fichte to the objective idealisms of Schelling and Hegel. Yet this is getting ahead of ourselves. Regardless of whether this type of eliminative materialist project is Spinoza's own (it is almost certainly not), Fichte must address the threat it poses. He aims to do so by precluding the materialist alternative. If the not-I can be deduced from the I, Fichte argues, then the ground is cut from under the materialist. There can be no beginning a philosophical system with the not-I and explaining (away) the I. Yet, if Fichte's project fails, then eliminative materialism is a live possibility.

At least in the early *Wissenschaftslehre*, Fichte's argument for advancing from the I to the not-I invokes logic. From a Hegelian perspective, this suggests a further instance in which transcendental philosophy's inability to noncircularly self-justify requires it to dogmatically rely on the formal logic of the day. In this tradition, the most basic law of logic is the law of identity: A is A, or A=A.[24] This is the law that explains why analytic truths are always true. The reason is that they can all be reduced to identities through a method of substituting equivalent concepts. For example, the analytic truth a bachelor is an unmarried man can be reduced to the identity an unmarried man is an unmarried man through this method of substitution.

---

[24] See Leibniz's essay "Primary Truths": "The primary truths are those which assert the same thing of itself or deny the opposite of its opposite. For example, A is A, A is not not A" (Leibniz 1989: 30).

As Fichte formulates it, the first principle of philosophy ("I am I") is just the first and most basic instance of the logical law of identity (A=A) obtained when we apply that law to the Cogito (I am). It is the "material" version of this "formal" principle. The law of identity simply says that if anything exists then it is self-identical, but it does not imply that anything exists. It is a hypothetical, rather than an apodictic, statement. As Fichte writes, "In insisting that the above proposition is intrinsically certain, we are not insisting that A is the case ... On the contrary, what we are saying is 'if A exists, then A exists.'" (WL I: 93/SK 94). Yet the Cogito differs, since it states that I, the thinker of this thought, am. Hence, the Cogito can be used as a foundation on which the logical law of identity rests. Without the Cogito, the law would simply have the form of a conditional: if A, then A. Yet with the addition of the Cogito, it is a categorical: A is A. Put another way, the I-concept furnishes the first and most basic instance of the logical law, A=A. That is why Fichte combines them in a statement of his system's first principle: I=I.

How, then, do we deduce the not-I? Fichte appeals to the next most basic law of logic, noncontradiction, $A \neq -A$, which he regards as equivalent to the law of identity (its "negative version") (SW I: 101–102/SK 101). If it is equivalent, then the I am I implies that the $I \neq -I$. In other words, it entails a form of subject–object dualism. This may be a successful strategy, but it suggests that the foundational principles of Fichte's philosophy stand in some type of complex relation of interdependence with the laws of formal logic.

Hegel holds that there is no clear, compelling reason that the I entails the not-I, none given by Fichte anyway (WdL 21: 64/SoL 54). In particular, Fichte's "logical" reason is not a valid one. It relies uncritically on the logic of the day, something Hegel maintains critical philosophers should not do. Hegel suspects that the true source of Fichte's conviction that this second step follows the first is not what he claimed it is. Fichte relied instead on the empirical fact that we are confronted with a world of objects distinct from us that affect our sense organs. Yet if the second step of the deduction is an empirical principle, then Fichte's ambitious strategy of argument fails. Recall that this strategy involved beginning with a principle indubitably certain and then showing that it entailed others no less certain than it. However, no such entailment has been shown to hold between the I and the not-I. If there is a not-I, then this is a type of empirical fact of which I am aware. It is a contingent truth, rather than a necessary one. It is not certain, even if highly probable. Hence, its ability to render all subsequent principles certain is undermined.

2.4 Surmounting the Swimming Objection 2, toward a Post-Kantian Ontological Argument: Jacobi, Hegel

Hegel will break with Fichte's Cartesian conviction that philosophy ought to begin with a claim to certain knowledge and defend an alternative that aligns him much more closely with the figure Fichte thought of as idealism's main opponent: the dogmatist Spinoza. Yet it is no part of Hegel's Fichte-critique to deny that the Fichtean version of the Cogito (I am I) is genuinely certain or indubitable. On the contrary, Hegel concedes this: "In the need to begin with something absolutely certain, i.e. the certainty of oneself ... these and other similar forms can be regarded as what must be the first" (EL § 86A). As we saw, however, the problem with Fichte's approach was not that its starting point was uncertain but that it was unable to advance a single step beyond this starting point.

Hence, Hegel will propose a different first principle, Being, one whose claim on our attention differs. Far from being especially secure, such a principle is insecure – arguably uniquely so. It would not be quite right to say that Being is uncertain, since it lacks the form of a proposition, so it cannot be affirmed or denied. Yet we could say that no sooner has it been introduced it is overturned and its opposite adopted: nothing. As long as we bear in mind that these are pseudo-propositions, we could say that the claim, the Absolute is Being, has been replaced by the counterclaim, the Absolute is Nothing. Admittedly, we do not yet know what either even means, let alone what argument would take us from the first to the second. However, it should be clear that the argument in which they figure has a different structure than Fichte's does. In this structure of argument, the inadequacy of our first principle is not a hindrance, as it might be in Fichte's more Cartesian system. On the contrary, it is what allows us to advance to the second step, from Being to Nothing, something Fichte could not do. Why, though, beyond the ability to advance in this way, would we want to begin with a first principle that is vulnerable to being overturned in this way?

Another reason is that this principle is more primitive, conceptually speaking: "the absolutely first, most abstract" (EL § 86 A). Being is presupposed by the Fichtean starting point of I am I, the Schellingian principle of identity, the law of identity A is A, and so on (EL § 86 A). All are concepts of beings or entities of some type and so presuppose some understanding of the concept of what it is to be anything at all. In the case of Fichte's first principle, the priority of being is especially clear. To say that I *am* I or that A *is* A is just to employ the identity relation, itself the relational version of the nonrelational category of being.[25] What, though, is it for anything to be at all? This is a prior question. If our aim is certainty, Fichte's I=I must be philosophy's first principle. Yet if it is conceptual primitiveness, then Hegel's Being deserves that title. Evidently, Hegel holds that certainty is less important than conceptual primitiveness, and it is not difficult to imagine what his argument for this might have been. We can only be certain of some proposition if we know what it means and therefore what the concepts deployed in it mean. Yet the only theory that can settle our doubts about meaning, especially the meanings of a priori concepts or categories, is one that starts from a primitive concept and explains all others in terms of it. This is precisely what Hegel's theory of the categories is meant to provide, and it is why he breaks with the Cartesian-cum-Kantian starting point of Fichte's system.

Yet there is an additional reason that Being has a claim to be philosophy's first principle, beyond the fact that it is conceptually primitive. Being is not only the most fundamental concept that there is but also the most comprehensive. Being and other concepts like it purport to comprehend everything that there is. Outside of them, we are told, there is nothing at all. Everything is a being or entity. Anything that was not would not exist. In other words, it is not simply the German Idealist search for a foundational "first principle" that informs Hegel's choice of Being. It is also the Spinozistic ideal of a form of philosophy that comprehends the whole of what is (the *hen-kai-pan*, "one and all").

However, we need to distinguish four distinct ways in which Being might comprehend the whole of what is.

The first is simply that Being is the whole of what is by virtue of being immediate. As the indeterminate, Being is not one being among others, distinguished from them by some determination. It is, rather, the only thing. More accurately, it is *at most* the only thing. As we will soon learn, Being could be nothing at all. What Being is most certainly not, however, is a particular being.

The second reason is that Being is the whole of what is by default. Particular beings simply are not part of the story yet for a reason that is as much semantic as metaphysical. The categories for such beings are not yet available: something, the finite and so on. These are categories of determinate being, which is not at issue at this early stage. Determinate being is a combination of being and negation: *omnis determination est*

---

[25] This is likely inspired by Hölderlin's critique of Fichte in the fragment *Urteil und Sein* (1962). See Henrich (1965/66).

negatio. Even negation, however, in its most primitive form, nothing-ness, has not yet appeared.

Strictly speaking, this would be the most faithful way to read Hegel's first principle, especially if one wants to adhere rigidly to the strictures of his method. However, it seems to me not entirely illicit to anticipate the advent of particular beings and the categories used to describe them. Some authors, intent on producing a commentary scrupulously faithful to Hegel's method, disagree.

Let us, then, consider a third possibility. Being might be a concept that comprehends multiple instances, the beings. Indeed, it would compre-hend every conceivable instance, since everything is being. On this view, Being is instantiated in all of the beings. Even this is somewhat infelici-tous, as the Concept too is a later discovery. Yet it does capture the way in which Being is what all have in common. However, this one-over-many structure does not, I think, suffice for Hegel's purposes. It suggests that the plurality of beings and Being are equally real, and I do not think this is the case for Hegel.

However, I will ultimately defend a fourth and final view. On this view, Being is a distinctive type of whole whose (proper) parts are the beings. Indeed, this would be a whole that is prior to its parts, not unlike space as Kant understands in the Transcendental Aesthetic. In just the same way that all particular spaces are "negations" of the one infinite space, obtained from it by drawing lines around a part of it, so too all particular beings would be "negations" of Being, obtained from it in a broadly analogous way. Of course, the critical-era Kant thought that this structure could only be found in the objects owing to the forms of intuition: space and time. A form of intuition, as itself an intuition, is a singular object with parts, whereas the relationship between a concept and its instances differs. (Unlike particular spaces, in relation to space, particular dogs are not nec-essarily parts of a single, all-encompassing, dog.) Each form of intuition, as a whole prior to its parts, is a "*totum analyticum*," as opposed to a "*totum syntheticum*," a totality rather than a sum.[26]

Given that this is a generic structure that each specific form of intuition bears, however, it should be possible to form a general concept of it: It is simply the general structure each of these forms, space and time, instanti-ate. Indeed, the critical Kant did at one point in *Critique* entertain the possibility of a conceptual version of such a totality: the *omnitudo realitatis* or *ens realissimum*, that is the God of the ontological argument. It too

---

[26] Al Azm (1972: 9).

is a *totum analyticum*, a whole prior to its parts, an unlimited being of which all further beings are just so many limited forms. What is more, the precritical Kant, more friendly to the ontological argument, insisted that such a being would furnish "the only possible basis for a proof of the existence of God." Given its importance to the ontological argument, which I believe lies at the center of Hegel's thought, it is this final version of Being's comprehensiveness that I choose.

In Chapter 4, I will discuss Hegel's relationship to this Kantian idea in more detail, but it is noteworthy here that Hegel equates his first definition of the Absolute, pure Being, with the *omnitudo realitatis* or *ens realissimum*.

> When being is expressed as a predicate of the absolute, this provides the first definition of the latter: the absolute is being ... It is the definition of the Eleatics, but at the same time also the familiar one that God is the sum total of all realities. The point is that one is supposed to abstract from the limitedness inherent in every reality, so that God is nothing but the real in all reality, the supremely real. Insofar as reality already contains a reflection, this idea is expressed more immediately in what Jacobi says about the God of Spinoza, namely that he is the principium of being in all existence. (EL § 86A)[27]

Here, it is significant that Hegel cites not only Eleatic monists such as Parmenides, and modern ones such as Spinoza, but also the language Kant used for the God of the ontological argument. As Harrelson has shown, Hegel here refers to the "*Inbegriff aller Realitäten,*" a German phrase for the *omnitudo realitatis*, or sum total of all realities.[28] I would here add that Hegel also uses the term "*Allerrealster,*" a German term for *ens realissimum*. Finally, the references to Spinoza and Jacobi are significant. Jacobi had argued that space, on Kant's conception, resembled Spinoza's God. He had further connected both to the *omnitudo realitatis* and to the *ens realissimum* of the Transcendental Dialectic. He had done this with a polemical intent. If Kant was prepared to recognize two totalities, space and time, why was he reluctant to recognize another, God? Of course, Kant would insist that when we are thinking of objects of possible experience, by means of the categories, we progress from parts to whole and not the other way. However, it is precisely this Kantian claim that the idealists are calling into question.

---

[27] Cf. Jacobi (1994: 323).

[28] Most others writing on the ontological argument in Hegel ignore this. See the otherwise excellent Williams (2017). An exception is Harrelson (2009).

This brings us to yet another distinctive feature of Being, which qualifies it to serve as the point of departure for Hegel's system. A concept such as Being is not only the most fundamental as well as the most comprehensive but also one that could not possibly fail to be instantiated. If any concept is instantiated in the world, then the concept of Being must be.[29] Everything is a being or entity, and in this sense a limitation of the unlimited Being. In this regard, Being has something in common with the I-concept as Fichte understood it in his version of the Cogito argument. Both are concepts that are necessarily nonempty.[30] However, this is for a different reason in each case. In the case of Being, it is because of the relationship between Being and beings or entities. The former is the unlimited being in comparison with which the latter are mere limitations. In the case of the I-concept, it is because the act of its use in thought or speech of the knowing subject automatically secures for it an object: the knower or speaker himself or herself.

As is so often the case in Hegel, we have a similar structure of argument to those employed by Kant and Fichte, but with a crucial difference. Hegel has completely stripped it of any psychological or epistemological association whatsoever. He has redeployed it in the form of Spinozism. Put another way, at the outset of the logic, the I, subject or thinker, must *not* "posit" but, rather, completely annul himself or herself. This he or she must do at least provisionally if the standpoint of self-determining subjectivity or idealism is to ultimately prove superior to that of Spinoza's substance or dogmatism.

Hegel himself was well aware of the analogy between these two classic arguments from early modern philosophy, the Cogito and the ontological argument. He draws a parallel between them himself in the *Encyclopedia* in the section entitled "Third Position of Thought towards Objectivity: Jacobi." The context is a discussion of the role of both Cartesian arguments in Jacobi's thought, and Hegel makes clear that he regards them as having a parallel structure:

1. The plain inseparability of thinking and the being of the thinker – *cogito ergo sum* …
2. Similarly, the inseparability of the representation of God and his concrete existence. (EL § 76)

In the surrounding sections, Hegel argues against Jacobi, a figure who maintained that it is faith rather than reason that justifies our belief in

---

[29] Cf. Redding and Bubbio (2014: 478).
[30] Cf. Redding and Bubbio (2014: 475).

the most fundamental truths. It would be easy to dismiss the Jacobian approach as unworthy of serious consideration, and Hegel's own discussions of it occasionally create this impression (he describes it as opening the door to relativism, irrationalism, subjectivism and so on).

Yet this would be overhasty, since, by faith, Jacobi primarily means those forms of justification that are noninferential. Seen in this light, Humean empiricism is a defense of faith. Humean empiricism shows us that our beliefs about causal connection are products of custom, rather than reason ("more properly felt than judged of"). Yet in a way, this improves their standing rather than undermining it. It shows that they are subject to a fundamentally different set of standards from those of reason, standards they may be more successful in meeting. It is therefore unsurprising that, after Spinoza, Hume is the philosopher about whom Jacobi wrote the most. Seen in this light, Jacobi's aim is not to reject philosophy in favor of folk-religion but, rather, to uncover overlooked continuities between the two.

In this context, Jacobi's significance for Hegel is in leading him to appreciate a connection between the cogito and the ontological argument. Jacobi identifies a wide range of beliefs that he claims can only be upheld by faith, because they cannot be justified inferentially. Among them are our belief in our own existence as well as our belief in God, both beliefs that earlier rationalist philosophers had attempted to prove through argument (EL § 64). Here, Jacobi follows Kant, who had shown that the Wolffian versions of these arguments based on syllogistic inference fail. Hegel appreciates the connection Jacobi has drawn between these beliefs and also regards them as closely related. Still, he responds by attempting to show that these beliefs, though not supported by syllogistic inference, are based on more than faith.

In part, Hegel is here siding with Descartes himself and against his disciples in the Leibniz–Wolff school. True, the Cogito is not a syllogistic inference, as Hegel himself points out in this discussion (EL § 64). If it were, it would not be sound. The major premise, anything that thinks exists, is not indubitable in the way that the claim "I think, I am" is (EL § 64). Nevertheless, this claim is upheld by more than faith, because it involves a transition in thought that is rationally necessary. This is the transition from the presence of a thought to that of a thinker who is its author. Regardless of whether the argument is ultimately successful, the important point is that it is an argument and not a brute assertion.

Hegel argues that something broadly similar is true of the ontological argument. Here too Hegel concedes that the argument is not syllogistic and sides with Jacobi against the Scholastics. Here too there is no general truth one can assume as a premise without begging the question. The major premise "Anything whose essence is to exist, exists" presupposes what is to be inferred as the conclusion: "God, whose essence is to exist, exists." Not only the Cogito but also the ontological proof cannot be recast in syllogistic terms. However, Hegel is unwilling to regard the latter as a product of faith. Though no syllogism, it involves a rationally necessary transition in thought from the idea of something whose essence is to exist to the impossibility of its nonexistence. In this way, Hegel hopes to win over his Romantic anti-rationalist opponents by showing that traditional rationalist forms of philosophy have more resources than they appreciate.

We might expect Hegel to uphold the claim of an infinite category such as Being to encompass the whole of what is. Precisely not. Nearly always, Hegel will argue that the claim cannot be upheld. The claim gives rise to a type of incoherence that renders it unacceptable. Famously, Hegel argues that this is true of the first such definition of the Absolute. In order for Being to be everything that there is, it would have to be devoid of any determinate (specific, particular) properties. Yet if that were so, then it would effectively be nothing at all. However, this does not mean that Hegel simply abandons the aspiration to know the Absolute comprehensively. Famously, the incoherence we are confronted with is of a certain specific type that allows us to move forward, rather than simply abandoning the search. The discovery we make is that if the concept were all-encompassing in the way it claims to be, it could not be all-encompassing in that way. In each case, however, Hegel will attempt to resolve the paradox so that the claim to comprehensiveness can be upheld. In the case before us, the result will be a better definition of the Absolute that combines Being and Nothing in a non incoherent or paradoxical way: Becoming. This is a concept defined as a type of transition from non-Being to Being. The transition would be analogous to that from not being an adult to being one, though the case that concerns is more abstract.

The concept of Being is instantiated in the world, if anything is – but what if nothing is? This is a problem for any thinker who argues for the existence of God via the conditional "If anything exists, then God does." The possibility that nothing exists is explicitly considered by Hegel. It is the one he raises immediately after considering Being and turns to an alternative definition of the Absolute as Nothing. Hegel claims that this is a standpoint like that occupied by the "Buddhists" for whom none of the objects we take to exist in our ordinary lives does, in fact, exist (EL § 87; cf. WdL 21: 325/SoL 283).

Understanding how Hegel rebuts this view requires us to take account of a less well-known aspect of his position. Famously, Hegel claims that Being and Nothing are the same, but it is too seldom realized that this claim is something like a biconditional. In other words, it is not merely that Being, devoid of all determinate properties, cannot be (distinguished from) Nothing. The reverse is also true, though the reason is harder to state. I understand it to be a variation on "the problem of Plato's beard," popularized by Quine but originally from the *Sophist*.[31] This is the problem of how we can deny that something fictional or imaginary exists: for example, "Plato's beard" or Pegasus. If there really is no such thing, then there is nothing of which we would deny existence. Yet if there is such a thing, denying its existence is ruled out from the outset.

I take Hegel's claim that Being is Nothing to be a version of the paradox of nonexistence, albeit applied to an indeterminate entity rather than ordinary determinate ones. Being is indistinguishable from Nothing, but the reverse is also true. Nothing is indistinguishable from Being. Indeed, and as others have pointed out, it is not just that we cannot distinguish them but that there is no distinction. That is why Hegel rejects nihilism, the belief that nothing exists. It is no less a nonstarter than the monism of Being.

In claiming that the concept of Being has these three distinctive properties, fundamental, comprehensive and necessarily instantiated, Hegel takes himself to have revived an older argument from the history of philosophy: the ontological argument. Like the proponent of the ontological argument, Hegel has claimed there is something whose definition entails its existence. Needless to say, this does not imply that Hegel endorses all versions of the argument, let alone those made by traditional theists. Hegel's version assumes a nontraditional God, closer to Parmenidean Being or Spinoza's substance. Although not often remarked upon in the literature, there are many signs of this in Hegel's discussion of Being. As we have already said, in the *Encyclopedia* he equates it with the *omnitudo realitatis* or *ens realissimum*, the Spinozist deity whom the precritical Kant thought would furnish "the only possible proof for the existence of God." In the *Science of Logic*, he also appends to the main discussion of this first category, Being, one of his most in-depth discussions of the ontological argument. In the passage, which I will quote and examine at

---

[31] Quine (1948).

length later, he claims that if Kant had employed the example of something infinite such as Parmenidean Being and not that of something finite such as a hundred dollars he would never have rejected the ontological argument (WdL 21: 75–77/SoL 65–66). Being may not be a real predicate in the case of ordinary entities, such as a hundred dollars. Yet matters are different in the case of those like Being itself. The important point for our purposes is the way in which things have come full circle. A reconstituted version of Kant's project has turned out to require the rehabilitation of a deeply un-Kantian argument closely associated with dogmatic metaphysics.

How does this opening argument of the *Logic* relate to the opening argument of Fichte's *Wissenschaftslehre*? Hegel has effectively taken the first step in Fichte's argument (I to not-I, I am to it is not me) that he finds unconvincing and altered it decisively. He has offered a more abstract version of it (Being to Nothing or non-Being, is to is not), a version divested of any reference to the self. The opening of Hegel's logic is simply the opening of Fichte's *Wissenschaftslehre* purged of the vocabulary of epistemology or psychology and rendered in the more austere idiom of ontology. If Hegel's argument succeeds where Fichte's failed, then he will be in a position to confront Fichte with a dilemma. Either Fichte "succeeds" in taking his argument's first step from the I to the not-I, in which case he has actually taken the first step in Hegel's argument from Being to Nothing. Or, alternatively, he does not succeed, in which case we have additional reason to consider an alternative.

If that is so, then we can see that the insecure status of the *Logic*'s "first principle" is a help rather than a hindrance. It allows Hegel to take a version of the step that Fichte could not. Yet it also requires us to divest the argument of any psychological material, even material from transcendental psychology. Ultimately, this is for the sake not only of a more satisfactory opening but of a more satisfactory conclusion as well. The standpoint of subjectivity will receive a superior vindication by virtue of having been renounced, if only provisionally, at the outset.

In the final analysis, Hegel's response to the swimming objection differs dramatically from that of his predecessors Reinhold and Fichte. It will completely decouple category theory from the idea of an investigation into our faculty of knowledge. This is reflected in the passage in which Hegel presents his response. The response discusses how a theory of the categories can be given that avoids the swimming objection. However, it omits entirely any mention of how the faculty of knowledge will figure in the theory:

Consequently, the activity of the forms of thought and their critique must be joined in knowing. The forms of thought must be considered in and of themselves [an und für sich]. They are themselves the object as well as the activity of the object. They themselves examine themselves and they must determine for themselves their limits and point up their deficiency in themselves. This is the activity of thinking that will soon be specifically considered under the name of dialectic, about which a preliminary remark must here suffice, namely that it is to be regarded not as something brought to bear on thought-determinations from outside of them, but instead as immanent in them. (EL § 41 Z1)

As it is described here, Hegel's theory of the categories will adhere to a method of argument that divorces category theory from faculty psychology.[32] It does not in any obvious way require recourse to the prior claim that we are investigating the faculty of knowledge or any account of what that faculty would be. We simply begin with the first category: Being. We then proceed by using this category and each one subsequently, as both the object of evaluation and the standard of evaluation. We will consider a category, along with its definition, asking whether there could even be such a category as the one before us, whether this definition is coherent or not. Is the idea of simply Being, as opposed to being this or that thing, coherent?

Hegel's famous answer is that it is not, since anything that existed in this way would be so devoid of determinate properties as to be indistinguishable from nothing. When we find that it does give rise to an incoherence, the incoherence will, as it were, be internal to the category or definition itself. Once it is resolved, we will have a new category, along with its definition. At which point the process repeats. At no point would it have helped to have a philosophical psychology in the background. From the perspective of Hegel's category theory, Kant's faculty psychology is superfluous. If transcendental philosophy consists in the conviction that philosophy must begin with an account of our faculty of knowledge, then Hegel has left transcendental philosophy behind. Yet if Hegel's theory of the categories is not pursued under the head of some form of faculty psychology, then what area of philosophy does it concern?

Here, as already noted, I follow other commentators in arguing that Hegel's theory of the categories is a contribution to general metaphysics (ontology). This is the area of traditional philosophy tasked with examining what can be said of any being or entity insofar as it is one. Yet if Hegel's theory of the categories is traditional in its basic aspirations, it is

[32] See, once again, Nuzzo (2016).

not in the methods it uses. Hegel makes clear that all subsequent definitions of the Absolute are refined version of the first. They are "sublations,"
canceling but also preserving and improving upon their predecessor. I take
this to mean that we are simply at work refining our conception of what it
is for anything to be at all.[33]

As Hegel himself makes clear, his is intended to be a distinctly postcritical form of ontology that will avoid the impasses of earlier varieties (EL
§ 30). However, Hegel dissents from Kant's diagnosis of the flaw in earlier
approaches. For Hegel, the problem with precritical ontology was that
it rested its account of the fundamental forms of being on an uncritical
appeal to ordinary language and common sense.[34] It lacked a more systematic way of deducing these categories like that which Hegel's presuppositionless method provides:

> In its well-ordered form, the first part of this metaphysics was constituted
> by ontology … [but] a principle was lacking for these determinations. For
> this reason, they had to be enumerated empirically and contingently and
> their more precise content can be based only on the representation, on the
> assurance that in thinking one associates precisely this particular content
> with a given word, or perhaps on etymology as well. In all this, it can be
> a matter merely of the correctness of the analysis (agreeing with linguistic
> usage) and of empirical completeness, not the truth and the necessity of
> such determinations. (EL § 35)

Significantly, Hegel does not follow Kant here in claiming that the older
ontology erred because of its transcendental realism, the naive belief that
we can know things as they are in themselves. Indeed, this seems to be the
one error he does not accuse it of making.

Hegel, then, embraces a form of general metaphysics (ontology). This is
the attempt to use empirically unaided thought to understand the nature
of Being, being-qua-being. Its topic is beings or entities just insofar as
they are beings or entities, and not beings or entities of a particular (sub)
type. At the end of the Analytic, Kant will conclude that this enterprise is
moribund. "The proud name of ontology" must yield its place to Kant's
more modest analytic of the understanding (A 246/B 303). Kant's Analytic
has shown that (synthetic a priori) knowledge is possible for us only if
we restrict our attention to appearances. We know that the concepts
employed in pure thinking, the categories, must apply to any object of
possible experience. Yet we have no comparable assurance in the case of

---

[33] Houlgate (2006: 116), Doz (1987: 23–24) cited in Houlgate.
[34] Horstmann (1990: 19).

things-in-themselves. Ontology is a type of attempt to know things as they are-in-themselves and therefore goes beyond the bounds of what can reasonably be known.

In Hegel's view, Kant has not earned the right to reject ontology in the way that he does. The main justification for restricting our knowledge to appearances is that this is the only way to guarantee universality and necessity. If there were some other away to guarantee this, then there would be no need. *Contra* Kant, Hegel puts forward this system as one that will give us categories that ground the possibility of nontrivial, universally and necessarily valid knowledge. These categories are the forms of being, rather than the forms of self-consciousness unity, forms of unifying a sensibly given manifold.[35] Ultimately, then there is no reason they need be restricted to appearances, rather than things-in-themselves.

However, there is a catch. The universality and necessity in question are not to be understood numerically, as applying to all beings considered as a sum. They are to be understood, instead, in terms of an all-encompassing whole or totality of which all beings are "negations."

Although I have only reconstructed Hegel's critique of Kant's Metaphysical Deduction, his critique of the Transcendental Deduction requires brief comment as well. Notoriously, the young Hegel dismisses it as "shallow" in his treatment of Kant in the early essay *Faith and Knowledge*. This is a shocking claim, though Hegel would later have more favorable things to say about the deduction. In any case, I would like to propose an explanation of why he might have made such a dismissive claim in the first place. My point of departure is an addition from the 1831 *Encyclopedia*:

> This, then, is what Kant calls pure apperception ... With this, the nature of all consciousness has, to be sure, been correctly articulated. Human beings' striving is directed generally at knowing the world, appropriating and submitting it to their will, and towards this end the reality of the world must, so to speak, be crushed, that is, idealized. At the same time, however, it needs to be noted that it is not the subjective activity of self-consciousness that introduces absolute unity into the manifoldness. This identity is, rather, the absolute, the true itself. (EL § 42 Z1)

---

[35] Houlgate (2006:126) also argues that Hegel's *Logic*, when approached as an ontology, provides a superior grounding for synthetic a priori knowledge ("general existence claims"). A slightly different version of this point is made by Stern (2009) ("Introduction: How is Hegelian Metaphysics Possible?"), who thinks of Hegel's "conceptual realism" as offering an alternative to the Kantian strategy for justifying synthetic a priori knowledge.

For Hegel, as we have seen, Kant's project in the Metaphysical Deduction must yield its place to a more traditional theory of the categories, a form of general metaphysics (ontology). Hegel can therefore concede the correctness of Kant's subsequent analysis from the Transcendental Deduction of the manner in which the mind unifies sensible representations into a coherent experience of a world structured by categories such as cause and substance. Still, Hegel would be justified in arguing that the importance of this analysis is severely diminished once we reject the Metaphysical Deduction. For Hegel, Kant's Transcendental Deduction no longer explains how the world acquires its categorial structure. The task of doing so now falls to general metaphysics (ontology). At most, then, claims such as those from Kant's deduction concerning the transcendental imagination, synthesis and so on supplement ontology's account of reality's own categorial structure. They do so by explaining the precise cognitive mechanism by which beings with minds like our own retrace the world's ontological structure in thought. They cannot, however, serve the role they did in Kant's philosophy of explaining how the world (of experience) acquires that structure in the first place.

In the Transcendental Deduction, Kant asks: What gives us the right to apply the categories to the manifold of sense experience? He calls this the *quid juris* as opposed to the *quid facti* (B 116/A 84). Yet, for Hegel, this question only makes sense in relation to finite categories, those that can conceivably fail to apply. It therefore only makes sense to treat that question as fundamental if we assume that finite categories are the only (or the most important) categories that there are. Ordinarily, it would make sense to ask whether a concept the thinking subject employs actually has instances in the objective world or not. The definitions of most ordinary concepts leave the question open as to whether they have instances or not. Assuming their definitions are even so much as coherent or noncontradictory, then it is an open question whether these concepts apply, and if so how widely. However, "infinite" categories differ. The definitions of these concepts do not leave this question open but rather settle it. Assuming their definition is even coherent, then they have instances. Indeed, they apply in every instance. For example: Being is present not just in some real thing but in every real thing.

* * *

Is there, then, no place at all in Hegel's *Logic* for a theory of the categories like that found in Kant's transcendental logic? To be sure, Hegel's categories are products of (conceptual) thinking as well, but the reason this is so differs profoundly from why it is so in the critical philosophy. As I argued in Chapter 1, Hegel does not begin from the premise that the categories are products of our thinking, as opposed to deriving from sensibility or some other source. That is what they are, and this is a fact that must obtain if we are to do Hegelian philosophical logic. However, this fact is not the first premise of the argument. As Hegel told us earlier, it matters a great deal to us as readers if the categories are products of thinking, but not at all to the *Logic*, at least not at the outset. Instead, Hegel will simply begin with the first category, Being, and proceed to refine it.

I go further than other commentators in debarring certain descriptions of this starting point. Even to call this a category, a concept, thought determination, an instance of thought reflecting on itself and its necessary determinations, would be premature. To be sure, Being, as the indeterminate, constitutes the necessary object of pure thinking: thinking that has abstracted from all sensible intuition and therefore from everything determinate. However, the idea that Being is the necessary object of pure thinking is not one we are in a position to vindicate until the close.

The reason Hegel does not want to presuppose that the categories are forms of thinking is that he wants to be in a position to prove this. It is not a premise of the argument but its conclusion. However, this does imply a fundamentally anti-Kantian conception of why, and in what sense, the categories are products of thinking. Originally, the categories are necessary forms of being. *Eventually, however, we discover that thinking is among being's necessary forms.*[36] Indeed, this is true of the type of thinking in which we were engaged when we discovered being's necessary forms: self-determining thinking, thinking thinking thinking.

Here, it is important to remember that future categories sublate "being," not necessarily determinate beings. Hegel's logic is not simply a further specification of what it is for any particular being to be but what Being as a whole is. Self-determining thinking, or thinking, thinking, thinking, as the successor to Being, remains a whole prior to its parts. Of course, it has other features that distinguish it from the type of whole that interests Parmenides and Spinoza, but Hegel acknowledges this part of their legacy.

Ultimately, then, we do eventually arrive at an epistemological explanation of how the knowledge we acquire in the preceding metaphysics is possible for us. We do not arrive at an account that would explain its possibility away, however – as if Hegel's metaphysics were always epistemology

---

[36] Houlgate (2006: 122). See also Nuzzo (2016).

in disguise, and this is what we learn at the close of the book. If that were the case, then Hegel would have effectively cut away the ground beneath his own feet. That is so because the metaphysics of the first part is necessary to give the account of subjectivity in the second. Hegel has a metaphysics of epistemology, an account of the structure relating the knower to the known in cases of knowledge. He has an explanation of how this structure fits into the world, where it has a footing no less secure than that of chemical reactions, law-governed matter, and self-reproducing species of living thing. Indeed, knowledge, theoretical and practical, even in its finite guise, arguably has a more important place in reality than any of these other phenomena. Just why this is the case is not my topic here, but I do want to emphasize that the turn to the subject at the close of the *Logic* is not Kant's Copernican turn. It is not a relativization of the ontological theory of the categories in the first part to the standpoint of the knowing subject as described in the second.

2.5   Conclusion: The Ontological Proof as "the True Critique of the Categories and of Reason"

To conclude, I want to note that Hegel's objection is provocative from a Kantian perspective. On the one hand, Hegel has effectively proposed to out-do the critical philosophy at the project that lay at its very foundation: providing a derivation of the categories without uncritically relying on the logic of the day. On the other, Hegel proposes to rest his derivation of the categories on an argument that it was the culminating gesture of the critical philosophy to rebut: the ontological argument. Hegel has, in effect, inverted the critique, proposing an argument rejected at the end of the critique, in the Dialectic as the key to a rehabilitated version of the Analytic's opening argument. This is what is required if we are to successfully carry out the project of a Metaphysical Deduction from the beginning of the Analytic ("Logic of Truth"). In particular, Hegel has claimed that the first principle from which the categories will derive is one that vouchsafes its own existence, like the God of the ontological argument.

Hegel himself presents his project in exactly this way with the bold declaration that the ontological argument is "the true critique of the categories and of reason."

> This criticism [Kant's criticism of the ontological proof – JM], because of its popular example, has won universal plausibility. Who does not know that a hundred actual dollars are different from a hundred possible ones? This difference is easily demonstrable in the case of the hundred dollars:

therefore, the concept, that is, the determinateness of the content as empty possibility, and being are different from each other; therefore, the concept of God and his being are also different, and just as I cannot extract from the possibility of the hundred dollars their actuality, I can just as little "extract" God's existence from his concept. The ontological proof consists precisely in thus extracting God's existence from his concept. Now, though there is of course truth to the claim that the concept is different from being, God's difference from the hundred dollars and other finite things is yet greater. It is the definition of finite things that in them concept and being are different; that the concept and reality, soul and body, are separable; that they are therefore perishable and mortal. The abstract definition of God, on the contrary, is precisely that his concept and his being are unseparated and inseparable. *The true critique of the categories and of reason is just this: to acquaint cognition with this distinction and to prevent it from applying to God the determinations and the relations of the finite.* (WdL 21: 77/SoL 66, italics mine)

At first the parallel to the ontological argument may seem slight. To be sure, Hegel claims there are certain concepts that, by definition, must have instances: for example, Being, the *omnitudo realitatis* or *ens realissimum*. Thus far, however, we have only considered the potential of such concepts to figure in a type of theory of the categories. We have not as yet said anything about mounting a defense of theism, either of an orthodox or of a heterodox variety. In spite of this, it seems clear that this is where Hegel's account is headed.

Kant himself will explicitly reject this type of project in the Transcendental Ideal, denying that a concept could be defined in such a way that it contained its own existence within itself. For now, Hegel should simply postpone responding to Kant's objections, since the question of whether Hegel is justified in embracing some version of the ontological argument is premature at this stage. Hegel has only sought to respond to Kant's Analytic, not the Dialectic. He has argued that a derivation of the categories superior to Kant's own is possible. However, it can be given by beginning with "infinite" categories, such as Being, categories of which some version of the ontological argument is true.

If Hegel has succeeded in this endeavor, then he has already won a significant victory over Kant. At the very least, he is raising the stakes of rejecting the ontological argument. Hegel's proposal is that a complete derivation of the categories of the type Kant himself and his immediate followers sought is only possible through the ontological argument. Even taking the first step into the Analytic ("Logic of Truth") will require qualifying the critique of rational theology that occurs at the close of the

Dialectic ("Logic of Illusion"). Hence, embracing Kant's critique of it will be more costly than previously anticipated. Clearly, a definitive verdict on the question of whether Hegel's version of the ontological argument succeeds will have to await his treatment of Kant's critique of metaphysics in the Dialectic.

I have already commented on the irony of Hegel rehabilitating an argument Kant ridiculed so that he can achieve a project Kant could not; however, I want to conclude here by commenting on a way that this irony is compounded, and in so doing connecting this discussion to our broader topic ("the logocentric predicament"). Hegel is led to this project by Kant's mishandling of the categories of transcendental logic, as well as, and more fundamentally, of the forms of judgment found in general logic. Hence, we can predict that the new system he proposes will offer a new foundation, not only for the categories of idealism and ontology but also of the very laws of thought recognized in "the former logic." The ontological argument is the true critique of reason and the categories, but it is also the first step toward a solution to the logocentric predicament.

CHAPTER 3

Hegel's Critique of "the Former Metaphysics"

3.1 Introduction

As I have sought to show, Hegel accuses the traditional Aristotelian logic of complacency. He further accuses Kant's transcendental logic of compounding the problem through its complacent relationship to tradition. Resolving these issues will require a rehabilitation of a form of metaphysics Kant repudiated. However, it would be mistaken to assume that Hegel simply intends to restore pre-Kantian metaphysics unchanged.

Hegel is ambivalent about the metaphysical tradition. On the one hand, he fully admits that precritical metaphysics gave rise to the impasses Kant identifies. In particular, he agrees that this tradition found itself plagued by intractable controversies, for example antinomies. On the other hand, he denies that any form of realist metaphysics would have to do so. He therefore blocks Kant's inference to the conclusion that we must reject transcendental realism in favor of idealism if we are to avoid the tradition's impasses. Hegel hopes to demonstrate that Kant has misdiagnosed the problem with precritical metaphysics. In Hegel's view, the errors Kant identifies (paralogisms, antinomies and so on) are by no means the result of transcendental realism, the assumption that we can know reality as it is in itself. Instead, they result from the use of a crude set of logical tools to achieve this otherwise legitimate aim,[1] tools furnished by the traditional Aristotelian logic: for example, the judgment of subject–predicate form and the syllogistic inference.

This alternative diagnosis opens up the possibility of arguing that a realist form of metaphysics remains a possibility for us, provided it uses a different set of logical tools. This would be a distinctly postcritical metaphysics, traditional in its aspiration to know the unconditioned if not in the logical means it employs in attempting to achieve that end. If Kant overlooked the true source of the problem with precritical metaphysics,

[1] Horstmann (1990: 24).

locating this source in its realism rather than its logic then this is unsurprising. After all, Kant was no less indebted to traditional logic than the figures he criticized.

I am, in this chapter and in Chapter 4, following Bowman, who makes a version of this point in his reading of Hegel.[2] From a Hegelian point of view, Bowman argues, *both* precritical metaphysics and Kant are pre-Hegelian in their logic. This, I think, furnishes a rejoinder to the common Kantian accusation that Hegel and the tradition are precritical in their metaphysics. However, I do slightly disagree with Bowman about what, in particular, is at issue in this "logical" dispute. For Bowman, it is the nature of the categories: the ten or twelve finite categories of the Aristotelian tradition and Kant versus the infinite categories Hegel prefers. Here, Bowman follows Fulda for whom Hegel's logic constitutes a bracing critique of the categories ("Logik ohne Ontologie").[3]

However, I regard the theory of the categories as a topic whose status as part of logic ("the common logic") was extremely ambiguous. While I will turn to the topic of finite categories in Chapter 4, I propose to consider here the role of two more classically logical topics: the natures and forms of concepts, judgments and inferences, as well as the fundamental laws of thought (noncontradiction, identity, excluded middle and so on).[4] The possibility I want to explore is that Hegel is led by his critique of metaphysics to the idea that a truly self-critical philosophy must jettison not just the theory of the categories (transcendental logic) but even the more elementary logic ("general logic"). A more radically self-critical form of thought will have to embrace that seemingly paradoxical thing, a form of rational argument unregimented by the rules of formal logic: the dialectic.

In pursuing this route, I also follow Houlgate, especially his treatment of Hegel's critique of judgments of subject–predicate form and his account of the dialectic as a method of argument whose chief virtue is its radically non-presuppositionless character. Especially in my treatment of immanent critique, I will emphasize the nondogmatic nature of the procedure. However, I believe resolving the philosophical problem that interests me here, the logocentric predicament, requires more than Houlgate provides.[5]

---

[2] Bowman (2013: 8).
[3] Bowman (2013: 36 n. 13).
[4] Once again, I here follow Hanna (1986).
[5] In fact, Houlgate does, in passing, describe formal logic itself as one of the presuppositions speculative logic must do without: "[W]e do not assume that thought should be governed by the rules of Aristotelian logic or that the law of noncontradiction holds, or that thought is regulated by any principles or laws whatsoever" (2006: 30).

It is no small feat to prove that a method of argument is free of the logical laws and materials that are commonly considered presuppositions of any legitimate argument whatsoever.

In the first place, we must further demonstrate the way the dialectic is free of any reliance not only on this particular type of judgment but on *any*. Pace Houlgate, even the speculative judgments, often said to be Hegel's stock in trade in the *Logic*, would not do for the purposes of the problem I would have him solve.[6] This non–formal logical interpretation of Hegel's speculative logic requires a thorough purgation of any of the laws and materials of what Kant called pure general logic.

Moving down one level of logical complexity, I will further seek to show that Hegel's account does not presuppose the existence even of concepts, said in logic to be the basic constituents of judgments. Moving up one level, I am also interested in extending Hegel's critique of judgment to include inference and showing why the same shortcomings would present them there. Finally, and at a still broader level, I will need to show that the method of argument Hegel embraces, given its status as non–formal logical, does not rely on the laws of logic: chief among them, noncontradiction. In treating the opening arguments of the logic as non–formal logical, and in all of these respects, I may risk approaching them as exercises in Romantic irrationalism. Yet as before I insist this is not my aim, since I seek in these opening arguments an expanded conception of reason capable of addressing the Romantic critique of enlightenment.

3.2 The Role of Formal Logic in Precritical Metaphysics

3.2.1 *Predicative Judgment*

The first of these tools I will consider is the tradition's reliance on judgments of subject–predicate form, "S is P." In precritical metaphysics, it was assumed that the judgment is the primary vehicle of "truth." As Hegel writes, "There was [in the tradition – JM] no investigation as to whether . . .

---

[6] Houlgate (2006: 93–98) treats "speculative propositions" as important to Hegel's *Logic*, whereas I hope to show that the argument itself takes place in a prepropositional form of thought (at least at the outset).

Here, I follow Koch (2018: 46; 2019), who rejects Pippin's claim that, for Hegel, pure thinking is originally judging. What is needed is not a *special* form of judgment, free of the ordinary forms of predication, but a type of thought that is wholly *nonjudgment based, prepredicative*.

the form of judgment is capable of being the form of truth (EL § 28)"[7] In order to see why the form of judgment was so important to the tradition, we should recall the following. Like any science, traditional metaphysics defines itself by its subject matter: God, the soul, and the world. Hence, it must begin with definitions of these items. Only in this way can it secure a subject matter for the science, which would otherwise be empty.

Once these definitions are in place, we can certainly pose and answer questions about God, the soul, and the world. In logical terms, we can do so using judgments of subject–predicate form. More specifically, we can ask of a subject concept whose definition has now been secured whether a certain predicate concept applies to it or not. Does God, on some widely accepted definition, exist or not? Is the soul, as it is commonly understood, mortal or immortal? Is the world-whole, as we usually understand it, finite or infinite in its age or size? In order to adjudicate these disputes, these figures would then construct syllogistic arguments for the thesis and antithesis claims. Admittedly, relying on judgment and syllogistic inference may seem innocuous. However, Hegel will argue that this logical apparatus is inherently dogmatic, at least when it is considered from the point of view of his own theory of the categories.

For Hegel, the tradition's ability to raise questions of this kind and explore them in depth required ignoring others. To judge of some subject concept that a further one can be predicated of it, we must either treat as settled or not treat as settled the question of the subject concept's meaning.

If we treat it as settled, then we are being dogmatic – positing meaning as self-evident.[8] As Hegel writes: "When we ask for the predicate that belongs to such subjects, the required judgment must be based on a concept that is presupposed" (WdL 12: 54/SoL 551). Precritical metaphysicians may have been content to defer to, for example, the Christian religion's definitions of terms such as God, the soul, and the world. Hegel is not, since in that instance the debate becomes arbitrary: "It is, therefore, the mere representation that in fact makes up the presupposed meaning ... and ... it is a mere accident, a historical fact, what is understood by a name" (WdL 12: 54/SoL 551). Hegel therefore concludes that the dispute would be "nothing more than verbal" (WdL 12: 54/SoL 551).

---

[7] "In this connection, we must observe right at the beginning that the proposition, in the form of a judgment, is not adept to express speculative truths" (WdL 21: 78/SoL 67).

[8] Cf. Horstmann (1990: 34), who provides a slightly differing account of the problem drawing on Moore's paradox of analysis.

That leaves the alternative of not treating the question as settled. If we do this, however, then we are not employing a judgment in the logical sense at all. This is so even if, grammatically speaking, our claim seems to have the form of a judgment. A judgment asserts a connection between two concepts. Yet in such an instance, we are only asking about the definition of one. If we decide not to treat the question of the meaning of our concepts as settled, as it seems we must if we are to avoid dogmatism, then we are no longer employing a judgment in the logical sense. In this way, Hegel's objection that judgment is inherently dogmatic is effectively conceded.

Even admitting that a nonjudgment-based inquiry into our concepts would avoid dogmatism, it is far from clear what form such an inquiry would take. Yet Hegel thinks there are clear cases of this from the history of philosophy. Inquiring into the meanings of our concepts without relying on the form of judgment is what Hegel thinks the characters are doing in Plato's dialogues when they pose and answer the question "What is X?" Here, the aim is not to assert a connection between two concepts, as a judgment in the logical sense does, but only to inquire into the content of one. It is also why Hegel denies that Plato is a dogmatic metaphysician, something that must sound very strange to Kantian ears. The following passages are representative:

> This kind of metaphysics was not a free and objective thinking, since it did not allow the object [*Objekt*] to determine itself out of itself but presupposed it as something ready made. As concerns Greek philosophy, it thought freely, but not scholasticism, since the latter likewise took up its content as something given and, indeed, given by the Church. We moderns, through our entire way of education, have been initiated into *representations* [of things] ... which it is exceptionally difficult to overcome. (EL § 31 + Z)
> Earlier philosophers and notably the Scholastics provided the material for this metaphysics ... Plato is not this kind of metaphysician, and Aristotle even less so, although it is usually believed that the opposite is the case. (EL § 36 Z)
> "... step forward that these universalities have been brought to light and made the subject of study on their own, as was done by Plato, and after him by Aristotle especially. (WdL 21: 12/SoL 14)

Although not a clear-cut case of the approach Hegel favors, Spinoza is meant to be doing something similar. Hegel believes that Spinoza's system contains the seeds of a profound logical innovation, though one concerning judgment rather than the law of noncontradiction. It is an innovation Hegel calls "the speculative proposition" (PhS § 61). This is a larger topic then I can discuss here, but I do want to draw attention to its Spinozistic provenance: in particular, its nonjudgmental, non–formal logical and therefore antidogmatic character.

In discussing the "speculative proposition," Hegel chooses an example that is undeniably Spinozist: the judgment "God is being" (PhS § 62). When Spinoza claims this, he is not making a judgment in the logical sense. He is not asserting a connection between two separate concepts whose received definitions are assumed as unproblematic: for example, definitions of God and nature as creator and created. Instead, Spinoza is thinking freely, which for Hegel means interrogating the meanings of our concepts. Accordingly, Spinoza is proposing a new concept, with a new definition. It is a hybrid concept, compounded out of two old ones: God and nature (*deus sive natura*).

If this is right, then Spinoza may not be a dogmatist either, at least when judged according to this logical criterion. Unfortunately, there are additional sources of dogmatism in Spinoza. The *more geometrico*, for example, requires us to stipulatively define our terms and postulate certain truths so that the propositions of the science can be derived from this starting point. Hegel would oppose this, urging that we employ a nondogmatic method of deduction to generate any and all conceptual resources our science draws on. Hence, he says of Spinoza's starting point:

> These concepts, however profound and correct, are definitions that are immediately assumed in the science from the start. Mathematics and other subordinate sciences must begin with something presupposed that constitutes their element and positive substrate. But the absolute cannot be a first, an immediate. (WdL II: 366–367/SoL 472–473)

I will return to this issue subsequently, arguing that it is a mistake to classify Spinoza alongside other rationalist metaphysicians as a precritical, dogmatic metaphysician. Once again, this will sound strange from a Kantian point of view, especially Kantian-idealist interpreters of Hegel. Not unlike Kant himself, they have tended to tar all pre-Kantian metaphysicians with the same brush.

3.2.2 Syllogistic Inference

In response, a defender of the tradition might point out that metaphysicians rely not only on judgment as the primary vehicle of truth but also on syllogistic arguments as the primary means of proving true. Since giving an argument for something is an alternative to dogmatically asserting it, this might seem to mitigate the problem of dogmatism. Yet far from resolving the problem posed by the dogmatism inherent to the form of judgment, syllogistic argument exacerbates it.

We are apt to think of such arguments as containing two or more judgments that are treated as premises from which some conclusion can be validly drawn. For example, consider the following syllogistic argument for God's existence. God is all perfect, existence is a perfection, therefore .... Here, however, we must consider a further component of Hegel's conception of the syllogism. Rather than think of syllogistic arguments as connecting two or more judgments of subject–predicate form, it would be better to think of them as connecting three or more concepts. This is reflected in the way types of syllogistic inference are, for Hegel, represented in terms of the way they connect three concepts: for example, "the second figure, P-S-U" (WdL 12: 99/SoL 597). A syllogism simply introduces a further concept, beyond the original two, whose role will be to mediate between the subject and predicate concepts connected in a judgment.

For example, take the judgment God exists, and the syllogistic argument for it just given. All the syllogism does is introduce a third concept <perfection> meant to mediate between two others connected in the judgment, the concepts of <God> and <existence>. On this view, judgments are simply two-place relations between concepts, and syllogisms the exact same relation, extended to three or more places. That is why Hegel always represents the syllogistic figures using a notation made up of a middle term and two extremes.

Since all that a syllogism does is further extend a connection between concepts already made in a judgment of subject–predicate form, it cannot help us transcend the limitations of this logical structure. At best, it postpones the task of interrogating the meanings of the subject concepts used in the judgments themselves. At worst, it forecloses the possibility of doing so. To the dogmatically assumed meanings of the first two concepts deployed in the judgment, we now add a third as soon as we construct a syllogism.

For Hegel, it is no coincidence that Scholasticism, the main form of precritical, dogmatic metaphysics, relied on the logic of the Aristotelian tradition. According to him, it is the two main tools of logicians in this tradition, judgment and syllogism, which, at least in part, explain the metaphysical tradition's dogmatism (as we will see in a moment, Christianity also has a role).

By contrast, Kant, who has a more favorable attitude toward the traditional logic, does not implicate it in the shortcomings of metaphysics. In the B preface, his famous words of praise for this science are intended to present it as an example metaphysics should emulate. Yet, from Hegel's perspective, Kant does not attend sufficiently to the way precritical metaphysics everywhere relies on the older logic. Since Kant relies on this logic as well, it is not at all surprising from a Hegelian perspective that he should have misdiagnosed the problem.

3.3 The Role of Religion

As we have seen, Hegel believes that the traditional logic confronted precritical metaphysicians with a dilemma: either treat meaning as self-evident in a way that is dogmatic or else abandon this logic entirely. Hegel believes that precritical metaphysicians attempted to resolve the dilemma in a way that involved an appeal to the Christian religion.

> This kind of metaphysics was not a free and objective thinking, since it did not allow the object [*Objekt*] to determine itself freely out of itself but presupposed it as something ready-made. – As concerns thinking freely, Greek philosophy thought freely, but not scholasticism, since the latter likewise took up its content as something given and, indeed, given by the Church. (EL § 31 + Z)

Ultimately, Christianity was the source of these metaphysicians' conceptions of the meanings of terms such as God, the soul, and the world. However, Hegel argues that the appeal is in the final analysis dogmatic. In order to understand why, we must consider Hegel's claim that this approach required earlier figures to employ resources drawn from the sphere of representation (*Vorstellung*).

> But objective logic comprises within itself also the rest of metaphysics, the metaphysics which sought to comprehend with the pure forms of thought such particular substrata, originally drawn from the imagination, as the soul, the world, and God ... Logic, however, considers these forms free of those substrata, which are the subjects of figurative representation. (WdL 21: 49/SoL 42)

Representation (*Vorstellung*) is a well-known term of art from Hegel's philosophical psychology, but for our purposes it will suffice to say the following. Hegel distinguishes between representation, a mode of thought in some way informed by concrete sense experience, and abstract conceptual thought (*Begriff*), which has been completely purified of any association with that form of experience (EL § 20). Importantly for our purposes, Hegel believes that representation is the medium of religion whereas conceptual thought is that of philosophy. Explaining this adequately would require a more extensive detour through Hegel's philosophy of religion as well as his philosophical psychology than is possible here. However, I offer the following in the way of background.

As I interpret him, Hegel thinks that traditional religious teachings on the nature of God, the soul, and the world are not literally true. However, he concedes the possibility that they might be so in a different way, figuratively. On this view, religion expresses, in a figurative way, truths that philosophy can state literally. Religion does so using imagery, whether this is verbal, pictorial or some other type. Images represent ideas that can be conveyed more directly and literally using concepts or words.

Still this confronts us with the question of what the literal content of these religious metaphors might be? What, exactly, do the metaphors of traditional religion stand for? Unless we confront this question concerning traditional religion, Hegel thinks, we will not make progress in philosophy. Part of the reason is that Hegel believes the content of these metaphors to be none other than his own speculative philosophy. For example, he thinks his definition of the Absolute as the Concept, a tripartite structure, is reflected in the doctrine of the Trinity (EL § 161+Z). He also describes the movement from the category of Something to that of Nothing as a more rigorous account of Christianity's *creatio ex nihilo*. It is, he says, the definitive refutation of the ancient pagan doctrine of the eternity of matter, which rested on the principle *a nihilo nihil fit* (WdL 21: 71/SoL 61). However, our topic here is Hegel's diagnosis of the problem with precritical metaphysics, rather than the prescription he recommends. How, then, does the metaphorical content of traditional religion explain the impasses of traditional metaphysics?

Lacking any clear understanding of the literal truth these metaphors express, people will vary widely in their assessments of what consequences for philosophy follow from them. In logical terms, each will begin with a subject concept, defined in an idiosyncratic way, and then reach divergent views about which predicate concepts can be attached. The extension of this structure, beyond judgment to inference, will only exacerbate the situation. This amounts only to the addition of a third term beyond the original two, and it further obscures the first. In the background is Hegel's belief that the medium of sensible intuition lends itself to content that is private and incommunicable in a way that of the conceptual does not, inasmuch as it allows for expression in a public language:

The representations of soul, world, God seem at first to offer thinking a *firm hold*. However ... the character of particular subjectivity is blended in with them and ... on account of this, they can have very different meanings, [meaning that] they first need to receive their firm determination through thinking. (EL § 31).

In passing, Hegel mentions what he calls the Eastern doctrine that God has infinitely many names, no one of which is sufficient (EL § 33). Yet it is clear that he views this less as a solution than as a confirmation of the problem. At least in precritical, dogmatic metaphysics the end result is an impasse. More specifically, we reach a conflict between opposed answers to some metaphysical question. It is a conflict made particularly intractable by the fact that the root of the disagreement is obscure to the parties involved. It is the intellectual equivalent of the wars of religion, as Kant himself implies with his metaphor of "the battleground of metaphysics."

***

Returning to the main stream of the argument, we can now combine Hegel's account of the role of formal logic in precritical metaphysics with his account of the role of religion. Our aim is to understand why they give rise to dogmatism. In Hegel's retelling, traditional logic and an uncritical appeal to religion combine to wreak havoc for precritical metaphysics. If the judgment or inference-based logic of the tradition discourages a critical interrogation of the subject concepts in metaphysical claims, then religion only does so further. The former encourages us to look at a higher level of logical complexity – and therefore in the wrong place. The latter ensures that even if we did examine the concepts themselves we would not discover their true content. One need only be glancingly familiar with Scholasticism to know of how the sham rigor of formal logic can disguise the complacency of religion about its subject matter. This is a fitting diagnosis, since, as we have seen, precritical metaphysics is, for Hegel, essentially the use of formal logic to reason about religion's subject matter. This, then, is Hegel's alternative diagnosis of the tradition's impasses.

What is needed is not further research into the questions of traditional metaphysics but a critical interrogation of the basic concepts metaphysicians deploy unthinkingly: God, the soul, and the world. In logical terms, we must abandon the question of which predicates attach to a given subject and turn to the prior one of how those subject terms ought to be defined. Yet this will require abandoning the medium of representation and embracing that of conceptual thought.

In proposing a critical interrogation of the concepts of God, the soul, and the world, Hegel is arguably more radical a critic of metaphysics than Kant. At least in this dispute, Hegel is disappointed to find that Kant is on the side of precritical metaphysics. According to Kant, the three objects of special metaphysics (God, the soul, and the world-whole) are a priori Ideas of reason itself. To at least this extent, critical metaphysicians were justified in their decision to promote them to such an important place. To be sure, Kant is critical of attempts by earlier metaphysicians to employ these Ideas uncritically. For Kant, they can only be used to regulate our pursuit of scientific knowledge, not to yield a distinct type of metaphysical (theoretical) knowledge. From Hegel's perspective, however, Kant is still too charitable toward the tradition. His critique concerns the specific use that is made of these concepts, rather than the concepts themselves. As regards traditional religion's influence on philosophy, both precritical metaphysicians and Kant are insufficiently wary, at least according to Hegel.

Worse still, Kant's attempt to show that these Ideas spring from reason itself only reentrenches the recurrent problem of his uncritical reliance on the logic of the day. In other words, Kant's attempt to avoid one form of precritical dogmatism, the religious, lands him in another, the logical. As with his deduction of the categories from the Analytic, Kant's deduction of the Ideas of reason in the Dialectic appeals to the logic of the day, this time the table of forms of inference. Kant draws the parallel himself:

> The transcendental analytic gave us an example of how the mere logical form of our cognition can contain the origin of pure concepts a priori, which represent objects prior to all experience, or rather which indicate the synthetic unity that alone makes possible an empirical cognition of objects. The form of judgments (transformed into a concept of the synthesis of intuitions) brought forth categories that direct all use of the understanding in experience. In the same way, we can expect that the form of the syllogisms, if applied to the synthetic unity of intuitions under the authority of the categories, will contain the origin of special concepts a priori that we may call pure concepts of reason or transcendental ideas, and they will determine the use of the understanding according to principles in the whole of an entire experience. (A 321/B 378)

The representations of metaphysics are Ideas of *reason*, after all. Yet the logical, as opposed to the real, use of reason is to form syllogistic inferences. Hence, each of reason's three Ideas can be traced back to a different form of syllogism: the soul from the categorical syllogism, the world from the hypothetical, God from the disjunctive. As before, the strategy of argument is based on Kant's conviction that this logic is complete. If these

are all the syllogistic forms that there are, then these Ideas must be all that
there are as well.

As he did before, Hegel rejects this claim. He denies that the table of
forms of inference is itself complete. Here too he does on the grounds that
the logic from which it derives is empirical. Odd as it may sound, this
claim is a constant refrain in Hegel's critique of Kant. It becomes slightly
less odd-seeming if we recall its meaning. This is merely that this logic is
based on intellectual experience, not the sensible variety.

> [T]hese Ideas are again derived from *experience, from formal logic*, according
> to which there are various forms of the syllogism. Because, says Kant, there
> are three forms of the syllogism, categorical, hypothetical, and disjunctive,
> the Unconditioned is also threefold in its nature. (VGP/LHoP v. 3 Kant:
> "Critique of Pure Reason," italics mine)

Kant's failure to prove completeness at the outset of the Dialectic is a point
of vulnerability Hegel will exploit. It leaves open a possibility Kant must rule
out if his critique of metaphysics is to succeed. I mean the possibility that a
distinct set of concepts, beyond those Kant considers, which could allow for
a new, superior form of metaphysics. If that were so, then there would be
no need to reject realist metaphysics in the name of transcendental idealism.

3.4   Truth

Ultimately, then, Hegel traces the dogmatism of the metaphysical tradition
to a logical source: Aristotelian logic. The tradition (and Kant) relies uncritically on the form of judgment, assuming that it is the sole "vehicle of truth,"
as well as the form of inference which the tradition (and Kant) regard as
the primary means of proving true. Hegel's alternative proposal is that individual concepts are themselves vehicles of truth and admit of being used on
their own in philosophy. For Hegel, we should no longer ask, as both precritical metaphysics and Kant did, whether a certain judgment is true, that
is whether the connection it asserts between a subject concept and the predicate concept in fact holds good. Nor should we pursue an answer to this
question through the less direct route of constructing syllogistic arguments
from which such a judgment can be drawn as the conclusion to a prior
set of premises. We should, instead, ask the more fundamental question of
whether the concepts themselves are true, in some sense of that term. This is
a question the tradition did not ask, though this is perhaps understandable.
Hegel recognizes that we are not accustomed to treating individual concepts
as truth bearers. What, though, can Hegel mean in suggesting that they are?

> The question whether being, existence or finitude, simplicity, composite-
> ness, and so on are *in and of themselves true concepts* must seem odd to
> someone who believes that there can be talk only of the truth of *a sentence*.
> The only question can be whether *a concept* is being truthfully *attributed* (as
> it is called) *to a subject* or not, and that [form or variety of – JM] untruth
> depended on the contradiction that might be found to exist between the
> subject of the representation and the concept to be predicated of it. But
> the concept as something concrete (and every determinacy in general) is
> essentially in itself a unity of diverse determinations. Hence, if truth were
> nothing more than the lack of contradiction, the first thing that would have
> to be considered for every concept is whether it did not of itself contain
> such an internal contradiction. (EL § 33)

Minimally, truth requires the absence of contradiction, and Hegel's conception of truth is usefully approached with this condition in mind. The
condition is reflected in a traditional definition of truth that Hegel will
alter in a decisive respect. On that traditional definition, truth, whatever
else it may be, requires at the very least the absence of contradiction
between the subject and predicate concepts united in a judgment. For
Hegel, truth can pertain to a single concept, since it is possible for individual concepts to contradict themselves. This is true of the very first
concept Hegel considers in the logic. Being, in terms of its lack of any
determinate (specific, particular) quality: "Being, pure being – without
further determination [*ohne alle weitere Bestimmung*]" (WdL 21: 68/SoL
59). Yet this means it is identical with its opposite, Nothing, defined in
the same way. Hence, Being, the simplest concept that there is, contradicts itself.

Yet this type of self-contradiction is especially common once we move
beyond the first few concepts of the *Logic*, and encounter others with a
more complex internal structure. As Hegel says, these subsequent concepts
are "unities of opposed determinations" (EL § 33). Hence, these concepts
can contradict themselves when the determinations they contain contradict each other. For example, consider the concept of an infinite quantity,
an instance of what Hegel calls "the bad infinite" (WdL 21: 239/SoL 207).
Hegel adheres to a traditional definition of a quantity on which it is something that always admits of increase or decrease. As an infinite quantity,
however, the quantity before us is meant to be the greatest quantity of all.[9]

---

[9] Hegel attributes this conception of the infinite to Kant, whom he criticizes. The context for these
remarks is a discussion of the first antinomy. However, the argument in question is older. It can be
found in Leibniz (1989: 25), who speaks of "the fastest motion, which is an absurdity." An overview
of its long history can be found in Priest (1995).

Yet because it can always be increased, such a quantity cannot be the greatest. So it both is and is not the greatest. Hence, the contradiction.

This idea concerning the ways in which individual concepts can be untrue reflects a broader Hegelian conception of truth. On this conception, truth is not a matter of correspondence between our representations and a reality independent of them. Hegel denounces this as mere correctness, rather than truth in the full-fledged sense. Instead, truth is a specific type of correspondence that a given reality exhibits with itself.

> Correctness and truth are very frequently considered to mean the same thing in ordinary life and one accordingly speaks of the truth of some content where it is a matter of mere correctness. Correctness generally affects merely the formal agreement of our representation with its content; however this content may be otherwise constituted. The truth consists, by contrast, in the agreement of the object with itself, i.e. with its concept. (EL § 172 Z)

This conception of truth as something "in the world" rather than a relation of language or thought to the world goes back to Plato and can be found throughout the history of philosophy. Yet Hegel gives it an unfamiliar twist. He argues that the type of self-correspondence he calls truth obtains when a thing satisfies its constitutive norm.[10] Hegel finds traces of this use of the term "truth" in expressions such as "a true friend" and "a true work of art" (EL § 24 Z1).[11] If that is so, then there is no reason to ascribe truth to judgments but withhold it from concepts. A judgment asserts a connection between subject and predicate, so it is true when that connection obtains. Similarly, a concept, though it does not assert anything, is meant to have a content. A concept is true when it has a coherent content and untrue when it does not.

3.5   Overcoming Dogmatism: Immanent Critique and Determinate Negation

This notion of truth gives Hegel the basis for a new method of philosophical reflection on our concepts that will enable him to avoid the dogmatism of precritical metaphysics. This is Hegel's dialectic, which employs the twin strategies of immanent critique and determinate negation.[12]

---

[10] See Alznauer (2016), who also draws on Wolff (1981).

[11] Cf. WdL 21: 17/SoL 18.

[12] The idea that the dialectic involves these twin strategies is particularly important to Rosen, whose discussion I follow here. See Rosen (1982: "2. Determinate Negation and Immanent Critique").

In the first step, sometimes known as "immanent critique," a concept is used as both the object and standard of evaluation. It is shown to be untrue in Hegel's sense of the term, self-contradictory. Part of the reason that the concept itself must be used as the standard is that any other would beg the question. We would face the question of what justifies the application of any "external" standard. Yet in the case of an internal one, this question does not arise.

Then, in the second step, sometimes known as "determinate negation," we find some way to resolve the contradiction. If we do, we will be left with a new concept that is contradiction-free and therefore an improvement upon the old. At the same time, this new concept is a refined version of the old. After all, it is the product of performing a certain operation on the old. Yet the mere fact that it is free of the contradiction that afflicted its predecessor does not mean it is wholly unproblematic. It will give rise to a contradiction of its own, at which point the process iterates. We know we have concluded it only when we return to the beginning. This requires that the last category be one that returns us to the first.

Admittedly, it is less often individual concepts than more complex structures that are subject to dialectical criticism in Hegel's writings. Here, we might think of the "configurations of consciousness" (*Gestalten des Bewußtseins*) from the *Phenomenology*, each of which involves a knowing subject, an object known, and a relation between them, knowledge. A conception of philosophy as the immanent critique of such "configurations of consciousness" was Hegel's earliest response to the swimming objection.[13] As we saw in Chapter 2, the objection was that evaluating claims to know by appealing to an account of the nature and limits of our cognitive faculties is question-begging or circular. We have already considered the mature Hegel's solution in the *Logic*, but the young Hegel's solution differs. It is that we can evaluate a claim to know with reference to an account of the nature and limits of our faculties *implicit in that very claim*, rather than one imported by the philosopher from elsewhere. For example, and famously, the protagonist of "Sense-Certainty" (*Die sinnliche Gewißheit oder das Diese und das Meinen*) makes a claim to know "this, here, now." Yet implicit in this claim is a corresponding conception of the knowing faculty as possessed of the faculty of sensibility, defined as immediately related to the singular object that is given to it. Unlike the *Logic*, then, the *Phenomenology* does not completely renounce an earlier subjective-idealist

---

[13] Habermas (1971) and Bristow (2007).

conception of critique as based in (some form of) philosophical psychology. It only renounces a particular version of this project, a version based on "external" rather than "internal" critique.

Beyond the opening arguments of the *Phenomenology* and the configurations of consciousness this work considers, we encounter other structures that are still more complex. We might also think of the "shapes of spirit" from that work, each of which is a different social and historical world (Ancient Greece, Rome, the Enlightenment and so on). Hegel's influential critiques of these forms of life only serve to distance his famed strategy of immanent critique further from the more austere subject matter of the *Logic*: quantity, quality and so on. The subsequent reception of Hegel's approach has done so as well. Certainly the most influential legacy of Hegel's idea of immanent critique is not its application to individual concepts, as in the logic,[14] but to social institutions. This is the role it plays in the Marxist tradition, where capitalism is criticized in terms of ideals and aspirations internal to it: for example, maximal productivity or efficiency. Be that is as it may, I wish to suggest that, in this foundational portion of Hegel's system, immanent critique operates at a more primitive level.

At least in the *Logic*, Hegel's dialectic is not just defined by a certain mode of progression but by a starting point. As we saw in Chapter 2, Being is the "first principle" of Hegel's philosophical system. It is not the only concept or proposition that has been proposed for that role. Yet Hegel defends his choice on the grounds that this concept is more primitive than any other. Every concept is the concept of a being or entity. However, we cannot assume in advance that the reverse is the case. That every being or entity is such as to be conceptualized or conceptualizable would be an unnecessary presupposition. Certainly, other candidate first principles name beings: the I=I, identity, the One and so on ("Being can be determined as I = I as the absolute indifference or identity, etc.") (EL § 83). To employ any of them would be to beg the question. In particular, it would be to assume that we already understand the concept all these further ones presuppose, Being. That is why there can be no skipping the first step and moving on to some other.

What is most important for our purposes is how the dialectical method, understood in this way, allows Hegel to avoid the form of dogmatism he finds in precritical metaphysics. The crucial point is that the dialectic,

---

[14] See Zambrana (2015) and Redding (1996) for interpretations of the *Logic* that stress "social" themes more than mine.

understood in this way, gives us a justification for defining and using our concepts in the way we do. In each case, the justification is always that this is the definition required to resolve a contradiction in the predecessor concept. Here, it should be noted that this justification is an a priori philosophical argument. The argument itself is not based on any appeal to ordinary usage, philosophical tradition, or any other external source. (It is possible these have some less significant role to play in the argument, such as making it comprehensible or relating it to other pertinent material.)

The argument is strengthened considerably when we realize that its starting point is Being, the most fundamental concept that there is. Every other concept is the concept of a being. If a concept purports to be a priori or a category but cannot be extracted from this first one using the procedure Hegel suggests, then it fails to secure this status. In a way, this is the fate suffered by traditional religious concepts of God, the soul and the world. At least in their traditional versions, they do not appear in the dialectical procession. Unlike Being, Substance and the Idea, and so on, their fate is to be unmasked as pseudo-concepts.

In some respects, Hegel could not have less in common with logical positivism/empiricism and ordinary language philosophy. Yet his criticism of rival philosophers and metaphysicians as effectively talking nonsense does seem to anticipate these developments. The difference of course is that Hegel mounts this assault on traditional metaphysics from the direction of a bold new form of it. He does not do so from an anti-metaphysical direction. This bold new form of metaphysics will be couched not in ordinary language but in a rather extraordinary one.

Moreover, a dialectical theory of concepts gives us a further standard by which to judge their use in philosophy, a standard precritical metaphysics lacked. This theory articulates a type of hierarchical order between these concepts that must be respected. If each solves a problem its predecessor could not, then this implies an order of rank between them. Criticisms of opponents for misusing concepts, using them out of their proper order or in ways that fail to respect the hierarchy between them are extremely common in Hegel.[15] This is certainly an odd mode of engaging with one's opponents, inasmuch as it does not directly involve criticizing their claims or the specific arguments for them. Yet this does explain why Hegel's chosen mode of engagement is so often this unusual one.

---

[15] See, for example, Hegel's criticism of a Kantian conception of concepts as belonging to the form of thought, rather than its sensibly given matter (EL § 160 Z1). His criticism is that, by the time we reach the standpoint of the Concept, the contrast between form and matter has been overcome.

3.6   Toward a Non–formal Logical Logic

In closing, I would like to explore the possibility that the dialectic is a radical alternative to a received view of philosophical discourse found in formal logic. Unlike formal logic, Hegel's *Logic* operates wholly at the level of individual concepts rather than at the level of judgments. It occupies a prepredicative standpoint rarely taken up in philosophy.[16] It takes up this more logically primitive standpoint to avoid the dogmatism of precritical metaphysics. Yet if that is so, then there is a further respect in which it differs from philosophy as traditionally practiced. Concepts combine into judgments, judgments into syllogistic inferences. By operating at this more primitive standpoint, Hegel's *Logic* is also noninferential. Especially in passages where he explains his dialectical method of argument, Hegel is scornful of what has usually passed for argument in philosophy. Whatever exactly the famed opening argument of Hegel's *Logic* is supposed to be – the argument taking us from Being to Nothing to Becoming – it should be fairly clear that it is not a syllogistic inference. This means that the dialectic is not only nonjudgmental but noninferential as well. It is at two levels of remove from the logical standpoint of precritical metaphysics, so as to more effectively avoid dogmatism. Hegel's *Logic* is therefore that rare thing, a work of philosophy entirely free of the type of claim and argument traditionally considered the philosopher's stock in trade. The uncanniness of this approach is lessened somewhat when we realize that judgment and inference are not the only type of claim and argument in philosophy. Nor does every stretch of written language that has the superficial appearance of a judgment or inference have the underlying logical structure. Hegel undeniably has a version of the distinction between surface grammar and logical form so important to later analytic philosophy. This would be one way of understanding his repeated insistence that not every fact-stating proposition (*Satz*) is a judgment (*Urteil*) in the logical sense.[17]

There is an important caveat to this, however. For Hegel, each concept that is considered in the *Logic* can be treated as a definition of the Absolute, and, therefore, as a judgment of subject–predicate form. "Being" becomes "the Absolute is Being," "Nothing" "the Absolute is Nothing," "Becoming"

---

[16] Cf. Koch (2019).
[17] Of course, Hegel's idea of what constitutes logical form would differ. Briefly, he seems to distinguish propositions and genuine judgments are classificatory, normatively laden, even essentialist: "Caesar was born in such and such a year" is a mere proposition, whereas "this is a healthy plant" is a "paradigm case of judgment."

"the Absolute is Becoming" and so on. Yet as Hegel makes clear, these are not judgments in the logical sense, claims asserting a connection between two distinct concepts. They are mere pseudo-judgments, since they in fact only involve one concept. In these pseudo-judgments, the Absolute is little more than an empty placeholder.[18] After all, it is only in the predicate that we learn what the definition of the subject is supposed to be.

> Being itself as well as the subsequent determinations, not only those of being but also the logical determinations in general, can be regarded as the definitions of the absolute, as *metaphysical definitions of God* ... [but] if the form of definitions were used, this would entail envisaging a representational substratum. For even *the absolute*, what is supposed to express God in the sense and in the form of thought, remains merely an *intended* thought, i.e. a substratum that as such is indeterminate, relative to its predicate as the determinate and actual expression in thought. *Because the thought, the basic matter solely at issue here, is contained only in the predicate, the form of a proposition, like that subject, is something completely superfluous.* (EL § 85 A)

Why, though, does Hegel take this approach? Here, Hegel's reference to a "representational substratum" is crucial. As we saw earlier, representation is the medium in which religion moves. It is also the medium in which religious concepts such as God, the soul and the world are found. Finally, it is also the source of the subject matter of precritical metaphysics. Logically speaking, God, the soul and the world are representations that pre-critical metaphysics relied upon to invest the subject terms of its judgments with meaning. Here, Hegel's claim is that if we were to treat the subject term as anything else than an empty placeholder, we would have no choice but to rely on representation for its meaning. Yet we would then find ourselves in the impasses of precritical metaphysics. Hence, the Absolute must be an empty placeholder. This is all that the subject term, the Absolute, can be if we are to avoid the dogmatism of precritical metaphysics.

In addition to its nonjudgmental, noninferential character there is a third respect in which the dialectic is nonlogical. The laws it adheres to in moving from one step to the next are not those of logic. They cannot be if Hegel is to later deduce those laws (a deduction I discuss later in Chapter 5). Those laws are not available to be appealed to at this early stage. If they were invoked, this would beg the question. It would make any deduction offered later circular. This is especially true in the opening

---

[18] Here I follow Koch (2019), for whom the Absolute is a "dummy subject" and these propositions "pseudo-propositions."

argument of the *Logic*, the Doctrine of Being. The laws of logic enter at a later point in the *Logic*, the Doctrine of Essence. As we later discuss in greater depth, the Doctrine of Being concerns of nonrelational concepts rather than relational ones, or concept pairs. In the Doctrine of Being, we do not yet have access to the "determinations of reflection" such as contradiction and identity that become relevant at a later point in the Doctrine of Essence.

Yet if that is so, we confront an obvious difficulty. The dialectic, as we have seen, does operate by identifying and then resolving contradictions. How, then, can it be independent of logic? Surely, it relies on at least one law of logic: the law of noncontradiction. Otherwise, there would be nothing that the contradictions that arise offended against. There would be no reason to resolve them in the way the dialectic does.[19]

The answer implicit in Hegel's argument is that contradictions in the logical sense and those that arise in his dialectic differ. A logical contradiction is richer in structure, and therefore in a sense downstream of those that interest Hegel – protocontradictions, as we might call them. For Hegel, the distinctly logical notion of contradiction pertains to judgments of the form S is P. This means that logical contradiction presupposes a certain structure with three components – a subject concept, a predicate concept and the copula that relates them. It is the connection between one and two asserted by three that gives rise to the contradiction. Yet the conflicts in which Hegel is interested arise before any of these components is available. We never get so far as even defining one concept, let alone two, or one in terms of the other. Indeed, we do not get as far as asserting a connection between them by means of the copula. In the case we have considered, the particular concept whose definition eludes us just is the one from which the copula "is" derives: the concept of being. Finally, I think it worth noting that there is nothing formal about these inconsistencies in the way there is for logical contradictions. Each arises because of the unique content they treat, not because of the form of statement made about it. Similarly, each is sui generis, rather than a token instance of some general type. I therefore think Hegel has good grounds to claim that the line he draws between dialectical contradictions and those of formal logic is nonarbitrary. However, I think a more definitive verdict would have to

---

[19] This problem is related to the more well-known one Henrich discusses in his essay "Anfang und Methode," namely that of how Hegel can claim Being and nothing are *identical* when this is a "determination of reflection" (1972). In both cases, the worry is that Hegel will have helped himself to conceptual resources to which he is not yet entitled to.

be based on whether this line is one we draw today. Certainly logicians of Hegel's time are not alone in claiming that judgment is the most basic truth bearer. This view is expressed in Frege's "context principle," from the *Grundlagen*, as well as in his idea of concepts as "unsaturated expressions."

A final respect in which Hegel's dialectic is non–formal logical is that, despite being nonempirical, it cuts across a common way that logical and extralogical truths are distinguished: the analytic/synthetic discussion. For Hegel, the knowledge that the dialectic gives us is *both* analytic and synthetic at once.[20]

> The philosophical method is as much analytic as it is synthetic, yet not in the sense of a mere juxtaposition or a mere oscillation of these two methods of finite knowing. It is instead such that it contains them as sublated in itself and accordingly behaves in each of its movements both analytically and synthetically at the same time. (EL § 238 Z)

Analysis of one concept does not simply demonstrate what it contains or what its definition is. It also gives rise to another concept distinct from and, indeed, in contradiction with the first. In Kant's terms, it is both "explicative" and "ampliative," rather than either/or (A 10). Finally, the resolution of this contradiction leads to their synthesis in a new concept, at which point the process repeats. We have, then, a necessary connection between two distinct concepts. Yet it is, as it were, a product of these two concepts themselves rather than of the knowing subject. One produces the other, conflicts with it, and then resolves the conflict by uniting with its opposite.

Like Quine, the great twentieth-century critic of the analytic–synthetic distinction, Hegel urges us to overcome the dichotomy between truths about the world and truths of language or logic. Unlike Quine, however, the truths about the world that interest him are not empirical or natural-scientific ones but a priori or metaphysical truths. There is a world of difference between rendering (formal) logic continuous with natural science and rendering it continuous with metaphysics.

This suggests that Hegel's answer to Kant's great question "How is synthetic a priori knowledge possible?" must differ from Kant's own.[21] For Kant, the synthetic a priori truths are possible because of "the possibility of experience." Since the subject concept does not contain the predicate

---

[20] I here follow two others who have made versions of this point: Rosen (1988: 258) and, more recently, Werner (2018).

[21] Burbidge (2006: 39–40) also argues that Hegel, unlike Kant, recognized the possibility of a purely intellectual synthesis.

concept, a "third thing, X," is necessary to unite them (B 194/A 155). We later learn that this third thing is the forms of intuition and the categories. Moreover, this third thing is contributed by the subject, the sensible and intelligible conditions on the possibility of experience.

However, no such "third thing" is required in Hegel's dialectic, at least not in the same sense. The first concept genuinely contains the second, but they contradict one another. They are then brought together with the resolution of the contradiction, though not through the addition of any other element – therefore not through the addition of one by the subject, as transcendental idealism maintains.

3.7 Conclusion: Concepts "under Erasure"?

I have suggested that Hegel's critique of metaphysics leads him to a method of thinking that is unconstrained by formal logic: the dialectic. I have sought to exhibit this form of thinking as nonjudgment based, non-inferential, even as operating independently of the law of noncontradiction. Only by dispending with these resources can Hegel overcome the dogmatic relationship to logic found in the metaphysical tradition, as well as pave the way for his own resolution of the logocentric predicament.

However, there may remain a respect in which Hegel's method is residually logical, which is that it operates upon concepts. Here too, however, Hegel will insist that what appears to be a presupposition is in fact a result. The following passage from the lectures is representative:

> In the science itself it will be seen that the universal for itself, on its own account, is necessary, that the other forms revert back to it, that it is what is true. The universal is the product of thinking, but [in this preliminary exposition] the universal form is taken up merely empirically. We represent thinking to ourselves as an activity. (LL 7/9–10)

Our "empirical" grasp of concepts as they arise in ordinary experience and scientific thought is all that is needed to understand Hegel's preliminary characterization of his science. The proof that this science's subject matter is and has all along been conceptual emerges later, however.

Much as I have done for judgment, inference, and other of logic's laws and materials, I deny that any contentful account of concepts is presupposed by Hegel's logic. We certainly do not need to presuppose an account of concepts like that given by Kant when he describes them as the representations native to a particular faculty: the understanding. The Hegelian equivalent of this would be to describe concepts as "thought determinations." More fundamentally, however, we do not need to presuppose an account of the concepts themselves as universals, one-over-many and so on. Supposing one insisted to the contrary it would hardly matter for the purposes of the argument. One might insist that the logic dealt with Fregean senses or "modes of presentation," Husserlian Noema(ta), Aristotelian categories, Kantian ones, Platonic/substantial forms or some other such item. Such misconceptions would hardly affect the argument that being and nothing, as immediate indeterminates, are the same. The point here is that no account of the psychological, semantic, epistemological or metaphysical vehicle we are operating with is in any way relevant to this particular argument. We can, crudely speaking, factor out or divide through by any such conception of the logic's subject matter. It is completely incidental to the matter at hand. This is not because there is no way to misconceive the subject matter of the logic but because no (mis)conception would matter much to the argument itself. Or, better, none would matter *at the outset*. The argument would resolve any such misconception *by its close*. After all, this is a science that culminates with insight into itself and its subject matter. I have sought to supplement this received idea with a further, more controversial, one that no such insight is necessary for the science to commence.

Another anachronistic way to put the point would be that, when we claim that Being and Nothing are the same, we are "using," rather than "mentioning," these concepts.[22] The only way to ask whether they are in fact concepts would be to cease doing so. What is more, misconceptions of the vehicles we use will be overturned when the argument concludes, and we learn that we have all throughout been thinkers thinking thinking. If one were to speak of the logic as studying concepts, one would need to make clear that nothing about these concepts is being presupposed. Yet this would be as good as to revoke one's statement that it is about concepts at all.

One is here reminded in the Continental tradition of those like the later Heidegger and Derrida who write certain terms "under erasure" (*Sous rature*), or, in the analytic, of Wittgenstein's ladder that one throws away once one climbs it. Much in the way so-called "resolute" readers of Wittgenstein are unflinching about the need to cast aside so much of the *Tractatus* as "nonsense" (*Unsinn, sinnlos*), so too am I a resolute reader of Hegel.[23] I am (or aspire to be) unflinching about the inadequacy of his

---

[22] Quine (1951: 23).
[23] Crary and Read (2000).

statements about his project to what that project, in fact, is. This would include both preliminary statements, in prefaces and introductions, as well as asides in the main text.

The difference is that, in Hegel, the suspension of belief about the subject matter of one's study is only provisional. At the close, one is in a position to grasp the justification for these beliefs and so "recapture" the initial standpoint. By doing so, one has a superior justification for occupying it than one could have possessed at the outset, and, indeed, a justification in terms of rational argument. At least some of the figures just mentioned may have been more content to claim that our entitlement to what is most fundamental in thought and language is a kind of mystery. Yet Hegel, a foe of all "mysterianism," insists this entitlement can be vindicated by thought itself.

CHAPTER 4

Hegel's Response to Kant's Critique of Metaphysics

As I have argued, Hegel's attitude toward the Kantian critique of metaphysics is complex. Hegel agrees with Kant that precritical metaphysics is a failed enterprise but not that transcendental idealism is the best alternative. Instead, Hegel advocates a new form of realist metaphysics that employs different logical resources or tools. I will focus on another of the crude logical tools Hegel thinks hindered the precritical tradition: finite categories. I here set aside the issue raised earlier about the ambivalent position of category theory vis-à-vis logic. I am far from the first to suggest that Kant's critical philosophy and precritical metaphysics alike were compromised by their reliance on finite categories.[1] However, I will offer a novel interpretation of this accusation, emphasizing Hegel's affinity for monist versions of the ontological proof.

What substantive issue lies behind this somewhat technical dispute over which categories to employ, finite or infinite? To answer this question, we should recall Hegel's suspicion that Kant lacks the conceptual resources to adequately grasp the nature of the infinite and is therefore not in a position to critically evaluate forms of metaphysics organized around this notion. We have already considered an instance of this criticism, Hegel's provocative claim that a "true critique of reason and the categories" would uphold, rather than condemn, the ontological argument (WdL 21: 77/ SoL 66). In the present context, however, a component of this provocative claim stands out more clearly. Hegel further maintains that this "true critique" would give the infinite its due, rather than conceiving of it using logical tools that are incapable to grasping its true nature: In particular, it would refrain from applying "determinations and relations of the finite" to God, or the infinite. As we will see, versions of this criticism are made of Kant's critique of rational psychology and cosmology as well, not only of his critique of rational theology.

[1] Bowman (2013).

In this respect, Kant is no less "uncritical" than his predecessors in the precritical tradition of dogmatic metaphysics. They too lacked the conceptual resources required to adequately grasp the infinite. Of course, they did not share Kant's dim view of the prospects for metaphysics, but their efforts were compromised by this oversight. To this extent, Kant's account of the impasses of the tradition is sound. In particular, Hegel agrees that its three branches (rational psychology, cosmology and theology) gave rise to three characteristic types of error (paralogism, antinomy and Ideal). Yet Kant's diagnosis of the sources of these impasses is unsound, at least from Hegel's perspective. For Hegel, these impasses result from a lack of infinite categories, not transcendental realism. Hence, Hegel must engage in a creative retelling of Kant's critique of metaphysics. This is a retelling in which the cause is finite, rather than infinite, categories and the cure is a project more continuous with the tradition than Kant's transcendental idealism.

What, then, does it mean to grasp the infinite? One does so by means of infinite categories, though this is not especially informative. Infinite categories are best understood negatively, via the contrast with the finite categories that, according to Hegel, predominate in Kant and the tradition. As we will see, there are two distinct respects in which such categories are finite, paralleling the two respects in which the thought forms of traditional logic were finitude: finite vis-à-vis one another, on the one hand, and finite vis-à-vis the world, on the other. I will occasionally refer to these forms of finitude as semantic noncomprehensiveness and real. They denote, on the one hand, a failure to exhaust the space of possible meanings and, on the other, a failure to exhaust reality – or even to find any foothold there at all.

As I hope to show, there is a complex division of labor between the three different parts of Hegel's response to the Kantian critique of metaphysics. In order to see this, it is important to realize that there are two distinct ways in which a category can be finite (or fail to be): finite vis-à-vis other categories, and finite vis-à-vis the world. Once we realize this, we will see that overcoming one form of finitude (vis-à-vis other categories) is the task of the first two parts of Hegel's discussion concerning Kant's critique of cosmology and psychology in the antinomies and paralogisms. Overcoming the other form of finitude (vis-à-vis the world) is the task of the third, concerning Kant's critique of rational theology, the Ideal. For complex reasons, seeing how these parts of Hegel's account work in concert will be crucial to appreciating the power of his argument against Kant, which can often appear uncharitable and even simple-minded.

Hegel would appear to favor a metaphysics organized around something maximally comprehensive and necessarily instantiated. This suggests a discrepancy between Hegel's view of traditional metaphysics and that of Kant. Both Hegel and Kant are critics of the tradition, but their critiques differ. Unlike Kant, Hegel does not appear willing to tar Spinoza and the Leibniz–Wolff school with the same brush.[2] He does not seem interested in denouncing both as precritical, dogmatic metaphysics but, rather, in separating the Spinozist wheat from the Scholastic-Aristotelian chaff. I return to this point concerning the Hegelian historiography of philosophy at the close, focusing for the remainder of the chapter on the substance of Hegel's position.

4.1   Finite and Infinite Categories

According to Hegel, Kant shares one of the same logical blind spots as the tradition he rejected: relying exclusively on finite categories and neglecting the infinite variety. What, then, are finite and infinite categories? Without a clear answer to this question, Hegel's critique of Kant will seem unconvincing. To be sure, the categories that Kant considers in the Analytic are finite (limited) in a certain sense of that term. As it turns out, they only yield knowledge of appearances and not of things in themselves. Yet it is simply unfair to claim that Kant simply overlooked the possibility of categories that are free of this limitation. Rather, he has a principled reason for doubting there are any such categories, many such reasons in fact. They could be summarized in the broad thesis that only categories that are limited in the way Kant describes ("finite") can truly yield knowledge: more specifically, the type of synthetic a priori knowledge found in mathematics and natural science.

The Analytic aside, Hegel's criticism seems even less persuasive when it is directed at Kant's Dialectic. After all, categories that are, in some sense, infinite figure prominently there. For example, consider Kant's critique of rational cosmology in the antinomies section. There Kant does consider the possibility that the world is infinite in age or size but denies we can know this. He further considers the possibility that the world is infinite, not just in the large but in the small. Pace Hegel, Kant does not overlook but carefully considers and then rejects the possibility that we could acquire theoretical knowledge by means of infinite concepts, or as

---

[2] The superiority of Spinozism, from a German Idealist point of view, to other schools of "precritical" dogmatic metaphysics is a theme in Franks (2005).

Kant would call them "Ideas of reason." Hegel's criticism that Kant lacks infinite categories, and remain confined to the finite variety, can therefore appear to be based on a simple misunderstanding.

However, none of the different senses of the terms finite and infinite that are at work in Kant's first critique can adequately prepare us for what Hegel has in mind. Put in Hegelian terms, Kant's infinites are finite infinites, bad or counterfeit varieties rather than genuine ones. To this extent, Hegel is right that the possibility he explores is one Kant never considered with sufficient care. Here, I want to return to the idea, developed in Chapter 1, that Hegel recognizes two types of finitude when it comes to "thought determinations," interconceptual and extraconceptual. Presumably, this includes not only concept, judgment and syllogism of traditional logic but also the categories.

4.1.1 Finitude vis-à-vis Other Categories

I begin with a first form of finitude: finitude vis-à-vis other categories. A category is finite vis-à-vis another if it meets its boundary, border or limit in at least one other category. This bounding, bordering or limiting occurs at a purely semantic level (here, we should recall the dialectical context and, more specifically, that Hegel is debating an opponent who cannot be assumed to share his view that "thinking and being are one"). This first semantic form of finitude can be identified independently whether the category in question finds application to reality.

Consider one of Hegel's favorite examples of a finite category: the category of a creator God, familiar from orthodox religion. This is a finite category because it is bounded by another, the category of God's creation understood as in some sense separate from its creator. Whereas the creator is "over here" creation is "over yonder," Hegel says, mocking adherents of this view for allowing spatial metaphors to creep in to pure thinking.

Crucially, the designation of this theological category as a finite one stands even if such a God does not exist. Perhaps acosmism is true: God is the hen-kai-pan ("one and all"), Spinoza's substance. Hence, the created world, as traditionally conceived, does not exist. Or perhaps atheism is true. Hence, no creator God exists, and all that does is an uncreated world. In a sense, however, the mirror-image threats of atheism and acosmism are irrelevant. Whether it finds a foothold in reality or not, the category of a creator God remains finite. It is noncomprehensive, at least semantically speaking. Of course, it would be really noncomprehensive as well, if it did exist. Traditional religion's God is a creator, set apart from his creation. Finitude in the conceptual domain finds its correlate in the domain of the real.

With this in mind, we can see that Kant's categories and ideas are finite for reasons quite independent of their restriction to the domain of appearances and their nonapplicability to things-in-themselves. Kant's twelve categories too are finite or semantically noncomprehensive. Each meets its border, boundary or limit in the others. True, each is a concept of an object in general. At the very least, however, each describes a different aspect of the object: a different property or relation in which it stands to other objects. This finitude of the categories would remain, even if they did apply to things-in-themselves. That they do not simply adds insult to injury.

The same is true of Kant's Ideas, even granting his claim that they represent "the unconditioned" condition of everything conditioned. So defined, they remain semantically noncomprehensive. Minimally, they are finite vis-à-vis one another. Yet they are also so vis-à-vis the conditioned things they condition. Unlike the categories, the Ideas do not afford us cognition of even objects of possible experience. They serve a purely regulative role. This further downgrading they suffer in relation to the categories is lamentable from a Hegelian point of view. However, it does not exhaust the problem of finitude, which would still arise even if somehow the Ideas did yield theoretical knowledge. From a Hegelian point of view, Kant's position concerning the Ideas is even further from the target than his position concerning categories.

A paradigm instance of a finite category is one with an opposite. Very often, a finite category comes in a pair with another, each member of which is defined as what the other is not.

> Predicates such as these are, for example, *existence,* as in the sentence *'God possesses existence; finitude* or *infinity,* as in the question whether the world is finite or infinite; *simple* or *composite,* as in the sentence "the soul is simple"; also "the thing is *one,* a *whole,"* and so on. (EL § 28)

Why are opposites preeminent in the pantheon of finite thinking? Because they are the closest a finite category can come to being infinite: occupying one half of the available semantic space. The simple is a finite category because it has its opposite in the category of the complex, and the same is true of the free and the determined, the finite and the (bad) infinite. As we will soon see, these finite categories are the categories used by precritical metaphysicians, such as those of the Leibniz–Wolff school.

By contrast, Being, the One, the (true) infinite and so on are not necessarily finite categories in Hegel's sense because they purport not to have opposites. Often, their claim to be infinite is not upheld – meaning we are here concerned with infinite purport, rather than infinitude per se. However, the case to be made for the infinitude of such categories is meant to be that they could not possibly have opposites, since they exhaust the entirety of what there is. Outside of them there is nothing, and therefore nothing left to be comprehended by an opposed concept, or even just a distinct one. Unlike the finite categories of the Leibniz–Wolff school, infinite categories are typically the province of those outside the philosophical mainstream: pre-Socratics, heretics, freethinkers, mystics and so on.

Since some of these categories appear on our list of both finite and infinite categories, an important caveat is needed here. One and the same category may admit of being understood in either of these two ways, finite or infinite. For example, consider Oneness or unity. It is a finite category when it is used by the Medieval Scholastics or early modern rationalists to describe the soul. The soul is an indestructible unity, different in kind from material objects, which are destructible pluralities. Yet this category is infinite when it is used by Parmenideans to describe the whole of reality. Outside of the one, everything else (plurality, motion, change and so on) is completely illusory. The distinction between infinite and finite categories is not extensional.

Overcoming finitude of this first type ("semantic noncomprehensiveness") is valuable for the purpose of resolving the impasses of precritical metaphysics. That is because it removes the possibility of confronting a claim with its opposite in the way the disputants in traditional metaphysical controversies do.

> This metaphysics became *dogmatism* because, *due to the nature of the finite determinations*, it had to assume that of *two opposite assertions* (which is what those sentences were) one had to be *true* while the other was *false*. (EL § 32, some italics mine)

In logical terms, we could explain this in the following way. Let us suppose we are given pairs of finite categories, opposed categories, each of which is defined as what the other is not. If that is so, then there will be the possibility of formulating pairs of opposed claims, each of which denies what the other affirms. For example, it is only because a concept such as simplicity is finite, only because it has an opposite in the complex, that metaphysicians can debate whether the soul is simple or complex. Yet if we employed infinite categories, then these debates might not arise. Both of the competing views could conceivably be subsumed under a more comprehensive perspective. Not the "either/or" of understanding, Hegel says, supplying Kierkegaard with his famous turn of phrase, but the "both/and" of reason.

At first, it might seem that Hegel's approach only eliminates "local" forms of finitude, rather than more "global" ones. So, for example, one could eliminate the finitude vis-à-vis one another of predicates such as body and soul, freedom and necessity, unity and plurality. Yet one would be left with the finitude of the entity they qualify: the particular living or spiritual being in question. Here, we should recall that the categories are not being considered as predicates of possible judgments but in their own right. Hence, overcoming their finitude via one another is a more significant accomplishment than it might at first seem. If these categories were being treated as predicates, then another source of finitude would remain: the entity designated by the subject term could be finite. However, this is not the case, since Hegel's critique operates at a prepredicative level.

Still, there is one form of finitude remaining: finitude vis-à-vis the world. In order to see why the finitude vis-à-vis one another is insufficient, we should consider the following. By arguing in this way, the most that Hegel could show is that a certain concept would resolve the impasses of metaphysics *if it had application to reality*. Yet unless it does, in fact, apply, this is a hollow victory. Metaphysics is concerned with the ultimate nature of reality. It would not be content to exchange its concepts for others that are mere "figments of the brain."

Put another way, overcoming finitude vis-à-vis other categories is only the first step. This is a form of finitude that arises because a category is not completely comprehensive, albeit at a semantic level. It shares logical space with other categories. Yet it remains necessary to overcome finitude vis-à-vis the world. Only in this way will the merely semantic comprehensiveness of a category result in its real comprehensiveness. The former does not necessarily entail the latter. It is at least possible that the world as it is in itself does not in any way correspond to the space of meanings. Perhaps it is meaningless.

4.1.2   Finitude vis-à-vis the World

I explain this second variety of finitude more briefly. A concept is finite vis-à-vis the world if it is *possible* that it should fail to be instantiated in the world. Here our concern is with the definition of the concept and whether or not it allows for this possibility. A concept is infinite vis-à-vis the world if it is necessary that it be instantiated, impossible that it fail to be so. It is part of its definition to exist, and therefore impossible that it should fail to do so. Because this truth obtains simply in virtue of meaning, that is the meaning of the concept in question, it is not a contingent truth. It cannot just so happen that an infinite category apply. If it applies, it necessarily does.

Hence, there is an asymmetry between infinitude categories and finite ones. The latter may or may not apply depending on the circumstances. Their meaning or definition leaves this question open. If it is true that they apply, then this is not a truth of meaning but a metaphysical or empirical truth. Not so with the former type of category, whose meaning or definition settles the issue rendering further argument otiose.

As should be clear, Hegel's appeal to categories that are infinite in this second sense reflects his endorsement of the ontological argument for the existence of God. Kant, its most famous critic, responds "existence is not a real predicate."[3] It is not the type of property that can belong to a thing by definition at all. Later, I will consider Hegel's response to this Kantian counterargument, but for now the important point is simply the following.

If there are categories that are infinite not only in the first sense but in the second as well, then they can be used to rehabilitate a form of realist metaphysics. In the first place, they would allow us to resolve the impasses reached by rational psychology and cosmology. Infinite categories should allow us to show that the true view incorporates both of the competing perspectives in the age-old controversies of metaphysics. Yet we could revive a form of rational theology as well. The infinite categories, which resolve these impasses, also describe a necessary being.

A caveat is that we should not be surprised if Hegel emphasizes different infinite categories at different times for different purposes. At one time, he will invoke (the Idea of) life, at another being, at a third, the Concept or Idea and so on. It would therefore be legitimate to worry that the different good-making features Hegel claims for his own preferred definition of the Absolute are, in fact, parceled out among many such definitions. They are nowhere found in any one definition, though we can grant Hegel that it would be nice if they were.

Yet Hegel has a response to this worry. Because each category is a refined or "sublated" version of its predecessors, Hegel believes that the advantageous aspects of any of them will eventually be shared by all of them. Just as there is a division of labor between Hegel's different defenses of metaphysics against various forms of attack from without, so too is there such a division within Hegel's metaphysics itself. Yet the division of labor enriches all of the participants.

Ultimately, Hegel's idea of an infinite category gives him a different conception of the task of philosophy than Kant held. For Hegel, philosophy's

---

[3] "Being is obviously not a real predicate, i.e., a concept of something that could add to the concept of a thing" (A 598/B 626).

task is simply to attempt to identify an infinite category whose definition is coherent. As we have seen this is more difficult than it might at first seem since nearly all fail to meet this standard. In any case, nearly all further philosophical tasks can be subsumed under this one.

This can be clarified by recalling an oft remarked upon and unusual feature of Hegel's project. This is Hegel's conviction that the task of deducing the categories, in Kant's Critique a mere preliminary carried out in the Metaphysical Deduction, can take over virtually all of the other tasks Kant saw for philosophy. There is no separate step needed to show such categories apply to the sensibly given manifold, or the world of appearances, the step Kant took in the Transcendental Deduction. Nor is there a need for a critical examination of reason's efforts in metaphysics to apply them to a world that goes beyond that of our experience, the step taken in the Dialectic. All of these tasks are collapsed into one, and, as we will soon see, in such a way that reason's claim to know the unconditioned is upheld, rather than denied.[4]

4.2 Responding to Kant's Critique of Rational Psychology: The Paralogisms

According to Kant, paralogisms are flawed inferences, though the flaw is not merely logical. Certainly, it cannot be accounted for in the way ordinary logical errors can. Simply attending to the form of the argument and finding invalidity therein is not a possibility here – or, at least, not a possible way of dispelling confusion. Instead, a paralogism is an error arising from the subject matter of the argument or its content. More specifically, there is an equivocation between the way a certain term is used in the premises and in the conclusion. Here is an example of a paralogism:

P1. That the representation of which is the absolute subject of our judgments, and cannot be employed as determination of any other thing, is substance.

---

[4] I here follow others like Rödl (2007), Pippin (2018: 122) and McDowell (2009: Ch. 4) who claim that Hegel collapses Kant's Transcendental Deduction into the Metaphysical Deduction. Yet I differ from these interpreters in a significant respect. For them, the reason Hegel can make this innovation over Kant is that he avoids a "subjectivist" conception of the given, the forms of intuition, as well as the need for a thing in itself. However, for me the reason has to do with his rehabilitation of both general metaphysics and the ontological argument. Perhaps there is a way of reconciling these two readings, but I do not pursue it here.

P2. I, as thinking being, am the absolute subject of all my possible judgments and this representation of myself cannot be employed as determination of any other thing.

C. Therefore, I, as thinking being (soul), am substance. (A 349)

In the premises, we are told that the self has some characteristic in a merely logical respect, for example, being the implicit subject of all its judgments. However, a metaphysical conclusion is then said to follow from this merely logical premise. For example, a conclusion like that drawn by the Cartesian dualist, for whom I am a type of substance in which accidental properties inhere. Admittedly, Kant describes the errors of rational psychology as being of several different kinds: for example, attempting to know using only concepts what would require (intellectual) intuition. However, the conflation of logical and metaphysical aspects of the knowing subject will be our focus.

Although Hegel is in broad agreement with Kant's critique of rational psychology, he maintains that the project of a metaphysics of subjectivity remains a viable one. For Hegel, the failure of pre-Kantian rational psychology does not entail that of any metaphysics of subjectivity. This would only follow if the finite categories that rational psychologists employ and that Kant focuses on in his critique of this tradition were the only ones there were. Yet this is not so, according to Hegel.

> It is quite correct, moreover, that predicates such as simplicity, immutability, and so on, are not to be attributed to the soul, yet not for the reason given by Kant, namely that reason would then overstep the limit set for it, but because abstract determinations of the understanding such as the simple are too poor for the soul and because it is something quite different from what is simple, immutable, and so on. Thus, for instance, the soul is indeed simple identity with itself, but qua active it is at the same time distinguishing itself from itself within itself. (EL § 47 Z)

There are other categories, infinite categories, and they are much better suited to the task ("distinguishing itself from itself within itself" would be an example of their structure). As Hegel says, Kant speaks as if his categories were "too high" to comprehend the knowing subject, but in reality they are "too poor and mean."

> The form which Kant accordingly bestows on Being, thing, substance, would seem to indicate that these categories of the understanding were too high for the subject, too high to be capable of being predicated of it. But really such determinations are too poor and too mean for what possesses life is not a thing, nor can the soul, the spirit, the ego, be called a thing.

> Being is the least or lowest quality that one can assign to spirit, its abstract, immediate identity with itself; Being thus no doubt pertains to spirit, but it must be considered as a determination scarcely worth applying to it. (VGP/LHoP v. 3 "Kant: Critique of Pure Reason")[5]

As this last quotation indicates, Hegel will understand the soul in a broader sense than rational psychology does. For him, the soul pertains not only to the mind but also to organic life (as in Aristotle) and to what Hegel calls "spirit." Both life and spirit are infinite categories.

It is because of its reliance on finite categories that rational psychology remains plagued by insoluble controversies. A clue to why is contained in Hegel's claim that the categories Kant employs are "one-sided."

> What Kant generally has in mind here is the state of the metaphysics of his time which, as a rule, stayed at these one-sided determinations with no hint of dialectic; he neither paid attention to, nor examined, the genuinely speculative ideas of older philosophers on the concept of spirit. (WdL12: 194/SoL 691)

Suppose we remain restricted to these categories in formulating philosophical claims. If that is so, then disputes will arise in the following way. Each thesis, framed in terms of one such category, can always be met by the antithesis, framed in terms of its contrary. Is the soul simple or complex? Mortal or immortal?[6] By contrast, infinite categories, if legitimate, would allow for a different approach. On the one hand, they would reveal both sides of the dispute to be equally right, insofar as each captures an important facet of a multifaceted phenomenon. On the other, they would reveal both to be equally wrong, insofar as they assume the alternatives on offer are mutually exclusive. Here, the relevant infinite categories are not so much those from the Doctrine of Being but rather from the Doctrine of Essence and the Doctrine of the Concept. I mean especially the category pairs such as form–matter from Hegel's engagement with Aristotle, as well as the later version of it, body–soul from Hegel's discussion of the

---

[5] Another passage that says the same is as follows: "In any case, it should be deemed a good result of the Kantian critique that philosophizing about spirit has been freed from the soul-thing, from the categories and thus from the questions concerning the simplicity or compositeness, the materiality, and so forth, of the soul. – However, the true viewpoint regarding the illegitimacy of such forms, even for ordinary human understanding, will surely not be that they are thoughts, but that such thoughts in and of themselves hold no truth" (EL § 47A).

[6] Here, I have to admit that Hegel is less scrupulous than he might be about distinguishing between the problems afflicting rational psychology, paralogisms, and those afflicting cosmology, antinomies. The two appear to be bleeding into one another in his presentation, inasmuch as he seems to be suggesting that the problem Kant saw with rational psychology was a type of antinomy.

Idea of life. In addition to these two, Hegel invokes his category of spirit here, which is also an infinite category. Because it is defined by its fundamentally nonalienated relationship to the natural world, including sensible impressions and desires, spirit is infinite vis-à-vis nature in a way that the Cartesian soul, being only contingently related to a material body, can never be. It is likely these categories from ancient philosophy that Hegel means to invoke when he refers to "the genuinely speculative ideas of older philosophers of spirit."

In contrast to the rational-psychologist's Cartesian idea of a soul substance, the Aristotelian conception of soul as the form of the living body can only be understood using infinite categories. Body and soul, understood as form and matter, are inseparable. Form is always the form of some matter, matter that of some form. Descartes' concepts of body and soul differ from the older Aristotelian ones. They are only contingently related and could exist apart from one another. If we reorganized discussion of the soul and subjectivity around infinite categories, then we could reframe each of the opposing positions in rational psychology as capturing only one side of a more complex two-sided phenomenon.

For Kant, the solution lies in recognizing that metaphysical claims about the subject hold good only if they are recast as more modest logical ones. Hegel rejects Kant's solution, but the reason he gives is perplexing. He does so on the grounds that these logical claims would be "empirical" – perhaps in a way that would prevent them from being satisfying replacements for those of rational psychology (EL § 47). Why, though, does Hegel hold this view? Clearly, Kant intended to weaken the claims of rational psychology, but not by replacing them with claims from empirical psychology. Yet Hegel seems to equate Kant's appeal to logic with a Humean or empiricist perspective on the self:

> As can be seen, this critique expresses nothing but the Humean observation mentioned above in § 39 that the thought-determinations in general, namely universality and necessity, are not to be found in perception and that the empirical is different, in terms of content as in terms of its form, from the thought-determination. (EL § 47)

> What Kant generally has in mind here is the state of the metaphysics of his time which, as a rule, stayed at these one-sided determinations with no hint of dialectic; he neither paid attention to, nor examined, the genuinely speculative ideas of older philosophers on the concept of spirit. In his critique of those determinations he then simply abided by the Humean style of skepticism; that is to say, he fixes on how the "I" appears in self-consciousness, but from this "I," since it is its essence (the thing in itself) that we want to cognize, he

removes everything empirical; nothing then remains but this appearance of the "I think" that accompanies all representations and of which we do not have the slightest concept. (WdL 12: 194/SoL 691)

That Kant's critical philosophy is an unsatisfying halfway house between metaphysics and empiricism is a common trope in Hegel's Kant critique. Yet it is also one that has frequently seemed both uncharitable to Kant and unpersuasive as a criticism. To be sure, Kant makes concessions to empiricism. However, his distinction between the logical and metaphysical I would not seem to be among them.

Here, I argue that Hegel's claim can be approached in terms of a recurrent theme in his critique of Kant as I have reconstructed it here. I mean Hegel's conviction that many of Kant's claims about the knowing subject are drawn from the logic of the day and that this logic is empirical in a way that creates problems for Kant's account. From a Hegelian perspective at least, Kant's logical alternative to rational psychology may be logical in a much more straightforward sense than is often realized. On this Hegelian view, the term "logic" as it is used by Kant in this context does not simply mean abstract, formal, conceptual and so on. Rather, it refers to the area of philosophy that has gone by the name, logic. At first, we might balk at the idea that this field could have anything to tell us about the traditional topics of rational psychology: for example, the nature of the soul. However, Kant's logic is by no means independent of every form of psychology, even if it is independent of the empirical variety. This does not mean logic is tantamount to rationalist metaphysics, but it does mean they share a similar topic: the self, broadly construed. That is why Kant is able to present rationalist metaphysics of the soul as logic taken one step too far.

Why, though, would a logic of subjectivity, in this sense, be objectionably empirical? As we have seen, Hegel often denounces the logic on which Kant relies as empirical, and the criticism is no less apt here in the paralogisms. To be sure, logic's claims about the subject do not rely on sense experience.[7] Yet they do rely for their justification on a type of intellectual experience that we have when we abstract in the relevant way. This empiricist tendency may not imperil all of Kant's objectives, but there is one it does threaten. This is his aim of making claims about the mind that remain universally and necessarily valid, even if they are not metaphysical in the way those of rational psychology were meant to be. Unfortunately,

---

[7] Houlgate (2006: 15).

and as we have seen before, the problem of induction arises for all empirical claims, not just those based on sense experience. Hence, it arises here as well, and, as a result, logic cannot be a satisfying surrogate for rational psychology. For Hegel, the paralogisms reflect Kant's overestimation of the logic of the day and underestimation of the metaphysical tradition.

4.3 Responding to Kant's Critique of Rational Cosmology: The Antinomies

For Kant, the errors found in the field of rational cosmology are unique. Only in cosmology do reason's attempts to know the unconditioned lead it into conflicts with itself that Kant calls *antinomies*. The reason for this concerns the particular variant of the Idea of the unconditioned that is relevant in this sphere, the Idea of the world as a whole. The Idea of the world as a whole is unique in being "pseudo-empirical." Unlike the others, this Idea pertains to the empirical world or the world of experience. At the same time, it encourages us to think about the empirical world in a manner that goes beyond the bounds of possible experience.[8]

As a result of its pseudo-empirical character, this Idea draws two faculties into operation, faculties whose conflicting demands give rise to antinomy: reason and the understanding. The antinomial conflicts between reason and the understanding arise in the following way. Kant holds that the faculty of reason is driven by the principle "If the condition is given, then the whole sum of conditions is given, and hence the ultimate unconditioned is given" (A 409/B 436). Yet reason can conceive of the unconditioned in only two ways, a constraint that gives rise to the antinomies (A 417–418/B 445–446). It can consider the unconditioned to be the entire series of conditions itself or else consider it to be the final term in the series, the unconditioned condition.[9] Ultimately, then, antinomies will arise when reason's

---

[8] For the explanation of why the antinomies arise only in the field of rational cosmology, and also for other points given as background here, I am substantially indebted to the discussion in Grier (2001).

[9] Antinomies require two further conditions: (1) a *series*, rather than a mere *aggregate*, and (2) a *regressive* series, rather than a *progressive* one (A 409–413/B 436–440). Concerning the first condition, the timeline is a *series*, since moments in time are sequentially ordered. Parts of space, however, only form an *aggregate* because they are not sequentially ordered but are all given simultaneously. However, as Kant explains, space may give rise to an antinomy since we "finite" knowers must always think of its parts sequentially. In addition to requiring *series*, rather than an *aggregate*, antinomies also require a specific kind of *series*. They require one in which it is possible to *regress* from conditioned to its condition, rather than one in which we *progress* from condition to conditioned. That is why the past gives rise to an antinomy but the future does not. For this reason, there can be no future-directed analogue of the first antinomy. In other words, there can be no antinomy concerning whether the world has a future ending or will continue indefinitely.

idea of the unconditioned proves "too big" for the understanding, yet the understanding's prove "too small" for reason (A 487–488/B 515–516). The antinomies oppose a "Platonic" "dogmatism" that strays beyond the bounds of possible experience to an "Epicurean" "empiricism" that insists nothing lies beyond these bounds.[10]

As Michelle Grier (2001: 175 ff.) helpfully explains, Kant regards the "mathematical antinomies" as the result of a flawed inference. This inference involves an equivocation, or "ambiguous middle." It is as follows:

P14. If a condition is given, the wholes series of conditions is given, and therefore the unconditioned is given.
P15. Objects of the senses are given as conditioned.
C5. Consequently the entire series of all conditions of objects of the senses is already given.
(P14, P15)

The "ambiguous middle" results because the conditioned referred to in the first premise is not the same as the conditioned referred to in the second. In the first premise, the conditioned is used as a pure rather than as an empirical concept, meaning it refers to things in themselves rather than appearances. In the second premise, however, the conditioned is used as an empirical concept, referring to appearances. As a result, the conclusion reached is false, and for the following reason. In the realm of appearances, the givenness of the conditioned does not entail that of the unconditioned. The reason has to do with the nature of human cognition. Knowers like ourselves must engage in the successive synthesis of the elements in a series. We cannot comprehend the whole series at one stroke.

For Kant, however, the conflict arises only if we assume the truth of transcendental realism. Once we give up this assumption, the conflict is dissolved. If transcendental realism were true, then we would not be presented with spatiotemporal appearances but, rather, things-in-themselves. Since things-in-themselves are not part of the empirical world, it can be said of them that a given condition entails that the whole series of conditions, and therefore that the unconditioned, is given. Were transcendental realism true, we would face a genuine conflict over whether the unconditioned should be conceived of as the whole series or a single unconditioned condition. Yet once we abandon transcendental realism and

---

[10] Of course, it might be tempting to assume that Kant would endorse "empiricism" over "Platonism." Yet the denial that anything lies beyond the bounds of experience will turn out to be no less dogmatic than the opposing claim (A 471/B 449).

embrace transcendental idealism, the conflict is averted. This is because transcendental idealism reveals the inference upon which the thesis and antithesis are based to be faulty. As we saw, thesis and antithesis are based on the following inference: given the conditioned, the unconditioned is also given. Yet as we saw, this inference only holds when the conditioned is a thing-in-itself and does not hold when it is an appearance. However, transcendental idealism requires that the conditioned that is given to us as knowers is an appearance, meaning the inference is based on an equivocation. Hence, both the thesis and antithesis that are based upon it are false.

By contrast, Hegel maintains that the antinomies arise from the use of certain flawed categories, and compared to this simpler diagnosis Kant's can seem positively baroque.

> Kant's antinomies of reason amount to nothing more than that from a concept one of its determinations is laid down as ground at one time, and another determination at another time, both with equal necessity. (WdL 12: 97/SoL 595)

Accordingly, Hegel will attempt to show that all of the additional materials that go into the construction of Kant's antinomies are superfluous. For Hegel, the antinomies are little more than the complex guise in which other simpler conflicts appear. Hence, Hegel's strategy will be to strip away all of the additional material that goes into the construction of a Kantian antinomy, revealing a simpler conflict at its core. It would be reasonable to wonder what these further materials have in common, and answering this question will allow us to connect Hegel's critique of Kant's antinomies to the larger project. *Most of these additional materials have in common that they belong to "common logic" or the transcendental logic based upon it.* Hence, Hegel's critique of Kant's antinomies belongs to a larger critique of Kant for relying on the same logic as his predecessors.

In order to illustrate this strategy, I will focus on the second antinomy. Typically, Hegel reframes the conflict in terms of the abstract concepts he calls categories, rather than the subject matter it appears to concern.[11] In this case, he does so by arguing that the second antinomy only *appears* to be a disagreement concerning the divisibility and indivisibility of material substances. It is, in fact, little more than a disguised version of the more fundamental conflict between two opposed conceptions of quantity (as either continuous or discrete).

---

[11] See also Houlgate (2016a: 43–44).

> The dispute or the antinomy of the infinite divisibility of space, time, matter, and so on, has its origin in the nature of quantity, that it is this simple unity of discreteness and continuity. This antinomy consists solely in the fact that discreteness must be maintained just as much as continuity. (WdL 21: 179/SoL 157)

Whether something admits of being divided or not is always a reflection of whether it is continuous or discrete. The continuum is the as-yet-undivided and therefore the divisible. The discrete is the already divided and therefore indivisible. Hence, continuity and discreteness are prior to divisibility or indivisibility. When we argue about whether something is divisible or indivisible, we are actually arguing about whether it is present in a continuous or discrete quantity.

Hegel also criticizes Kant's involvement of Idea of the world as a whole in the framing of the antinomy, arguing that this particular Idea at any rate is irrelevant to what is genuinely at issue. The conflict between the two, continuity and discreteness, would arise in any realm in which the category in question, quantity, applied. Hence, the problem of whether matter existing in space and time is infinitely divisible constitutes little more than a specific, concrete instance of a more general, abstract problem. For Hegel, this is the problem of whether continuity or discreteness is definitive of quantity itself:

> Further, Kant did not pick the antinomy from the concepts themselves, but from the already *concrete* form of cosmological determinations. To capture it pure, and to deal with it in its simple concept, the thought determinations must not be taken as applied to, and entangled in, the representation of the world, space, time, matter, and so on, but must rather be considered purely in themselves, without this concrete material which has no force or authority here, for the thought determinations alone make up the essence and the ground of the antinomies. (WdL 21: 180/SoL 158)

In Hegel's view, the argument about whether "something" is divisible or indivisible, continuous or discrete, remains unaffected by what, exactly, that something happens to be: "The substrate given to these abstractions, namely these substances in the world ... bears no influence on the antinomy itself" (WdL 21: 181/SoL 159).

This dispute also has a logical dimension. Hegel must first show that the real conflict arises at the subpropositional level, within individual concepts rather than between pairs of judgments. For Hegel, the appearance that there is a conflict between two opposed judgments is also misleading. To be sure, we appear to be confronted with two judgments connecting some subject concept with a distinct predicate concept. Indeed, connecting two or more concepts in this way is the mark of a judgment in the logical sense, as opposed to something that merely seems to have that form because of grammatical or psychological considerations.

However, Hegel argues, these Kantian theses and antitheses are not judgments in the true sense at all. In fact, they simply repeat the same concept again, rather than connect two distinct ones. In this case, they simply assert the existence of the continuous or the discrete, not of finitely or infinitely divisible material substances. Here, Hegel tries to argue that the thesis and antithesis claims, seen in light of his earlier analysis, are tautologies. For example, it is tautologous to claim that a composite substance is made up of indivisible atoms, because this is just true by definition of composites.

> That the composite is not one thing in and for itself but is something only externally put together, that it *consists of something other*, is its immediate determination. But this something other than the composite is the simple. It is therefore a tautology to say that the composite is made up of the simple. (WdL 21: 181/SoL 159)

Having denied that these conflicts arise between opposed judgments, Hegel attempts to rule out the further possibility that they inherently involve something of even greater logical complexity: syllogistic arguments. Here, Hegel's strategy is to attempt to show that the arguments themselves are superfluous. This he does by attempting to show in each case that they are circular, presupposing what they set out to prove. I will refrain from discussing a specific example here, since this is fairly well trod ground.[12]

Diagnosing the true source of the problem by descending to this more logically primitive level is only the beginning. Remaining there to provide a more satisfying solution than Kant's own is the goal. Here, I differ from two broad approaches found in the literature. Some commentators, such as Winegar, approach Hegel's argument as if his main concern was resolving the antinomies themselves.[13] Others, such as Sedgwick, Ameriks and Rosen, argue that he was unconcerned with doing so – though this could either be deliberate on his part or the result of some type of mistake.[14]

---

[12] Sedgwick (2012) provides an in-depth and convincing account of Hegel's attempts to show that Kant's arguments are circular.

[13] Winegar (2016).

[14] Sedgwick (2012), Ameriks (2000: iv) and Rosen (1982).

In my view, these two broad approaches can be reconciled. On the one hand, Hegel's main concern was, indeed, resolving simpler problems lying at the basis of the antinomies, rather than the antinomies themselves. To this extent, those who think he was not directly concerned with resolving the antinomies are right. On the other hand, it is by no means true that Hegel was completely uninterested in resolving the antinomies either, even if he did not attempt to do so directly. Rather, I wish to suggest that Hegel's approach to resolving them is indirect. After all, the simpler problems that interest Hegel lie at the very basis of the antinomies. In resolving the former, he will resolve the latter as well.

Preliminarily, we should note Hegel's reservations about Kant's solution, before turning to the alternative he favors. Hegel does not accept Kant's solution to the mathematical antinomies, denying that it succeeds in resolving the contradiction. Let us suppose Hegel is right that the true source of the problem is a contradiction inherent to the category, for example of quantity. If that is so, then the problem should arise anywhere that this contradictory category is applied (WdL 21: 189/SoL 165). Therefore, the problem will remain, even if we accept that material substances are appearances, rather than things-in-themselves, phenomena rather than noumena. In other words, it will arise just as much in the realm of appearances as in that of things-in-themselves.

For Hegel, then, the true solution to the antinomies is to seek a refined version of the category in question that resolves the contradiction rather than to renounce transcendental realism in favor of idealism. As we have seen, Hegel maintains that we ought to abstract not only from matter but also from space and time. We must focus on the concepts of the continuous and the discrete themselves, which are more basic than their instances. Hegel's solution is modal in that it involves a distinction between possibility and actuality.

> From the standpoint of *continuity* ... [there] remains the *possibility* of parting, as possibility, without actually coming to the atom. Now, even if we stay with these oppositions as just defined, we see that the moment of atomicity lies in continuity itself, for continuity is the possibility of parting. (WdL 21: 187/SoL 164)

Hegel argues that the continuous always implies the possibility of the discrete, since dividing the continuous produces the discrete. It therefore implies the possibility of an infinite quantity of discrete units. Yet it does not follow from this that the continuous actually does contain this infinite quantity of discrete units already. The fallacy consists in conflating the possibility of infinite divisions with the actuality of an infinite number of divided things. This would follow only if the continuous depended on the discrete, as if it were by summing discrete units that one achieves continuous quantities. Yet for Hegel this is not so. Indeed, the reverse is the case, since it is only by dividing the continuous that one arrives at the discrete.

Once the solution is stated in its full generality, it can be applied to Kant's second antinomy. Matter is infinitely divisible but not actually divided into infinite parts. In this way, there is no contradiction between thesis and antithesis. However, this is not because we have renounced realism in favor of idealism. In particular, it is not because we have introduced a distinction between things as they appear to us and things as they are in themselves. Rather, it is because we have introduced a metaphysical distinction between the potential and the actual into reality itself. Especially in its traditional Aristotelian guise, but also in Hegel, ours is a distinction pertaining directly to the object, rather than one pertaining to the standpoint of the knowing subject. Ultimately, then, Hegel's solution is fully compatible with realist metaphysics, and in no way Kantian-idealist. If that is so, then the antinomies give us no reason to abandon that form of metaphysics – and certainly not to do so in favor of transcendental idealism.

A striking feature of Hegel's engagement with Kant's second antinomy, seldom mentioned in the literature on this topic, lies in Hegel's repeated comparisons between Kant's Dialectic and the positions of certain ancient philosophers. For example, Hegel regards Zeno's paradox of motion as the true problem at the root of Kant's antinomies. For failing to recognize this, Kant himself comes in for criticism. More surprising still, Hegel regards Aristotle's solutions to Zeno's paradoxes as the true solution to Kant's antinomies.

As Hegel writes, both the second antinomy and Zeno's paradox concern a contradiction within our concept of quantity, a contradiction between the continuous and the discrete.

> Infinitely more meaningful and more profound than this Kantian antinomy just considered are the dialectical examples of the ancient Eleatic school, especially those dealing with movement, *which are likewise based on, and find their solution in, the concept of quantity.* (WdL 21: 187/SoL 164)

Hegel is even more emphatic on this point in his *Lectures on the History of Philosophy*:

> This is the dialectic of Zeno; he had a knowledge of the determinations which our ideas of space and time contain, and showed in them their contradiction; Kant's antinomies do no more than Zeno did here. (VGP/LHoP v. 1 "Zeno")

In the *Logic*, Hegel does not explain the relationship between Kant's antinomy and Zeno's paradox. However, he notes that the task of doing so should be left to the distinct discipline of the history of philosophy.

> To consider them here also would take us too far afield; they have to do with the concepts of space and time and can be dealt with in the history of philosophy in connection with them. – These examples do the greatest honor to the reason of their discoverers. (WdL 21: 187/SoL 164)

Presumably, Hegel is referring to the history of philosophy as told by Hegel himself. It therefore seems warranted to examine Hegel's posthumously published *Lectures on the History of Philosophy* for clarification. The approach gains further support from the many striking parallels between the two discussions that draw on many of the same ideas. Most importantly, the *Lectures* seem to repeat the claims from Hegel's *Logic* concerning the relationship between Zeno's paradoxes and Kant's antinomies.

> This is the dialectic of Zeno; he had a knowledge of the determinations which our ideas of space and time contain, and showed in them their contradiction; Kant's antinomies do no more than Zeno did here. (VGP/LHoP v. 1 "Zeno")

Although Hegel considers four paradoxes, I will confine myself to one very well known one, concerning motion. As summarized by Aristotle, whom Hegel quotes, this paradox of Zeno runs as follows: "Movement has no truth, because what is in motion must first reach the middle of the space before arriving at the end" (VGP/LHoP v. 1 "Zeno"). The paradox may be illustrated by means of a thought-experiment. To move from its resting place to a destination, an object must move half the distance to the destination. In order to move from its resting place to this new half destination, the object must move halfway to that, and so on. The paradoxical conclusion seems to be that the object can never arrive at its original destination. In one version of the paradox, doing so is impossible because it would require the object to travel an infinite distance. That is, it would need to travel a distance equal to the sum of the infinite half distances, and halves of half distances, and halves of half distances.

Hegel has his own idiosyncratic analysis of Zeno's argument for the paradox inherent in motion, however. He claims it results from the contradiction between two different candidate definitions of the concept of quantity: continuity and discreteness. At the outset of the thought experiment, Hegel argues, we must assume space is continuous, rather than discrete. Space must be treated as divisible into parts, though not yet actually divided. As Hegel writes, "That what is in motion must reach the half is the assertion of continuity, i.e. the possibility of division as mere possibility" (VGP/ LHoP v. 1 "Zeno"). Were it divided, it would already be partitioned into units. Once it is actually divided, however, we assume space to be discrete. More specifically, we now have discrete quantities of space: the new region of space is half the length of its predecessor; these regions are also two in number. Put differently, space, once divided, is *dis*continuous, since there is a break in it. As he writes, "in the conception of a half, the interruption of continuity is involved" (VGP/LHoP v. 1 "Zeno"). However, the cycle can then repeat itself once more. Restricting ourselves to the new distance, we are led to assume continuity, since the new quantity of space, in being divisible, must not yet be viewed as divided or discontinuous. Once divided, however ... The cycle repeats itself *ad infinitum*.

In both the *Lectures on the History of Philosophy* and the *Logic*, Hegel turns to Aristotle's resolution of Zeno's paradoxes to illustrate the nature of his favored solution. He praises them as "genuinely speculative" and attempts to defend them from the criticisms of Pierre Bayle.[15] In essence, Aristotle's solution is the same as Hegel's own "modal" solution. Aristotle, it seems, drew on a central distinction of his ontology to resolve the apparent contradiction: the distinction between potentiality and actuality. Space is *actually* continuous, or divisible. However, it is therefore always *potentially* discrete, or divided into atoms, for reasons we have already considered.

> The solution that Aristotle gives to these dialectical tropes is contained in his truly speculative concepts of space, time, and movement, and merits high praise. The most famous of his proofs rest on opposing infinite divisibility (imagined as if it were actually carried out and hence as equivalent to infinite partition, the atoms) to continuity, which applies just as well to time as to space, so that the infinite, that is, abstract plurality is contained in this continuity only *in itself*, as *possibility*. The actual as contrasted to abstract plurality ... (WdL 21: 188/SoL 164–165)

This solution implies a subordination of the discrete to the continuous. However, Hegel argues this is required.[16] The innovation enables Aristotle to resolve Zeno's paradox. An object that traverses the continuous distance in space has not, in fact, traveled an infinite distance. To be sure, there are

---

15 The solution with which most modern readers are likely to be familiar is that provided by the calculus, and, in particular, the notion of a limit. For better or worse, this solution is unavailable to Hegel, since he is a critic of the calculus. Hegel regards the infinite approximation (alluded to in the idea of a limit) as an instance of "the bad infinite."

16 In subordinating the discrete to the continuous, Hegel also follows Spinoza, for whom discrete quantity is merely "imaginary" whereas the continuous is alone what the intellect grasps as true quantity. Hegel quotes this Spinozist doctrine at length and in the original Latin (WdL 21: 178/SoL 155).

infinite *potential* divisions in this region of space. There are not infinite *actual* divisions in it. Hence, the infinite divisions are merely *potentially* present in the distance traversed, not *actually* present therein. Put differently, this region of space is infinitely *divisible* but not infinitely *divided*. Hegel writes: "The general explanation which Aristotle gives to this contradiction, is that space and time are not infinitely divided, but are only divisible" (VGP/LHoP v. 1 "Zeno"). As Hegel observes, critics of Aristotle (in particular, Bayle) often argue that this must mean there are actually infinite divisions in space. Hence, Zeno's paradox is not solved. An object that traverses a certain continuous distance has, in fact, traveled an infinite distance, composed of an infinite number of discrete divisions. As Hegel observes, however, Aristotle's solution requires no such thing.

Although the parallel is seldom, if ever, noted, Russell also treats Kant's second antinomy as a version of Zeno's paradox and claims that modern solutions to the latter solve the former (Russell 2015: 359–360). He also argues, like Hegel, that these and other problems that have been thought to concern space and time are actually more abstract. Because he refers in other contexts to the pertinent parts of Hegel, Russell was probably aware of the parallel. Indeed, a striking facet of *Principles of Mathematics* is the frequency with which Hegelian opponents in the philosophy of mathematics crop up. Even Hegelians are often ignorant of Hegel's philosophy of mathematics, but Russell knows it well – and not just in general outline. I therefore think it likely that Russell was aware of the irony here. I mean that his argument, though anti-Hegelian in substance, was Hegelian in form. In the same work, Russell even mentions Hegel's solution to the paradox/antinomy, the solution based on the inseparability of continuity and discreteness. Yet he does so only to ridicule it:

> The notion of continuity has been treated by philosophers, as a rule, as though it were incapable of analysis. They have said many things about it, including the Hegelian dictum that everything discrete is also continuous and vice versa. This remark, as being an exemplification of Hegel's usual habit of combining opposites, has been tamely repeated by all his followers. But as to what they meant by continuity and discreteness, they preserved a discreet and continuous silence; only one thing was evident, that whatever they did mean could not be relevant … to the philosophy of space and time. (Russell 2015: 290)

***

As I indicated earlier, Hegel's critique of Kant only goes so far in overcoming the problem posed by the paralogisms. At most, it shows that Hegel is in possession of an alternative set of concepts that have a single promising feature. Specifically, these are concepts that are infinite in the first of the two senses we distinguished earlier. In other words, they are not limited by others distinct from or opposed to them. Once more, this is true of concepts such as the Aristotelian idea of soul and the German idealist idea of spirit in a way it is not of the Cartesian dualist concept of soul. It is also true of Hegel's concepts of continuous and discrete quantity. Yet just because Hegel has overcome the dualism between each of these concepts and its opposite does not mean he has shown they apply. At most, Hegel would have shown that these concepts would, if applicable, solve certain problems. He would not have shown that they do, in fact, apply and that these problems are in fact as good as solved. In other words, Hegel has not yet shown that these concepts are infinite in the other of these senses: infinite vis-à-vis the objective world. Yet for Hegel it is deeply important that the categories making up his *Logic* be infinite in both of these senses.

4.4 Responding to Kant's Critique of Rational Theology: The Ideal

For Kant, we are necessarily led to the Idea of a supreme Being (God) by our aspiration to achieve comprehensive knowledge of the object. Such a being would contain the "because" (*darum*) for every "why?" (*warum*) (A 585/B 613). Kant is concerned here with our aspiration to know the object in its full determinateness (specificity, particularity). In order to do so, we employ a certain standard or principle, the idea of the complete set of determinate (specific, particular) features or properties a thing could possibly have. This is the Idea of the *omnitudo realitatis*, the sum of all realities. We then imagine being able to compare any given object of our knowledge with this standard. This would involve determining in the case of each possible predicate that a thing could possibly have whether it in fact had or lacked that predicate. This is what it would be to know the object in its full determinateness. In a further and perhaps more questionable step, we then treat the *omnitudo realitatis*, the sum of all realities, as itself a further real thing, the *ens realissimum*. Indeed, it is called so because it is not simply a real thing, something over and above the sum of predicates and irreducible to them. It is the most real thing, the vast store of predicates in which every other real thing has only a limited share: "every thing as deriv[es] its own possibility from the share it has in the whole of possibility" (A 572/B 600). For Kant, there is no harm at all in employing this notion for heuristic purposes as a standard that all scientific inquiry should strive to approximate. However, the rational theologian wants to go further.

The rational theologian argues that the *ens realissimum* exists and that we can have theoretical knowledge of this. That is because we have a valid argument for this conclusion: the ontological argument. The ontological argument begins from the premise that God, the most real being, would contain all real predicates. It then proceeds to draw the conclusion that God exists via the further premise that existence is among the real predicates God would include. Famously, Kant denies that this is so ("being is not a real predicate"). Whether a thing exists or not cannot, in general, be inferred from its definition. Kant puts this in a number of different ways, but one is that existence claims are never analytic but always synthetic truths. Their denial is never a contradiction. Their affirmation is never based on conceptual containment. Put bluntly, I will not improve my finances by reflecting on my concept of a hundred dollars.

Hegel's response is the common one that Kant's objection to the ontological argument is question-begging (WdL 21: 76/SoL 65–66). To be sure, the definitions of most of the ordinary things that we encounter in our everyday lives and their existences are distinct. Yet, from this, we cannot necessarily conclude that there is nothing whose definition is to exist. There might be an exception to the rule "existence is not a real predicate," and the ontological argument, in effect, suggests this is true of God. One can, of course, reject this proposal but not on the grounds that it is not in general true that existence can be extracted from a definition. Nobody is disputing that it is not in general true, just that it is in all cases – including the unusual one of God.

This is a widespread response to Kant's critique of the ontological argument, but it has a significant limitation Hegel will need to overcome. It requires us to explain why, exactly, God is an exception to the rule, rather than just insisting that he is. Why should it be legitimate to treat existence as a real predicate in this case, if it is not in every other? We need a principled reason for exempting the concept of God from the rules that usually apply to concepts. Here, Hegel proposes a "logical" solution to this recurrent problem, invoking the distinction between infinite categories and finite ones.

For Hegel, infinite categories improve the prospects for the claim that God, by definition, exists. They do so even if we concede that existence does not work this way for ordinary entities, those describable using finite categories. Which, though, of the many infinite categories making up

Hegel's *Logic* can we use to test this hypothesis? Clearly, Hegel understands nearly all of them to be relevant to the ontological argument. Each time a new set of categories is introduced, Hegel discusses how they promise to improve prospects for the ontological argument. In Hegel's *Logic* there will be an ontological argument of Being, existence, reason (syllogism), objectivity and so on.

However, I will simply consider the very first of these categories from the *Logic*: Being. As we know, each such category doubles as a definition of the Absolute (God).[17] However, there is an additional reason Being is especially pertinent here. It is not just that, as we have seen, Hegel refers to it as the *omnitudo realitatis*, a clear reference to Kant's critique of the ontological argument. Nor is it that he also refers to it as the monist principle at the foundation of Spinoza's system, at least as interpreted by Jacobi, something that further aligns being with the Ideal. It is that Hegel makes this connection himself in the greater *Logic* and in a somewhat more direct way.

There, he does so in the remark appended to the section on Being (WdL 21: 70–77/SoL 60–66). In that remark, Hegel suggests that if Kant had been aware of infinite categories such as this one, he never would have rejected the ontological argument. As Hegel says, Kant ought to have focused on Parmenidean Being, not on his personal finances:

> [A] "hundred dollars" is nothing self-referring but something alterable and perishable. This thinking or imagining which has before it only a determinate being, existence, must be referred back to the previously mentioned beginning of science which Parmenides made – the one who purified and elevated to pure thought, to being as such, his own otherwise pictorial representations and hence also those of posterity, thus ushering in the element of science. (WdL 21: 75–76/SoL 65)

As Hegel goes on to explain, in a somewhat winding and tortuous set of passages, notions such as Being are counterexamples to Kant's claim: existence is not a real predicate (WdL 21: 76–77/SoL 65–66). The thought behind this proposal is the following. We can deny the existence of ordinary things, such as Kant's one hundred dollars. However, we cannot deny existence to the whole of existence itself, something described using infinite categories (Being, existence, the One, the infinite). The two cases are fundamentally different, and Kant has conflated them. Clearly, the version of the ontological proof that is taking shape will work only if we presuppose a Spinozistic conception God, rather than an orthodox one. Still, the

---

[17] Technically, this is only true of the first and third categories in each section. Yet this is a condition Being meets.

argument has the advantage of seeming almost trivially true.[18] How could being, or existence, fail to exist? Unfortunately, the argument does appear to rest on a questionable assumption. I mean the assumption that there is even any such thing as the whole of existence, as opposed to its constituent parts.

In his own critique of the ontological argument, Kant questions this assumption in a way that will prove extremely prescient. He does so in a criticism of the ontological argument that appears before the better known one ("existence is not a real predicate"). The criticism is directed at those versions of the ontological argument that presuppose a conception of God as the *omnitudo realitatis*. Kant describes such versions of the argument as resting on a fallacy. This is the fallacy of conflating merely distributive unity with collective unity (A 582–583/B 610–611).

> That we subsequently hypostatize this idea of the sum total of all reality, however, comes about because we dialectically transform the distributive unity of the use of the understanding in experience, into the collective unity of a whole of experience; and from this whole of appearance we think up an individual thing containing in itself all empirical reality, which then – by means of the transcendental subreption we have already thought – is confused with the concept of a thing that stands at the summit of the possibility of all things, providing the real conditions for their thoroughgoing determination. (A 582–583/B 660–661)

It arises in the following way. Suppose we grant that each existing thing exists. Existence is distributed or dispersed among them, in that each has an existence of its own. However, it does not follow that all of them taken together are a further existing thing. There is no collective existence in which all participate, no existence over and above that of each existing thing. The sum of all existing things is not a further existing thing. The *omnitudo realitatis* is not the *ens realissimum*. It is no more so than the sum of all dogs is itself a further mega-dog.

Yet this objection is less fatal for Hegel's version of the ontological argument than it might initially seem. Even Kant thought the problem could be partially overcome, a sign of his greater sympathy with Spinozist versions of the ontological argument. That may be why he does not make the error of conflating distributive and collective senses of existence his main objection to the ontological argument. It is a preliminary criticism that is

---

[18] I here follow Redding and Bubbio (2014), though they see Hegel as more dismissive of the proposal to base the ontological argument on Being.

dispatched early so that more threatening ones can be considered. As Kant correctly saw, all the rational theologian needed to do to overcome the problem was specify more clearly which kind of whole God was intended to be. It would need to be a whole that preceded its parts, rather than one that does not. It would need to be a totality, rather than a sum.

Fortunately, we have near at hand a model of the type of whole that this Spinozist God would have to be if we are to be able to run the ontological argument on it. It may be found in Kant's own conception of space from the Transcendental Aesthetic. Jacobi was the first to point out the connection when he accused Kant of Spinozism during the *Pantheismusstreit*.[19] For Kant, the whole of space precedes its parts. Every region of space is derived from the whole of space by delimiting the latter in a certain way. We begin with the whole of space and then bound or limit some portion of it by drawing lines. In so doing, we are left with a part. Importantly, there is no way to define a part except in reference to the whole. For this reason, the whole of space could not be derived from adding its parts together. Each of the parts is what it is by virtue of its relation to the whole. So we could not start with them and work up to the whole by constructing it out of them.

Kant proposes that the *ens realissimum* would have to be a whole of this kind, a whole prior to its parts. In explaining what such a whole would have to be, he invokes Spinoza's dictum "all determination is negation."

> If, therefore, reason employs in the complete determination of things a transcendental substrate that contains, as it were, the whole store of material from which all possible predicates of things must be taken, this substrate cannot be anything else than the idea of an *omnitudo realitatis*. All true negations are nothing but limitations – a title which would be inapplicable, were they not thus based upon the unlimited, that is, upon "the All." (A 576/B 604)

The analogy with Absolute space as Kant conceives of in the Aesthetic is helpful in illustrating the meaning for Kant of this dictum. We begin with the whole of space. Each specific ("determinate") part of it can be understood as its "negation." Each is simply a different way of not being the whole or failing to coincide with it, "negating" it. Only the whole truly is. Its parts are not it. Each is the result of partially "negating" the whole, discarding all in the whole that is not the particular part in question. Since the whole contains all of the parts, we could also say that each determinate part is the negation of all the others. Of course, Kant's aim in bringing

---

[19] Jacobi (1994: 218, n. 30).

up the analogy with space is to shield the ontological argument from this particular criticism (conflating the distributive with the collective), not from every criticism. After all, Kant is a foe of the ontological argument.

In spite of this, Kant may have been overzealous in his effort to improve the prospects of the ontological argument, especially when we consider it from a Hegelian point of view. In proposing this Spinozist amendment to traditional versions of the ontological argument Kant unwittingly makes a fatal concussion to his opponent. To be sure, all Kant means to be doing is making a minor improvement to the argument, so that he can be sure he refutes the best version of it. Yet Hegel thinks that Kant has unwittingly strengthened the argument so greatly that it will now survive Kant's own subsequent critique of it. That is because the Spinozist amendment to the ontological argument gives us a response to an objection Kant thought most fatal to it. I mean the objection that this argument treats existence as a real predicate.

For a Spinozist, such as Hegel, God by definition exists, but this is not for the reason usually given by proponents of the ontological argument. It is not because existence is among the predicate concepts analytically contained in this subject concept, as in classical versions of the ontological argument. Rather, it is for a more fundamental reason that Hegel can claim as his original discovery, though it is anticipated by others. At least at the outset of Hegel's *Logic*, God is being or existence itself. By contrast, all existing things have only some limited share in existence ("*omnis determinatio ...*"). It could not exactly be said that Hegel has improved the prospects of this argument solely by embracing a different conception of God. This conception works together with a new conception of Being or existence, as well as its relationship to ordinary things. Since this is the load-bearing feature of Hegel's ontological argument, it would be an interesting question to ask what justifies it. It would also be worth returning to the issue of what resources Kant has to respond to. Still, it seems to me that Hegel is well within his rights here; the only constraint on an ontological argument is that it have no empirical premise. Fortunately, a premise concerning the nature of Being itself, as well as its relationship to particular beings, need not be an empirical one.

Here, I comment only briefly on Hegel's responses to Kant's critiques of the cosmological and physico-teleological arguments. Kant had already claimed that all three of the traditional proofs were interdependent. More specifically, Kant held that the cosmological and physico-teleological arguments were dependent on the ontological argument. The main reason Kant gave was that no inference from an empirical state of affairs in the world to its cause could establish that this cause was of any particular kind, let alone that it was the God of traditional religion. Only with an independent line of argument that establishes the existence of a necessary being could we draw this inference. Yet an independent line of argument would be one that did not rely on empirical claims in the way these others do. In other words, it would have to be an a priori argument for the existence of God, that is the ontological argument.

Hegel must reject the cosmological argument, at least if this argument takes its traditional form. The cosmological argument would rule out Hegel's own nontraditional version of the ontological argument. As Hegel explains, the problem with the traditional versions of the cosmological argument is to have inferred God's existence from that of ordinary things (EL § 50 Z). The existence of these things is contingent, rather than necessary. Hence, they must have some cause distinct from them. As we have seen, this line of reasoning, even if correct, would not establish the existence of any particular type of cause. However, Hegel has a distinct worry – that treating God as a type of cause would render it finite, limited. Inherently, a cause is something limited, since it is distinct from its effect. As we have seen, however, Hegel holds that only a definition of the Absolute as infinite will allow the ontological argument to go through. For Hegel, any definition of God as finite cannot not rule out the possibility that God should fail to exist.

Yet if Hegel rejects the traditional version of the cosmological argument, he does not reject any version. Indeed, Hegel's ontological argument as I have reconstructed it here already is a type of cosmological argument. In Kant, the three arguments are interdependent, though distinct. Yet in Hegel they blur into one another. Admittedly, Hegel's argument does not progress from the effect to the cause, in the way traditional cosmological arguments do. Yet it does progress from grounded to ground, and this seems sufficient. More specifically, it infers from the existence of determinate things that of their indeterminate ground. Another difference between Hegel's cosmological argument and earlier versions concerns the role of negation in each. Whereas the traditional version works by inferring God's existence from that of ordinary things, Hegel's works by inferring it from their nonexistence. In Hegel's revised version, we do not infer God's existence from what Hegel calls determinate (specific) being. Rather, we argue that all determinate beings are negations or nonbeings in comparison to the indeterminate, being.

As Hegel explains, the conviction that negativity is integral to rational theology is Spinozist in origin (EL § 50Z). Indeed, it is what makes

Spinoza a pious thinker, rather than an atheist. The ordinary religious believer accepts the existence of God but also that of the world in its separation from God. The atheist denies the existence of God, affirming that of the world. Yet Spinoza has the most pious position of all since he affirms the reality of God and denies that of the world in its separation from God. He is the opposite of an atheist, an acosmist.

Although Hegel only hints at it briefly, there are indications that the resultant argument is meant to be physico-teleological as well. This is not because it argues for an intelligent designer on the basis of teleological organization in nature. Kant considered that inference flawed, but Hegel has a different complaint. It is not that we could never know for certain whether there is such a designer but that it would not help if we could. Living beings are self-organizing, meaning the analogy with products of design is necessarily incomplete. Of course, Kant thought this analogy was, more or less, the best we would do. Clearly, Hegel differs, but this is not relevant here. For our purposes, the important point is simply that one of Hegel's own definitions of the Absolute is the Idea of life or, speaking loosely, internal purposiveness itself. On this view, God does not design life, but is life.

> But setting aside the practice of presupposing some representation of God and judging a result according to such a presupposition, the above determinations are indeed of great value and necessary moments of the idea of God. In order to bring the basic content in its true determination, the true idea of God, before thinking in this manner, the point of departure must, of course, not be taken from subordinate content. The merely contingent things of the world are a very abstract determination. *The organic creations and determinations of their purposes belong to a higher circle, life.* (EL § 50, italics mine)

Nor should it be surprising that Hegel thinks of life itself as divine. For Hegel, as for Kant, living beings are yet another example of an entity in which the whole is prior to the parts. And Hegel thinks the ontological argument works best for such entities. This, I think, explains how Hegel can cite the argument from design as inspiration for his own. He is broadly sympathetic to the idea that organic life is relevant to proving the existence of God, even if not exactly in the way that precritical metaphysicians thought, that is by testifying to the existence of a higher intelligence.

Up to this point, we have only considered a claim Hegel makes on behalf of his first definition of the Absolute: Being. Why, though, should this be thought to carry any implication for subsequent definitions? Here, I have claimed that Hegel's decision to start with Being implies a broadly favorable attitude toward this definition of the Absolute. Yet on a more familiar interpretation, this decision underscores the impoverishment of Being in comparison to all subsequent definitions of the Absolute.[20] Be that as it may, Being is also the foundation for everything that follows. The claim Being raises to be necessarily instantiated is one all subsequent definitions of the Absolute will inherit. Here, we should recall that life, cognition and, indeed, all definitions of the Absolute subsequent to the first, Being, are refined versions of it ("sublations").[21] Unsurprisingly then, Hegel will reformulate the ontological argument every time a new set of definitions is reached. There is an ontological argument for the categories of existence, because it is a refined and more advanced form of the category of being. There is one for the object for the exact same reason.

4.5   Conclusion: Post-Kantian German Idealism as Metaphysical Monism?

At this point, it should be clear that Hegel's vision of the history of philosophy differs from Kant's in one important respect. From Hegel's perspective, excessive reliance on "representation" is found in even so-called rationalist metaphysics, as well as in transcendental idealism and, obviously, empiricism. Instances of this include the methods of mathematics, orthodox Christianity, ordinary language and, finally, my focus in these chapters, the received Scholastic-Aristotelian logic. All prop up a metaphysics whose rationalism is more aspirational than real.

Yet if it is true that Hegel, in his conception of philosophy's history often does not draw the *exact* distinctions between figures and schools Kant does, it is no less true that Hegel sees *other* distinctions to which Kant is completely blind. Something like this point is recognized by Pippin, who argues that Hegel, in rejecting traditional metaphysics, means the rationalist rather than the Aristotelian variety. Yet as Houlgate points out, in a response to Pippin, this claim is difficult to reconcile with Hegel's admiration for Spinoza.[22] If Houlgate is right, then, we must cut things even more finely than Pippin does. No less than metaphysics, "rationalist

---

[20] Some claim it is a "false start. See Redding (1991).

[21] Once again, I follow Houlgate (2006) and Doz (1987) here.

[22] Houlgate (2019). There are even now a number of interpreters who argue Hegel has affinities with the Leibniz–Wolff school, though I am not myself an adherent of this view. See Wolf (2019), who is following de Boer (2011) and Nuzzo (2018).

metaphysics" is simply too crude a category. Where, then, within the category of "rationalist metaphysics" does the further cut lie?

As I have argued, Hegel attributes the impasses of traditional metaphysics to finite thinking. Paradigmatically, this is thinking that employs finite categories, those that are semantically and really nonexhaustive. However, this charge would not clearly apply to Spinoza's substance monism. Substance is causally and conceptually self-sufficient. At the very least, it is an infinite category, if not the exact one Hegel prefers (the Concept, Idea, Spirit). Spinoza, quite correctly, draws from his monist conception of substance the implication that such a thing could not fail to exist. In other words, he is a proponent of the ontological argument. Spinoza has no use for finite categories such as soul and body of the Cartesian dualist. Indeed, he ridicules the categories of the Aristotelian tradition as so much Scholastic nonsense, though his reasons for skepticism likely differ from Hegel's. Of course, Hegel is critical of Spinoza's method, the more *geometrico*. This is largely because it requires us to use intuition to grasp the correctness of the axioms, definitions and postulates.

As we have seen, Hegel does not regard Aristotle and Plato as traditional metaphysicians in any pejorative sense, for example "dogmatic." Might Hegel have a similar attitude toward Spinozism?[23]

Unlike Spinoza, the Leibniz–Wolff school relies exclusively on the finite categories that go back to Aristotle. Initially, it is God and creation that meet their limit, border or boundary in one another. Yet this move is then repeated in the distinctions drawn between the type of created thing and individual tokens of those types. In place of Spinoza's anarchic blurring of the boundaries, we have the Leibniz–Wolff school's attempt to ensure that everything remains in its appointed place. In Scholastic-Aristotelian logic, the Leibniz–Wolff school has an "empirical" logic to complement its metaphysics of finitude.

These technical issues aside, it is not difficult to see in historical terms why one might distinguish between the metaphysics of the Leibniz–Wolff tradition and that of Spinoza.[24] The former school aspires to reconcile philosophy with orthodox Christianity and is in league with Church and State. Spinoza, however, is a freethinker and heretic who faces persecution and censorship. As Beiser notes, university professors in Germany swore an oath to the authorities when they took up their appointments, and publicly denouncing Spinoza was a customary way of proving one's

---

[23] Houlgate (2019).
[24] Beiser (1987, 2005).

loyalty. It may be for this reason that the Romantics were eager to rehabilitate Spinoza. Franks has argued that Spinoza's substance monism was the version of dogmatic metaphysics viewed as most likely to withstand Kant's critique of metaphysics. This point is strengthened when we note the differences between it and the metaphysics Leibniz–Wolff school. Hence it will not do to claim that Hegel rejects only rationalist metaphysics, and not all metaphysics: for example, Aristotelian metaphysics. Within rationalism, there remains the distinction between a traditional metaphysics of the finite and Spinoza's metaphysics of the infinite.

In this chapter and Chapter 3 I have considered Hegel's critique of traditional metaphysics. This critique is part of my account of the logocentric predicament in Hegel's thought, inasmuch as he believes that the errors of traditional metaphysics can be attributed to its failure to confront this dilemma. However, it also paves the way for an account of Hegel's positive project, namely, resolving the logocentric predicament by invoking a new nondogmatic form of metaphysics.

CHAPTER 5

Logical Contradiction and Real Opposition
Hegel on the Laws of Logic

As I interpret him, Hegel is a thinker who seeks an answer to one of the most fundamental questions in the philosophy of logic. I mean the question of how the laws of logic, presupposed by our attempts at justification in all other areas, may themselves be justified. As we have seen, there are two broad types of answer. There is the way of argument with its attendant risk of circularity and the way of brute fact with its attendant risk of complacency. In my view, Hegel's answer is of the former type – and he is not the only idealist to go this route. In proceeding in this way, however, Hegel breaks with the tradition and with Kant, whose approach was of the latter type. More specifically, pre-Hegelian philosophers sought to justify these laws through a form of self-reflection. Carried out appropriately, this form of reflection would, in turn, demonstrate that the laws of logic were the laws of thought. They were the constitutive norms of a certain psychological faculty, those internal to any exercise of it. What, then, is the type of argument Hegel favors over this traditional approach? Is it possible for him to avoid relying on the very laws he seeks to prove?

The answer I defend is that it is an argument drawn from his metaphysics. As I hope to show, Hegel proposes to ground the laws of logic in a general metaphysical (ontological) theory of the categories.[1] By general metaphysics, I mean an inquiry into being-qua-being. This is an inquiry that adopts a maximally abstract perspective on beings or entities. It considers them simply insofar as they are beings or entities at all rather than ones of a particular type. To concern oneself with being-qua-being in the way the philosopher does is distinct from concerning oneself with beings-qua-numbered or qua-natural in the way mathematicians and natural scientists do. A crucial point to bear in mind is that categories such as quantity and quality are promising candidates for principles describing

---

[1] Earlier, I argued that the metaphysics of Hegel's "Objective Logic" is simultaneously general and special, but here I will emphasize the former aspect.

being-qua-being. Traditionally, a category is a concept that can be predicated of every full-fledged being or entity.

Admittedly, it is far from clear what it would mean to ground logic in an ontological theory of the categories of this kind, but my basic proposal will be that this project is possible because both logic and ontology share a certain generality that allows one to found the other. The result is that logic achieves a metaphysical status in that its laws concerning what we are permitted to think are only valid on the condition that they reflect the correct metaphysical account of the way things fundamentally are. Of course, the obvious question for any such project is how we could have any access to the way things fundamentally are. Sense experience is irrelevant to the universal and necessary truths at issue in logic and ontology, but we lack intellectual intuition.

There is precedent for the general idea of a metaphysical basis for logic in the *Metaphysics*, Gamma 3, where Aristotle acknowledges the existence of both psychological and metaphysical versions of the law of noncontradiction. The metaphysical version states that a substance cannot both have and lack the same property (at the same time and in the same respect).[2] The psychological version states that we cannot think some subject both has and lacks the same predicate (at the same time and in the same respect).[3] Aristotle further suggests that the psychological version derives from the metaphysical version, since the former is just a special case of the latter. Admittedly, Aristotle's argument is extremely unpopular, not only in the literature on ancient philosophy but in recent philosophy as well.[4]

Still, my proposal is that a law of logic or law of thought might have some metaphysical basis is one Hegel will take up. To be clear, this would not be tantamount to reducing a law of logic to a law of nature (any more than it would mean reducing it to a law of psychology).

By proposing to ground the laws and materials of formal logic in the categories of general metaphysics, Hegel is in effect inverting Kant's conception of the relationship between them. At least on the reading I favor, Kant sought to derive his categories from pure general logic. Yet when it comes to Hegel's treatment of the laws of logic, he is (in this respect) deeply un-Kantian.

---

[2] *Metaphysics* (Gamma 3, 1005b19–20) in Aristotle (1984, vol. 2: 489).
[3] *Metaphysics* (Gamma 3, 10005 b22–25) in Aristotle (1984, vol. 2: 489).
[4] See Gottlieb (2019) who refers to it as a "bad argument." Kimi (2018): 1.3: 29) and Rödl (2018: 149–150) take up questions raised by Aristotle's discussion of the different versions of the principle of noncontradiction but reject the "metaphysics first" view defended here. In Peacocke's terms, their view is better characterized as "no-priority."

I oppose what I take to be a broadly Kantian-idealist interpretation prominent in the literature. On this interpretation, defended most prominently by Longuenesse, Hegel's objection is that traditional logic goes too far in the direction of metaphysics, and in so doing it fails to adequately ground the generality of logic: More specifically, the traditional approach is said to conflate logic with ontology. In my view, however, Hegel's objection is the opposite, that traditional logic does not go far enough in the direction of metaphysics and that this is why it failed to ground the generality of logic.

Once again, Hegel's approach will only seem regressive when judged against the backdrop of a certain (neo-)Kantian narrative of the history of philosophy – one that Hegel rejects. On this narrative, pre-Kantian logicians conflate logic and ontology, whereas Kant accords it the status of an autonomous science. This narrative will seem especially compelling if by logic one understands the theory of a priori concepts: "categories." After all, who could deny that, in the tradition, categories were studied under the head of general metaphysics (ontology), whereas, in Kant, they are adopted into transcendental logic? However, I challenge the association of logic with category theory. Historically, category theory was historically of uncertain status in relation to logic, whose topics classically include law concept, judgment and syllogism. With this shift from transcendental to general logic in view, we are in a position to challenge the neo-Kantian narrative. At least from Hegel's point of view, Kant's conception of logic as the study of the constitutive norms of a psychological faculty is continuous with that of Scholastic Aristotelianism. This constitutivism is not "psychologism," in Frege's terms, but it is psychological.

Is Hegel's project reformist or revolutionary? Descriptive or revisionary? Initially, it might seem that Hegel is simply attempting to come to the aid of the traditional logic. He is furnishing it with a new mode of justification for its findings but leaving those findings unchallenged. Yet matters are more complex, since Hegel is also mounting a type of challenge to traditional logic. How can he coherently claim to do both? Certainly, Hegel will equip the tradition with a better strategy of justification, but this will actually render it vulnerable to criticism. Adopting this new strategy of justification requires us to admit the possibility that some of the traditional laws will not admit of being justified in this new way and will therefore need to be abandoned.

Notoriously, Hegel seems to reject the law of noncontradiction, an unpopular move that even sympathetic commentators have struggled to defend.[5] In so doing, he embraces a view usually thought to be completely absurd on its face, the view that there are true contradictions. For some of Hegel's critics, this is all the evidence necessary to convict him of not being a serious philosophical thinker. Yet even for those of us more friendly to Hegel's philosophical project, his unorthodox views on contradiction are puzzling. Why would a thinker of Hegel's stature have held what seems to be such an apparently absurd position? A common approach to answering this question is simply to deny that Hegel did, in fact, hold as extreme a view as he is often thought to have held. If it seems that he did so, then this can only be because we are misinterpreting the relevant texts. It is easy to sympathize with this approach, since Hegel has so often been the victim of uncharitable interpretations at the hands of his critics.

Even so, it seems to me that in their zeal to rescue Hegel from the embarrassment of denying the law of noncontradiction interpreters have overlooked an interesting possibility. I simply mean the possibility that Hegel had a respectable argument of his own for why we ought to reject the law of noncontradiction. One reason to revisit Hegel's perspective on this issue is that it appears to have entered the mainstream. In the analytic tradition, interest in nonclassical logics is at an all-time high. What is more, the case contemporary logicians develop for this logic is not always technical. Often, it depends on examples of dialetheias or true contradictions, which are meant to be intuitive: for example, motion as understood in pre-Socratic philosophy, where there is a blurring, or cases of vagueness and indeterminacy. Evidently, certain analytic philosophers find Hegel's views less embarrassing from a contemporary standpoint than do many Hegel scholars.[6] This motivates me to explore the possibility of a revival of the traditional view that Hegel denies the law of noncontradiction.

An ancillary aim will be to argue that a metaphysical interpretation of Hegel's views in logic helps clarify his argument for why we should reject the law of noncontradiction. Drawing on his conviction that every candidate law of logic must be given a metaphysical basis, Hegel rejects the law of noncontradiction on the grounds that it is incompatible with what he takes to be the correct metaphysical theory of the nature of reality. This is a metaphysics in which reality is pervasively characterized by the

---

[5] It is among the Hegel myths and legends considered in an edited anthology of that name, Stewart (1996: Part V: "The Myth that Hegel Denied the Law of Non-contradiction").
[6] See, for example, Priest (1989 but also the more recent 2006). There is a small but growing literature that treats Hegel as some type of dialetheist. See Bordignon (2017), Ficara (2020a) and Moss (2020).

phenomenon Hegel calls opposition. We find it in any domain in which there are what we would conventionally call opposites. Hegel gives examples from mathematics (positive and negative numbers), physics (especially electromagnet phenomena, such as positive and negative charge, and forces), morality (virtue and vice), geography (north and south) and finance (assets and debts). Crucially, the existence of opposition is no contingent empirical fact but a necessary consequence of the correct theory of the categories.

Of course, the central question to answer in evaluating Hegel's argument is how he could have possibly thought that anything as exotic as true contradiction could be found in such a seemingly commonplace phenomenon as opposition. It has been thought that one would have to descend to the quantum realm to find anything as exotic as a true contradiction. Yet Hegel purports to find it in phenomena known to every child. What can his motivation possibly be? The crux of the issue, first raised by Trandelenberg, is that Hegel's examples seem to be tensions, rather than contradictions in a strict logical sense.[7]

Like all intelligent critics of the law of noncontradiction, Hegel believes its rejection is required to deal with paradoxes, ones that force upon us the conclusion that something is A if it is not A and vice versa. Yet unlike these critics, he does not invoke the famous paradoxes of self-reference, such as the liar. Rather, I shall argue, he discovers a novel metaphysical, category-theoretic paradox. This is a paradox concerning identity, the foundational category of the second division of his *Science of Logic*. It is, very roughly, as follows. If they are to be identical with one another, two things must be different from one another, in some respect. So if they are identical, they are different. The point is summarized well by two later philosophers, neither of whom is a Hegelian: Russell and the early Wittgenstein.

> The question whether identity is or is not a relation, and even whether there is such a concept at all, is not easy to answer. For, it may be said, identity cannot be a relation, since, where it is truly asserted, we have only one term, whereas two terms are required for a relation. And indeed identity, an objector may urge, cannot be anything at all: two terms plainly are not identical, and one term cannot be, for what is it identical with? (Russell 2015: 63)
>
> 5.5303 Roughly speaking: to say of two things that they are identical is nonsense, and to say of one thing that it is identical with itself is to say nothing. (Wittgenstein 2005: 62)

---

[7] A more technical version of this criticism is that Hegel conflates contraries with contradictories. See Ficara (2015) for an excellent overview of the history of this objection, which includes Trandelenberg, Croce, Adorno and others.

There is an interesting historical backstory to Hegel's concept of opposition, which may help to clarify the larger interest of his broader position on the law of noncontradiction. This is a story told by Michael Wolff, and frequently repeated in the literature today (1986: 115).[8] It is sometimes cited by commentators who find in it evidence of Hegel's debt to Kant's critique of metaphysics. Yet I hope to show that it can be approached in an alternative way more consistent with the metaphysical interpretation developed here.

In a precritical essay ("Attempt to Introduce the Concept of Negative Magnitudes in Philosophy"), Kant had given a theory of "real" opposition, citing many of the examples Hegel would later invoke.[9] For Kant, however, real opposition must be kept rigorously distinct from the logician's notion of contradiction. True, both involve a relationship of incompatibility or exclusion. Yet the former is a real phenomenon in the world, whereas the latter concerns a relationship between judgments or propositions. In realizing that there is a distinction here, Kant takes an important step beyond rationalist metaphysics. He undermines their conviction that the mere analysis of concepts can yield insight into the fundamental nature of reality. As Kant has shown, this is false in at least one central case. There is no route from reflection on the logical law of noncontradiction to the reality of opposition. A representative passage: "[I]t [real opposition] simply does not take place in virtue of the law of contradiction" (2003: 241/ AK 2:204). Later, these ideas will resurface in Kant's critique of Leibniz in the section of the first critique called the Amphiboly.

Some commentators treat Hegel as taking over Kant's position in the negative magnitudes essay more or less wholesale.[10] They do so because they regard Hegel as a critic of traditional metaphysics in the way that Kant was before him and rely upon a certain Kantian account of the history of logic. On my view, by contrast, Hegel agrees with Kant that logical contradiction and real opposition are distinct. However, he uses this insight to defend a novel form of metaphysics. This is one in which metaphysics is prior to logic, rather than the reverse. In our metaphysics we recognize real opposition, and in our logic we adhere to the law of noncontradiction. So far, so Kantian. However, Hegel argues that metaphysics is prior to logic in the following sense. Every law of (formal) logic must, ultimately, be reducible to the category-theoretic or ontological

---

[8] In addition to Wolff (1981) see Longuenesse (2007) and de Boer (2010a).
[9] Kant (2003).
[10] I believe this could justly be said of Longuenesse (2007).

principles that make up our metaphysics.[11] If that is so, then, Hegel will argue, we must reject the logical law of noncontradiction. For reasons we will soon consider, Hegel thinks this law is in conflict with the metaphysical principle that there is real opposition in the world. In making this metaphysical claim, Hegel does not claim nonsensible or intellectual intuition of things-in-themselves. Rather, he claims to have an argument for why opposition is a category, a predicate of any being or entity considered as such.

Yet if Kantian interpretations of Hegel are one-sided, it will be important to avoid a one-sidedly ontological interpretation as well. In my view, Wolff provides an example of one such interpretation. For Wolff, the contradictions that interest Hegel are *not* logical contradictions at all but are, instead, ontological.[12] Part of the reason is that the definition Hegel gives of contradictions is not syntactic, for example "p and not-p." It is, rather, ontological in that it defines contradiction in terms of the states of affairs in the world that it describes, for example the struggle between virtue and vice. Although I agree with Wolff that contradictions in Hegel have this "*de re*" dimension, I join others in denying that this is the whole story.[13] Both the ontological and the linguistic or syntactic definitions are important to Hegel, and once we see this we can also see that there is a definite order of priority between the two. As Bordignon convincingly argues, it is *because* of the ontological structure Hegel calls opposition that we find ourselves caught in logical contradictions.[14] The former have priority, but the latter remain significant.

5.1   Two Methods of Justifying the Laws of Logic

In his treatment of the laws of logic, Hegel rejects an approach to justifying them often taken in the philosophical tradition. At least according to Hegel, this traditional approach is based on a straightforward strategy:

> [These laws] were said to have the status of *universal laws of thought* that lie at the base of all thinking; to be inherently absolute and indemonstrable but immediately and indisputably recognized and accepted as true by all thought upon grasping their meaning. (WdL II: 258/SoL 354)

---

[11] I am here close to Bordignon (2017), as I explain in the next paragraph.
[12] Wolff (1981: 31–34).
[13] Bordignon (2017).
[14] As she writes, for Hegel "linguistic contradictions, therefore, testify to the existence of contradictions in the actual world itself" (2017: "II: Hegel's Notion of Contradiction"). See also the logician and philosopher Roy Sorensen (2005: 305).

Hegel's treatment of the laws of logic is intended to comprise part of his critique of Scholastic-Aristotelian logic that we considered in Chapter 1. Since the laws of logic are laws of thinking, the tradition argued, these laws can be justified through a process of intellectual reflection. This would simply be a process in which the relevant laws are shown to govern our thinking. In this process, we begin with a judgment, inference or some other such thing. For example, "All men are mortal, Socrates is a man …" We then focus on the contribution of thinking alone, abstracting completely from those of other faculties, such as sensible representation. In this way, we arrive at a formal principle, without sensibly given matter. In this case, "All As are Bs, C is an A …" We further find that this formal principle is impossible for us to deny. In this way, we discover the laws of how we necessarily do think when the faculty of sensibility does not interfere. We draw from these laws imperatives dictating how we ought to think, even under less optimal conditions. For the tradition, there is no need to argue for these laws, which is fortunate given that any argument would likely be circular. Instead, they are upheld simply by being reflected upon and found self-evident. In the method of abstraction, each principle is discovered on its own, apart from its connection to the others. Hence, the laws we discover will form an aggregate, rather than a system.

As we have repeatedly seen, the main problem Hegel identifies with this approach is that it is empirical, though the sense in which this is so requires clarification. The traditional approach may not rely on sense experience, but it does rely on a form of intellectual experience. However, this is irrelevant from the perspective of the Hegelian objection to traditional logic. As an empirical theory, its findings are no less vulnerable to the problem of induction than any other. Hegel believes that even the proponents of the traditional logic will have to concede this. None could seriously maintain that the findings of their science are universally and necessarily valid, given its status as empirical:

> As to the other confirmation of the absolute truth of the principle of identity, this is made to rest on experience … for anyone presented with this proposition, "A is A," "a tree is a tree," immediately grants it and is satisfied that the proposition is self-evident and in need of no further justification or demonstration. Nobody will want to say that the abstract proposition, "A is A," has actually been tried out on *every* consciousness. The appeal to actual experience is therefore not in earnest but is rather only an *assurance* that, if the said experiment were made, universal acknowledgment of the proposition would be the result. (WdL II: 263/SoL 359)

As Hegel points out, nobody seriously maintains that we could test the laws of logic on everyone, let alone that we have actually done so. Yet nobody appears to regard this as a problem for logic either. Hence, Hegel concludes, it must be that there is a different justification for these laws than what the traditional logician thinks.

Hegel's alternative is to treat the laws of logic as deriving from the general metaphysical (ontological) theory of the categories defended in his *Science of Logic*. The basic thought behind the deduction is as follows. A law of logic is a principle we must observe in all our thinking, regardless of its subject matter. The metaphysical concepts called categories, however, are those that apply to any being or entity, regardless of what type of being or entity it is. Here, Hegel cites with approval Aristotle's definition of a category: "A category, according to the etymology of the word and Aristotle's definition of it, is what is said and asserted of every existent" (WdL II: 259/SoL 355). If that is so, then the generality of a law of logic can be grounded in the corresponding generality of a category. Once we recognize this, we can formulate the law by using a certain formal strategy that Hegel later calls "express[ing]" a category in the form of a "proposition" (WdL II: 258–259/SoL 354). For example, Hegel maintains that we can formulate the law of identity, "Everything is identical (to itself)," by deploying the category of identity in this way.

That this is Hegel's approach is suggested by a provocative claim he makes concerning traditional logic. Hegel claims that traditional logic erred in restricting its focus to a small number of basic laws (identity, non-contradiction, sufficient reason). Strictly speaking, all of the categories in the Doctrine of Being imply correlative laws, not just the determinations of reflection from Essence:

> On the face of it, it is difficult to see why only these simple determinations of reflection should be expressed in this particular form and not also the rest, such as the categories that belong to the sphere of being. We would then have, for instance, such propositions as, "Everything is," "Everything has an existence," etc.; or again, "Everything has a quality, a quantity, and so on." (WdL II: 258–259/SoL 354)

Once we take Hegel's approach into account, we find that there are far more laws of logic than was traditionally thought. In principle, any category could be used to generate a logical law or law of thought of the form "Everything is X (= a category)." We would then be faced with far more logical laws than the tradition recognizes. This suggests an additional criticism of traditional logic to the effect that its focus on certain laws rather than others was arbitrary. As Hegel says, there should not only be a law of identity but also one of being, existence, quality, quantity and the like. In the tradition, the laws of logic form a natural set, but no longer in Hegel where they have been assimilated to general metaphysics (ontology).

At least in these more extreme moments, Hegel suggests that formal logic does not constitute a self-standing, independent domain of inquiry at all but is simply metaphysics (category theory) in a different guise. Hegel's position, then, can often seem to be not only reductionist but also eliminativist. This can be seen in Hegel's claim that the propositional form in which the laws of logic are expressed should be rejected entirely. Only in this way will the metaphysical categories from which the laws of formal logic derive receive their due. Hegel defends this eliminativist view by confronting the proponent of traditional logic with a dilemma:

> Now this propositional form is, for one thing, something superfluous; the determinations of reflection are to be regarded in and for themselves. Moreover, the propositions suffer from the drawback that they have "being," "everything," for subject. They thus bring being into play again, and enunciate the determinations of reflection (the identity, etc., of anything) as a quality which a something would have within – not in any speculative sense, but in the sense that the something, as subject, persists in such a quality as an existent, not that it has passed over into identity (etc.) as into its truth and essence. (WdL II: 259/SoL 355)

Let us consider two possibilities.

- The first is that propositional form adds nothing over and above the metaphysical category from which the logical law derives. If that is so, then propositional form is "superfluous" and can be safely ignored.
- The second possibility is that it does add something, and this seems to be closer to the truth. After all, the statements of the traditional laws have subject–predicate form. All invoke at least one other concept beyond the relevant category. For example, in stating that "everything is self-identical" the law of identity invokes not only the concept of identity but that of every being. Yet if that is so then we are failing to respect the hierarchical order that obtains among the categories. In this case, we are neglecting the way in which a category like being is subordinate to one like identity.

The reason for this is complex, and is one we will be in a position to clarify only in Chapter 6. However, it can be crudely summarized in the following way. Being is a nonrelational category of the Doctrine of Being, whereas the latter is a relational one of the Doctrine of Essence. The latter is more advanced than the former because it is free of a type of internal contradiction afflicting it. Using them together as if they were on a par is a mistake, a (partial) regression to a less advanced standpoint.

Yet Hegel's most significant innovation over the tradition is the type of system his approach makes possible. Logical laws derive from metaphysical categories, not from the form of intellectual self-reflection advocated by the tradition. This has an important consequence, anticipated earlier. Because the categories form a system, rather than an aggregate, the laws that derive from them do as well. Much in the way that each category gives rise to an internal conflict that its successor resolves, so too will each law. Hence, there will be deductive relations between laws and other laws. Lacking insight into the category-theoretic basis of the laws of logic, the tradition saw no such relations. Hegel's alternative approach has allowed him to achieve a deduction of the principles on which all deductive argument depends. My aim in this chapter is to chronicle Hegel's ambitious attempt to derive the laws of logic from one another. Essentially, this will require considering the sequence of categories from which those laws derive, as well as the deductive interrelations among these categories.

Here, the metaphor of the rhizome (mushroom) used in more recent Continental philosophy may help clarify Hegel's project. If the laws of traditional logic are like mushrooms dispersed across a field, then the categories of Hegel's ontology are like their roots reaching down into the soil.[15] Unlike the mushrooms, which appear to be distinct individuals, the roots are everywhere interconnected. Whereas the traditional laws confront us as disconnected, Hegel's categories derive from one another.

It is by taking this subterranean point of view that we learn where the nourishment for these mushrooms actually comes from. Again, characteristic features of the laws will turn out to be dependent on the categories. Yet it is also at this subterranean level where we discover that some of the laws of logic lack the firm basis of support we thought that they had. Some of these mushrooms are languishing in ways not visible on the surface and should be uprooted. For Hegel not only wants to preserve old laws but reject others and introduce new ones. New and stronger ones will grow up in place of the old.

---

[15] Deleuze and Guattari (1987) use the metaphor for a different purpose. They use it as an alternative to the arboreal (tree-based) one that philosophers like Descartes have used for the structure of human knowledge.

5.2   Hegel on the Laws of Logic in the Leibniz–Wolff Tradition: Identity (of Indiscernibles), Noncontradiction, Excluded Middle and Sufficient Reason

The five laws recognized by the formal logic of Hegel's day differ from those familiar to us today. Here, it is important to note that the form of Scholastic Aristotelianism of Hegel's time was heavily influenced by Leibniz. Its logic includes principles integral to Leibniz's thought. This is worth noting, since some of the laws are not ones we would typically consider logical today:

1. Identity: Everything is identical to itself (self-identical). A = A or A is A.
2. Diversity (identity of indiscernibles/indiscernibility of identicals): Nothing can be completely identical with anything else. Everything is different.
3. Noncontradiction: Nothing both is and is not itself. A ≠ A and -A.
4. Excluded middle: For every thing, A, and every pair of opposed predicates, F and non-F, every thing has either one or the other. A is either F or non-F.
5. Sufficient ground: Everything has a sufficient ground.

In keeping with Hegel's approach, understanding the basis of each of these laws will require that we examine the ontological categories from which they derive. Hegel begins with the category of identity, which is the basis of the law of identity. He then proceeds to derive a new category from it and therewith a new logical law. This comes about through the identification of a type of deficiency in the old that can only be resolved by the new. In this case, the new category is difference, and the successor law is the identity of indiscernibles. At this point the process repeats.

One peculiar feature of Hegel's method is its simultaneously constructive and destructive character. On the one hand, each law of logic receives from the Hegelian system a more rigorous justification than it could have in the tradition. On the other, each suffers a more bracing critique than would have been given in that tradition either. An analogue to this in non-Hegelian philosophy would be the practice of developing the best possible version of an opponent's argument – before rebutting it.

It would be natural to wonder why the laws of logic become relevant at this point in Hegel's dialectic and no earlier.[16] The answer, I believe,

---

[16] In the following paragraphs, I am close to Iber (1990: 245–246), though he views the break with Being as more radical than I do.

concerns the status of propositional form in the logic. Unlike some philosophers, Hegel regards the form of the proposition (*Satz*) as derivative
rather than primitive. Like all other conceptual resources, propositional
form must be justified. The justification is as follows.

Whatever else it might be, propositional form is a multiplace relation.
With one term, we do not yet have a proposition. Yet with two or more,
we do. Unless it is elliptical for something more complex, "Aristotle" is not
by itself a proposition. By contrast, "Aristotle was born in such-and-such
year" is a proposition. In deference to this, Hegel refers to propositions
as "reflected," playing on the connotations this term has of duality –for
example, when we envision the original item and then its reflection in a
pool of water or a mirror. Importantly, this is not the form of reflection
thought engages in but, rather, one found in the world.[17]

Accordingly, propositional form can emerge only mid-way in the *Logic*,
in the Doctrine of Essence. For it is there that we first come upon relational categories, or category pairs: whole and parts, cause and effect, form
and content, and so on. More specifically, propositional form can emerge
only when we have become convinced of the inadequacy of earlier nonrelational categories such as those from the Doctrine of Being.

Yet even if propositional form arises in this way, this does not yet explain
why a specific set of propositions, the laws of logic, become relevant at this
stage. Why are the first propositions we consider the law of identity, noncontradiction, excluded middle, sufficient reason and so on?

The answer I favor requires us to appreciate an additional facet of
Hegel's approach. Hegel tells us that the Doctrine of Essence will cycle
through the same material as the Doctrine of Being, though from a different perspective.

> Because the one concept is the substantial element in everything, the same
> determinations surface in the development of the essence as in the develop-
> ment of being, but in reflected form. Hence, instead of being and nothing,
> the forms of the positive and the negative now enter in, the former initially
> corresponding to the opposition-less being as identity, the latter (shining in
> itself) developed as the difference. (EL § 114 A)

More specifically, the Doctrine of Essence will consider relational versions
of the nonrelational categories from Being ("the same determinations ...
but in reflected form"). Next comes the crucial step. For Hegel, identity is
simply the relational version of the nonrelational category of being. Unlike

---

[17] Here, I follow Houlgate (2011).

most other writers who discuss the identity relation,[18] Hegel takes seriously the way that identity statements, those of the form "A is A," use a conjugated form of the verb "to be." Identity is to the Doctrine of Essence what Being was to the Doctrine of Being. That is why the law of identity becomes relevant only at this later stage.

What, though, of the other laws, for example noncontradiction? As we saw in our discussion of Fichte, the law of noncontradiction was considered a "negative" version of the law of identity in this tradition. It states that A ≠ -A. With this in mind, we can understand why Hegel chooses to discuss noncontradiction at this point as well. Moreover, we should note that a version of the same point about the Doctrine of Being applies here as well. If Identity is simply Being in the form of a relation, then difference is Nothing in the same form. When two things are different, one is not the other.

If that is so, then an intriguing possibility suggests itself, namely, that Hegel's famous argument for the opening of the *Logic* concerning Being and Nothing is repeated here, albeit in a slightly different form. Before, Hegel argued for the paradoxical claim that Being and Nothing, nonrelational categories, are the same. Now, he will argue that Identity and Difference, the corresponding relations, are the same as well. It is to this latter argument that I now turn, and, as I hope to show, it is this argument that holds the key to unlocking Hegel's critique of the laws of logic as they were traditionally understood.

5.2.1   Identity

Hegel holds that the logical law of identity is informed by a specific, and perhaps questionable, understanding of the category of identity: "the identity of the understanding."

> Such a thought will always have only abstract identity in mind, and … alongside it, difference. In its opinion, reason is no more than a loom intertwining warp (say, identity) and woof (say, difference), joining them externally; or, if it turns to analysis, now specifically pulling out identity, and *at the same time also* obtaining difference *alongside* it. (WdL 11: 261/SoL 357)

On this account, identity completely excludes difference. Examples of identity without difference are cases such as the following: "a planet is a planet," "magnetism is magnetism" and "the spirit is a spirit."

---

[18] An exception is Heidegger's *Identity and Difference* (1969).

We might call these examples cases of *strict identity*. In such cases, there is no difference at all between what is identified and itself. Even the slightest difference, such as the difference between an object at itself at a slightly later point in time, would be incompatible with Identity in this sense. So too would a merely notional difference, such as the difference between the object considered from one perspective and the same object considered from another. On this view, identity excludes difference of any kind.

Since this is the identity of the understanding, we should also briefly recall what Hegel means by this term. The understanding is defined by its tendency to draw distinctions, separating things from one another that should not be confused. In this case, it does so with identity and difference. Yet we should also recall that Hegel regards the understanding's perspective as superficial. Reason will ultimately show the distinctions it draws turn out to be less stark than it supposed. This will turn out to be the case with identity and difference as well.

For Hegel, the identity of the understanding is ultimately nonsensical. Identity does not exclude difference, but presupposes it. In other words, there can be no identity without difference. Hegel's argument for this is simple. Identity is a relation, and a relation presupposes two different things to relate. The difference can be very slight, or even merely notional. Yet without any difference at all, we could not identify the things with one another. There would not be different things to identify with one another, but just one thing. Matters are not helped significantly if we speak of numerical identity. Numerical identity is a relation as well. It obtains between two things when they are identical. Yet if there are two of them, they are not identical. The same problem arises at a different level.

Even the abstract formal principle that states the law of identity (A=A) is not truly an instance of the "identity of the understanding," at least not in the way it is often thought to be:

> More is entailed, therefore, in the form of the proposition expressing identity than simple, abstract identity; entailed by it is this pure movement of reflection in the course of which there emerges the other, but only as reflective shine, as immediate disappearing; "A is" is a beginning that envisages a something different before it to which the "A is" would proceed; but the "A is" never gets to it. "A is ... A": the difference is only a disappearing and the movement goes back into itself. – The propositional form can be regarded as the hidden necessity of adding to abstract identity the extra factor of that movement. (WdL 11: 264/SoL 360)

For Hegel, even the formal representation of identity presupposes that of difference. The subject–predicate structure of judgment itself provides for two different places in which the same concept can be placed (A is A). Hence, the ease of formalizing pure identity in this way is deceptive. We are, in fact, relying on a formal representation of difference. Difference has been moved elsewhere, but not eliminated. Indeed, it can never be eliminated as long as the identity relation holds. It is for this reason that Hegel focuses not on the apparent ease of formally representing identity but on the very real difficulty of explaining the meaning of the notion itself. Without recourse to empty formulae like A is A the inherent difficulties in defining this notion become apparent. Notoriously, identity is difficult to define in a noncircular way. We might claim that identity is that relation which something stands in only to itself and nothing else. But what is to count as "itself" and what as "something else"? This we can only determine with recourse to a notion of identity, the notion we hoped to define. However, the problem that interests Hegel differs, even if it is one that is also sometimes brought up in later discussions. It is that the notion of identity seems to be inherently self-contradictory, since one can only identify what is different.

Even using the questionable strategy of justification that the tradition favors, we cannot justify the law of identity. The relevant stock of judgments from which we might abstract to discover the law of identity simply does not exist. Nobody in ordinary life makes judgments of the form "a planet is a planet," "magnetism is magnetism" and so on. People may do so in philosophy, but that is only because they are already under the influence of the questionable logical theory whose credentials are here in question. For Hegel, then, there are no such judgments from everyday life from which one could "abstract" and discover the "formal" principle: A=A. Consequently, this principle cannot be deemed inherent to the form of thought as such, in contrast to its contingently given matter. It is not a law of thought in the weighty sense the tradition favors but a kind of contrivance. Hegel elaborates:

> If one maintains that this sentence cannot be proven but that *each* consciousness proceeds in accord with it and experientially concurs with it as soon as it hears it, then it is necessary to note, in opposition to this alleged experience of the school, the general experience that no consciousness thinks, has representations, and so forth, or speaks according to this law, that no concrete existence of any sort exists according to this law. Speaking according to this alleged law of truth ("a planet is a planet," "magnetism is - magnetism," "the spirit is a spirit") is considered, quite correctly, to be silly;

this is presumably a universal experience. The school in which alone such laws are valid has, along with its logic which seriously propounds them, long since been discredited in the eyes of healthy common sense and in the eyes of reason. (EL § 115 A)

To be sure, a certain process of abstraction has occurred in order to yield this law, but it is a highly dubious one. It is less a form of abstraction intended to reveal the form of the judgments we make in ordinary life than one intended to conceal their true form. The true form of the judgment is not "the identity of the understanding," or identity without difference, A=A, but rather a form of identity in difference. This is reflected in the subject–predicate form of the judgment that does not simply repeat the subject concept ("a magnet is a magnet") but predicates something differ-ent of it ("a magnet is charged").

Sometimes, it is suggested that Hegel's objection is little more than the common sense one that we do not regularly think and judge in the way traditional logic suggests. This is correct but misleading. It implies an attitude of deference toward common sense that is alien both to Hegel and to traditional logic. This objection only gains its force when we recall that traditional logic, though it did not simply defer to ordinary thought, did rely on it. More specifically, this logic employed a method of abstrac-tion intended to elicit the underlying structure of ordinary thought. Yet Hegel is denying the existence of the original stock of judgments there would need to be for this law to be discovered (as opposed to merely being invented). Hegel elaborates on this, essentially accusing logicians of altering the facts to fit their theory, rather than deriving their theory from the facts:

> *Formal identity* or *identity of the understanding* is this identity insofar as one fastens on it and *abstracts* from the difference. Or the *abstraction* is rather the positing of this formal identity, the transformation of something in itself concrete into this form of simplicity – be it that a part of the mani-fold on hand in what is concrete is *omitted* (through so-called *analysing*) and only *one* of the manifold parts is taken up or that, with the omission of its diversity, the manifold determinations are *pulled together* into one. (EL § 115 A)

Hegel puts the point a different way when he denies that the laws of logic or of thought are analytic, something the tradition tended to affirm. As he writes, "From this it is clear that the principle of identity itself, and still more the principle of contradiction, are not of merely *analytical* but of *synthetic* nature" (WdL II: 265/SoL 360). We can reconstruct Hegel's argument for this claim as follows. It is not contained in the very concept of an entity that this entity be identical with itself. In order to arrive at that conclusion, we need a further concept not contained in the first one, namely, the relational concept of identity. Only with the addition of this further concept can we get to the law of identity. That law connects the nonrelational concept of an entity with that very entity itself by means of a further relational concept: the concept of a relation of identity holding between an entity and itself.

This allows us to approach Hegel's point about identity and difference another way. Consider an actual state-of-affairs in which there were only a single thing that was in some sense plural or different from itself. For Hegel, this would be a state-of-affairs in which the identity relation, self-identity, would not be possible. We would simply have the entity, A, rather than a relation of self-identity, A=A. We would have entity and not identity.

Yet another argument Hegel runs is that his opponent's view is self-undermining. The reason is that identity and difference are interdefined. On Hegel's view, we cannot define identity except by contrasting it with difference. If that is so, however, then identity is inseparable from difference:

> They do not see that in saying, "*Identity is different* from difference," they have thereby already said *that identity is something different.* And since this must also be conceded as the nature of identity, the implication is that to be different belongs to identity not externally, but within it, in its nature. (WdL II: 262–263/SoL 358)

There is a further nuance to Hegel's argument that suggests the position he is arguing for is bolder than may at first have been apparent. Difference is required to define identity but not just because identity can only be defined contrastively with difference. There is a further reason. Difference is required to define identity because the contrastive relation just invoked in the definition of identity is itself a relation of difference. In other words, difference is not just one of the relata in the identity–difference dyad but the entire relation itself. *There is a relation of difference between identity and difference.* However, this relation is prior to its terms, in that it is required to define their meanings. Hence, difference is not just bound up with identity, but, in an important sense, prior to it.

This could be evidence for Priest's suggestion, made in passing in his "Dialectic and Dialethic" (1989), that Hegel's *Logic* involves a distinct class of paradoxes of self-reference, for example the liar and Russell's paradox. To develop this suggestion further, I would claim that Hegel's *Logic* contains conceptual paradoxes of self-reference. Here, the form of self-reference would differ. It would not be the reference of a sentence to itself, for example "this sentence is false," made possible by the language's inclusion of its own truth predicate. Nor would it be the inclusion of a set in itself, for example "the set of all sets that are not members of themselves." Rather, it would be the application of a concept to itself: more specifically, the application of a concept pair to that very concept pair.

For example, and to take another famous case from the *Logic*, consider the concepts of the infinite and the finite. The former is the lack of any limitations, the latter is the possession of one (or more). The former is what the latter is not and vice versa. So the infinite is finite vis-à-vis the finite. The concept pair, finite and infinite, when applied to itself, self-undermines. It does not self-justify, or self-comprehend. In much the same way that dialethists such as Priest regard paradoxes as counterexamples to the law of noncontradiction in its classical form, we could do so with these conceptual paradoxes. They push us toward conceding that a pair of concepts can be both identical and different.

In a further version of the argument, Hegel raises another problem for his opponent's position (WdL II: 264–265/SoL 360). Crudely summarized, the problem is that the inherent generality of the law of identity requires us to acknowledge that identity implies difference. The law "everything is identical with itself" has a certain inherent generality because it is meant to apply to every particular that there is. Yet inherent in the universal–particular relationship implicitly acknowledged by the law of identity is difference, namely, the difference between the universal law and the particular instances falling under it. Put another way, one can recognize the law of identity, everything is identical with itself, only if one already acknowledges the nonidentity between the law itself and the particular instances falling under it. That nonidentity between a law and the instances falling under it is part of what makes a law the distinctive sort of thing that it is. Hence, Hegel's broader strategy is to undermine the law of identity by showing that it is incompatible with a basic presupposition of the idea of law itself, namely, the difference between the abstract law and its concrete applications.

It is, perhaps, surprising that Hegel should be so dogged in his insistence that identity cannot be held apart from difference. Who has ever held otherwise, besides some forgotten logicians? Hence it is worth noting that Hegel's main opponent in his critique of the "identity of the understanding" or "abstract identity" is very likely Schelling.[19] Schelling endorses

---

[19] Cf. Iber (2016: 31, "5. Hegels Kritik der Ontologischen Fundierung bei Schelling").

"the identity of the understanding" because it is the form of identity his system requires. At least in one of its more influential versions, beginning with the 1801 "Presentation of my System of Philosophy" (*Darstellung meines Systems der Philosophie*) the Schellingian system accords identity a foundational role. It is the "first principle" of this system, much like the "I" is the first principle of Fichte's. By this, I simply mean that it is a principle from which all other claims in Schelling's system derive. Yet if identity is to be the system's first principle, then it cannot presuppose any other principle for the following straightforward reason. All other principles are meant to derive from it rather than the reverse. Hegel's claim that identity presupposes difference would therefore be profoundly threatening to Schelling's identity philosophy, which Hegel famously criticized even before the *Logic*.

5.2.2   *Identity of Indiscernibles*

"The law of diversity" is a version of Leibniz's principle of the identity of indiscernibles, and, once it is seen in this way, we can appreciate why it would follow from the law of identity (EL § 117 A, Z). The law of identity states that everything is self-identical: a planet is a planet, magnetism is magnetism and so on. However, it also implies that nothing is identical to anything distinct from it: a planet is not magnetism and so on. Reformulated, then, the principle states that every individual thing is different (from every other), sui generis.

Much as he argued that there can be no identity without difference, Hegel here argues that there can be no difference without identity. Preliminarily, Hegel argues that it is not possible for two things to simply be different. They would have to be different in at least one respect(s). The reason is that it is only by identifying the respect in which they are different can we cite the properties that differentiate them. If they are different in color, then that is because this one is blue and that one is red. For Hegel, then, there is no such thing as difference *tout court*. If two things were simply different, rather than differing in some specific respect, then we would be unable to identify the properties in virtue of which they were different. We would simply be able to say that they were different – which is not an effective way of differentiating them at all.

Having established that difference is always determinate difference, Hegel proceeds to argue that this entails identity. For Hegel, the prior claim is equivalent to another. I mean the claim that difference in some specific respect implies identity in some more general respect. The differing properties of each thing will always be determinates of some determinable. If two things are different colors, blue and yellow, then they are identical in respect of being colored, and so on. If they are numerically different, then they are, at the very least, both numbered. In this way, Hegel completes his demonstration of the mutual implication of identity and difference. Just as there can be no identity without difference, there can be no difference without identity.

5.2.3   Noncontradiction

Here, we should recall from our discussion of Fichte that, traditionally, the law of noncontradiction has been considered a version of the law of identity.[20] Hegel undoubtedly shares this traditional view. As he writes: "The other expression of the principle of identity, 'A cannot be A and not-A at the same time,' is in a negative form; it is called the 'principle of contradiction'" (WdL II: 265/SoL 360). At least in its traditional form, this law simply states that nothing that is identical to itself can, at the same time, differ from itself. It cannot be the case that A = A and also -A. As we saw earlier, this intrapropositional version of the law of noncontradiction, that is concerning a single proposition (judgment), is prior to the interpropositional version, that is one concerning contradictions between pairs of propositions (judgments).

Yet if the law of noncontradiction and that of identity are equivalent, then Hegel has already taken the decisive step in his rejection of noncontradiction. That is because his critique of the law of identity can double as a critique of the law of noncontradiction. That something can be both identical with itself and different from itself is exactly what Hegel asserts there. This is what he means when he claims that identity presupposes difference. Before he draws this conclusion, however, Hegel consolidates the results of his critique of the laws of identity and diversity. He does so by considering two additional sets of categories that respect the interdependence of identity and difference.

For Hegel, a superior set of categories that reflects the lesson of the critique of identity is likeness/unlikeness. Things are always alike in some particular respect(s) rather than in all respects. Yet this is to acknowledge that they are unlike in other respects. Similarly, things are always unlike

---

[20] See Leibniz, "Primary Truths" (1989). See also the earlier discussion of Fichte on the laws of identity and noncontradiction, where it was clear that Fichte relied on this Leibnizian conception of the laws as equivalent.

in some respect(s) rather than in all. Yet this is to acknowledge they are alike in others. To acknowledge this is to accept that identity and difference are inseparable and that there is no pure identity or difference. As Hegel writes:

> Likeness is an identity only of such as are *not the same,* not identical to one another, and unlikeness is a *relation* of what is not alike. Hence, neither falls indifferently outside the other into diverse sides or aspects; instead, each is a shining into the other [*ein Scheinen in die andere*]. Diversity is thus difference of reflection or *difference in itself, determinate* difference. (EL § 118)

However, the problem with the category pair like and unlike is a form of arbitrariness it introduces into our thinking. As Hegel explains, the standard relative to which the things are deemed like or unlike is distinct from the things themselves. This means that there are, in principle, any number of standards relative to which things could be deemed like or unlike. Relative to one basis of comparison, two things can be alike rather than unlike. Relative to another, they can be unlike, rather than alike. It seems inevitable that the standard will be arbitrarily decided upon by the subject rendering the comparison. Like and unlike, then, are too arbitrary and subjective to constitute a genuine "definition of the Absolute."

A new category, "opposition" (*Entgegensetzung*), is supposed to eliminate the arbitrariness, relativity and subjectivism inherent in diversity (EL § 119; WdL II: 279/SoL 374). In order to see why this is so we must first define this new category by defining what opposites are. This proves more difficult than might at first be apparent. Hegel's discussion is certainly not short on examples (the two poles of a magnet, those of the planet, acid and base, positive and negative charge, positive and negative numbers, virtue and vice, asset and debt, east and west, light and darkness, and so on). However, examples are not a definition.

An initial way to acclimate oneself to Hegel's idea of opposition is simply to realize that a great many things are different even though they are not opposites. As Hegel explains, moral innocence, like that which very young children or certain animals possess, and moral vice are different (WdL II: 384/SoL 379). Yet they are not opposites in the way moral virtue and moral vice are. Here, then, are a set of conditions some pair of things must meet to be opposites:

1. They are different.
2. They are interdefined.
3. They are negatively interdefined.

4. They cannot be combined without "cancellation."
5. Each is one of only two possible determinates of some determinable.
6. The opposites are, in a certain sense, compatible with (1), identical.

Let us illustrate these conditions by considering some of Hegel's examples. A negative number and the positive number that is its opposite, for example + 6 and – 6, are different (1). Moreover, they are interdefined, since each is defined in terms of the other (2). In particular, each is defined as not being the other (3). We can see that this is so when we recall that there is little more to define a positive number and its negative counterpart than the fact that each is not the other. Neither has an intrinsic characteristic marking it as positive rather than negative. We may, of course, use different signs for them (+, –). We may, alternatively, represent one as 6 hash marks left of the number 0 on the number line and the other as 6 hash marks to the right of it. Even so, these designations are arbitrary. All that distinguishes the two numbers is that each is not the other. In this case too, the opposites cannot be combined without cancelling one another. Their sum is 0. In other words, they oppose one another, perhaps in the sense in which two opponents in some sort of contest do. Hegel does not shy away from speaking of them as bent on mutual annihilation (4). In spite of the fact that these numbers are opposites, there is nevertheless some property they share in common. In this case, there is the quantity itself, 6, considered irrespective of whether it is positive or negative – the so-called "absolute value." Moreover, the positive and negative numbers are (the only) two ways to realize this absolute value. They are the only two determinates of one and the same determinable (5). Finally, Hegel draws from the foregoing the striking implication that the opposites are identical (6). He simply means the following. When we realize that each entails the other, we will realize that there is just one thing here comprised of two distinct parts. It is as if we are speaking imprecisely when we refer to a positive number or a negative one in isolation, since the existence of each always implies that of the other.

Another example is magnetism. The two poles of a magnet are different (1). Yet each is defined in terms of the other, since part of what it is to be a pole is to be one of a pair (2). In fact, each is only the particular pole that it is because it is not the other (3). One is called north and the other south because they correspond to the earth's poles. However, these designations are ultimately arbitrary. No intrinsic property here either. Although they are distinct parts of one and the same entity, the magnet, the two poles are opposed. They cannot be combined further. There is no mixing or blending of them together in the way there are of colors (4). Moreover, each pole, north and south, instantiates differently the same overarching property, namely polarity (5). They are the two possible determinates of a single determinable. Ultimately, the two poles are identical in a specific sense. Neither can exist without the other, so it makes sense to speak of one entity of which they are each distinct parts: the magnet.

Like diversity, opposition unites identity and difference, but it avoids the objectionable features of the latter.

> However, to say that the positive and the negative exist in themselves essentially implies that to be opposed is not a mere moment, nor that it is just a matter of comparison, but that it is the determination of the sides themselves of the opposition. (WdL II: 275/SoL 370)

Let us briefly recall why diversity left us with the problem of subjectivism, arbitrariness and relativism so as to better understand how opposition resolves this problem. In diversity, two different things could be compared on any basis whatsoever. As a result, they could be identical or different, depending on which basis was selected. Yet no basis seemed significantly better than any other. Which basis was selected seemed to be entirely down to the whims of an external observer. Yet once we move to the standpoint of opposition, the arbitrariness is removed. Henceforth, there is only one possible basis of comparison possible. For example, two opposite numbers are to be compared with respect to the two different ways in which they realize the same absolute value, two poles of a magnet with respect to the different ways in which they are charged and so on. In this standpoint, then, there is an objective fact of the matter about whether and to what extent the two are identical and different. It is not relativized to the subjective standpoint of any particular observer.

We are now in a position to understand Hegel's rationale for what is undoubtedly among his most controversial positions, his rejection of the law of noncontradiction. As I hope to show, the need for this rejection is a consequence of Hegel's definition of the Absolute as opposition. "Opposites entail contradiction" (WdL II: 288/SoL 383). As we saw, each category (pair) can be reformulated as a definition of the Absolute. In this case, "the Absolute is opposition." Once we recall that the Absolute is an empty placeholder, and that opposites are (inter)defined as the negations of one another, however, we get a contradiction. The contradiction: X is F and not-F.

In its more familiar form, the law of noncontradiction includes a crucial caveat that Hegel appears to flagrantly disregard. It only forbids ascribing opposed properties to a thing *at the same time and in the same respect*. For this reason, it is necessary to distinguish between the mere appearance of contradiction and genuine contradiction. Presented with an apparent contradiction, we ought to apply this qualification so as to find out if the appearance of contradiction can be explained away. If it can, there is no true contradiction. If not, then there is a contradiction. Yet Hegel appears not to do this.[21]

Here, I restrict myself to describing a few avenues of response I think worthy of being explored more than they have so far.

As we have seen, Hegel is part of a tradition that thinks of the law of noncontradiction as a version of the law of identity, A=A. The law of noncontradiction tells us that A ≠ -A, or A ≠ A and -A. Moreover, Hegel's rejection of the law of identity and therewith noncontradiction is reached through reflection on a type of paradox. This is the paradox that one only identify what is different. In this regard, Hegel resembles other critics of the law of noncontradiction, even if the paradox that interests them differs. If that is so, then perhaps it is here with the topic of identity that a defense could begin.

Why, then, would Hegel disregard the qualification? One immediate difficulty is that the qualification is question-begging. In attempting to explain away the possibility of a true contradiction, it invokes identity ("... *same* time ... *same* respect"). Yet identity is what gave rise to the appearance of contradiction in the first place. Far from eliminating an apparent contradiction, the qualification multiplies it. In attempting to specify what it means to describe one moment in time as the same as another, or one respect as the same as another, we will encounter the same problems that led Hegel to the notion of true contradiction. In other words, we will have taken a more elaborate detour to the same destination.

Another promising resource in Hegel's account is the idea that opposites are interdefined. They cannot be separated from one another, since each entails the other (no plus without minus, no positive without negative and so on). Once we realize that is so, we can discern a potential vulnerability in the proposed strategy for explaining away contradiction. This strategy effectively amounts to separating out the opposites from one another. They are either referred to separate perspectives or standpoints on the object or else said to occupy separate parts of it. Whatever the details of how Hegel's traditional opponent proposes to separate the relevant properties, that is effectively what her strategy entails.

---

[21] See Russell: "And as for Hegel, he cries wolf so often that when he gives the alarm of a contradiction we finally cease to be disturbed" (2015: 61).

However, separating the relevant properties from one another is exactly what Hegel has argued cannot be done in his account of opposites.[22] Admittedly, their inseparability is dictated by Hegel's metaphysics. When this metaphysics conflicts with a law of classical logic, a proponent of this logic might argue that the former should give way to the latter. Yet Hegel's metaphysics-first approach rules this out. Hegel regards logic as answerable to metaphysics, rather than the reverse. So the proponent of the tradition cannot respond in this way without begging the question against Hegel.

5.2.4   Excluded Middle

Hegel's main argument against the excluded third simply invokes his category of opposition. For Hegel, it is possible for something to have both of two opposed properties. Indeed, Hegel's claim is stronger. It is that things just are unities of opposed properties:

> Instead of speaking in terms of the principle of excluded middle (the principle of abstract understanding), one should rather say: everything is opposed. Indeed, neither in heaven nor on earth, neither in the spiritual nor in the natural world, is there any such abstract either/or of the sort that the understanding maintains. Everything that is some sort of thing is something concrete, something that is in itself thereby differentiated and opposed. The finitude of things consists then in the fact that their immediate existence [*Dasein*] does not correspond to what they are in themselves. Thus, for example, in inorganic nature, an acid is in itself at the same time a base, that is to say, its being is simply only this, to be related to its other. With this, however, an acid is also not something quietly perduring in opposition but instead is striving to posit itself as what it is in itself. Contradiction is what moves the world in general and it is ridiculous to say that contradiction cannot be thought. (EL § 119 + Z2)

Moreover, Hegel claims that in cases of opposition, A and -A, there is a third property that is neither. In other words, there is a third that we must not exclude. This third is the determinable of which each of the opposed properties is a determinate instance.[23] For example, there are the six dollars, as opposed to the six dollars in assets or six dollars in debts, the six miles, as opposed to the six miles from the east or the six miles from the west, and so on.

[22] I here follow Ficara, who calls the inseparability of opposites "the basic idea of Hegelian contradiction" (2020a: 175).

[23] Ficara (2020a: 192–193).

Difference in itself yields the principle: "Everything is something essentially differentiated" or, as it has also been expressed, "*Only one of two opposite predicates pertain to a particular something and there is no third.*"... The principle of *the excluded third* is the principle of the determinate understanding that wants to refrain from contradiction and, in doing so, contradicts itself. *A* is supposed to be +*A* or -*A;* but the third, the *A,* is thereby articulated, something which is *neither + nor –* and that is posited *just as much as* +*A* and as -*A* are. If +*W* 6 means 6 miles in a westerly direction and – *W* 6 means 6 miles in an easterly direction, and + and – cancel one another [*sich aufheben*], then the 6 miles of the way or space remain what they were with and without the opposition. Even the mere plus and minus of the number or the abstract direction have, if one will, zero as their third. But it should not be denied that the empty opposition of the understanding, signaled by +and –, also has its place in the case of such abstractions as number, direction, and so forth. (EL § 119 A)

As is well known, the law of excluded middle does not apply to "contrary" properties (blue and not blue, where not blue entails being some other color). That is because, if it did, there would be clear counterexamples. Some things are neither of the contraries. They are neither blue nor some nonblue color for the simple reason that they are not colored at all. If that is so, then we must adjust the law so that it only applies to "contradictories" (blue and nonblue, where nonblue does not entail being any color).

However, Hegel regards this new version as resulting in an incoherence of another kind. For Hegel, it is meaningless to describe something as nonblue. This is exactly the type of indeterminate difference Hegel rejects in the opening arguments of *Logic* when he denies that (indeterminate) Nothing is a legitimate definition of the Absolute. There is only ever determinate negation, never indeterminate: being some nonblue color is allowed, but simply being nonblue is not. More pertinently, and as we saw earlier, Hegel also denies that there is any such thing as (indeterminate) Difference, as opposed to difference in some respect. The upshot is the same in both the relational and the earlier nonrelational case. Here, Hegel elaborates on this claim. From his point of view, it would be nonsensical to say that spirit and blue are, in some sense, different but not specify in what respect they are different, such as different in color. Yet if something is no color at all, then we should simply refuse to attach any color predicate to it rather than claim that it has the color predicate nonblue.

5.2.5 *Sufficient Reason*

Philosophers of the Leibniz–Wolff school embraced the principle of sufficient reason (PSR) or, as Hegel calls it, ground: every thing has a sufficient ground, reason or cause for its existence. Perhaps surprisingly, they often viewed it as a principle of logic alongside those of identity and noncontradiction. To some commentators, this might appear to be yet another instance of the ontologizing tendency in traditional logic. This is a tendency they think Hegel must reject as inconsistent with Kant's Copernican revolution in philosophy. Here it should be remembered that even Kant acknowledged a logical version of the PSR, though he distinguished it from the "real" one. It is a *logical* truth that, presented with any judgment, we can always ask which judgments it follows from via syllogistic inference. It is the logical version of the PSR, treated as applying to things-in-themselves, which gives rise to reason's ill-fated attempt to know the unconditioned.

As I hope to show, Hegel does criticize the PSR but not from a Kantian-idealist direction. Moreover, he does not reject it wholesale but claims to have achieved deeper insight into why this law obtains and where it does. While for some of these figures the principle is brute or near enough so, Hegel disagrees. If the PSR holds, then this will be for the simple reason that it is the legitimate successor to the preceding logical laws. In this respect, Hegel is a successor of rationalist project of deriving the PSR from the principle of noncontradiction. Yet owing to his rejection of the latter, as well as his contrary view of the basis of logic's laws, Hegel's version of this undertaking is idiosyncratic. Before turning to Hegel's argument, I want to briefly explain the broader Hegelian perspective on the PSR it reflects.

Hegel confronts an orthodox opponent of the PSR with a dilemma, one that arises when we ask: What justifies the PSR itself? Hegel calls this "the demand addressed to … logic for a justification of the principle of the ground" (EL § 121 + Z). We could call this "meta-grounding," the grounding of the grounding relation itself.[24] For Hegel, this is equivalent to asking if there is a sufficient reason for the PSR itself.

Yet when we do, we confront two unpalatable alternatives. If there is a sufficient reason for the principle, then this implies that the PSR is not ultimate in the way it has often been thought to be. Rather, whatever principle explains it is ultimate. Alternatively, we may claim there is no

---

[24] I owe this formulation to Leonard Weiss.

sufficient reason for the principle of reason. This might allow it to remain ultimate. Yet its ultimacy would come at a serious cost. It would mean that the PSR was false. There would be brute facts for which no explanation could be given – and the PSR would be the main example of one. Approached from this direction, the PSR would be a counterexample to itself. Indeed, it would contradict itself. In spite of the drastic costs of this second avenue of response, Hegel thinks that it is the one most logicians of the day chose. They treated the PSR as a type of brute fact:

> This is then also the simple sense of the so-called principle [*Denkgesetz*] of sufficient reason … Formal logic, incidentally, provides the other sciences with a bad example, inasmuch as it demands that the sciences not allow their content to be immediately valid, and nonetheless sets up this principle without deriving it and pointing out its mediation. With the same reason that the logician maintains that our capacity of thinking is simply so constituted that we have to ask for a ground in every case, the physician, asked why someone who falls into the water drowns, could also answer that human beings are simply so constructed not to be able to live under water. So, too, a judge, if asked why a criminal is punished, could answer that civil society is simply so constituted that criminals are not allowed to go unpunished. But even if one is to set aside the demand addressed to the logic for a justification of the principle of the ground … (EL § 121 Z)

As he so often has before, Hegel accuses formal logic of hypocrisy. It omits an argument for the principles on which all rational arguments depend, in this case the PSR. In so doing, logic exempts itself from the requirement it rightly insists all other sciences meet. Moreover, Hegel here alludes to what we have seen is the main source logicians appeal to when they invoke brute fact: (philosophical) psychology. In particular, Hegel describes traditional logic's practice of maintaining that our faculties are just so constituted that we adhere to principles like the PSR in our thinking.

For Hegel, the PSR does hold good in certain spheres, but it is not a brute fact that it does. Rather, it is Hegel's theory of the categories that explains why this principle holds good when it does. More specifically, the explanation takes the form of a deduction of the category of ground itself from earlier categories. This deduction shows why ground is the necessary successor to the earlier ones. It therefore explains why the law of logic correlative with ground, the principle of sufficient ground, holds good when it does. More specifically, Hegel will show that ground provides the best resolution considered so far to the problem posed by the two preceding categories, identity and difference. This is the paradox that for two things to be identical they must be different and vice versa. Somehow, ground will unite the two in a nonparadoxical way. As he writes, "The ground is the unity of identity and difference; the truth of what the difference and the identity have turned out to be" (EL § 121).

In order to understand why the category of ground should have this relationship to its predecessors, those of identity and difference, we need to rehearse its definition. A sufficient ground is not just any cause or reason but one that is decisive. It is a cause that *suffices* for its effect. In short, a sufficient ground suffices to ground what it grounds. If a sufficient ground is in place, then no further supplementary ground is necessary for the outcome. Nor, it seems, can any other ground interfere to prevent the outcome. In short, it is logically or conceptually impossible that a sufficient ground should fail to suffice. How, though, can a sufficient ground be so reliably connected to what it grounds? After all, the causes or reasons with which we are familiar often seem not to be reliable in this way.

Enter identity in difference. For Hegel, the connection can reliably obtain only if there are not two distinct entities here at all, ground and grounded, but, rather, a single entity with two aspects. More specifically, Hegel proposes that ground and grounded are simply the same content in a different form. Only in this way can we explain why one should always accompany the other. Here, Hegel reprises his previous argument that identity and difference are inseparable. However, he applies it to the case of grounds. For example, consider the ground in question as a type of cause. A body strikes another, allowing it to gain momentum. If it is to be the sufficient ground of the gain in momentum, then it must itself have that same amount of momentum. The change, then, simply involves one body conveying its momentum to the other. One and the same content, two different forms.[25]

For Hegel, the problem with sufficient ground is that it gives rise to paradoxes of its own. "Diverse grounds can be put forward for one and the same content, a diversity of grounds that proceeds according to the concept of difference, then further to opposition in the form of grounds for and against the same content" (EL § 121). I here attempt to unpack Hegel's thought.

Just because a certain ground is sufficient does not mean that no other would be. In general, a sufficient condition need not be necessary, and this is the case here as well. Nor does it even mean that there could not be a sufficient ground for the very opposite of what was to be grounded.

[25] Later, this identity within difference of the ground and grounded will be on full display in Hegel's "identity theory of causation" (Meyer 2017).

That there is a sufficient ground for one thing does not rule out the possibility of a sufficient ground for the opposite. The paradoxical scenario that results is one in which there could be two grounds, each sufficient to ground the opposite outcome, each sufficient to ground an outcome incompatible with the other. If they are sufficient grounds, then both, in and of themselves, guarantee their outcome. Yet their two opposed outcomes cannot both occur. Indeed, this is as much a problem in the case of concurring sufficient grounds for a single event. This would seem to entail that the event occur twice, though many events cannot, for example death. It is precisely the possibility of such cases that has provoked the anxieties of those skeptical of mental causation.[26] They worry that mental causation would overdetermine its effect, since there would be physical causation as well. A common example is that of multiple members of a firing squad hitting their victim at the same time and in a fatal way. Arguably, there is a more abstract version of this problem, not at all concerned with the mind–body problem. This is the version Hegel considers.

Although it can sometimes seem like it, Hegel is not just making a commonplace observation about a type of scenario we are apt to encounter in our ordinary lives. I mean a situation in which we cannot ourselves identify a single sufficient ground for something, or even a situation in which there does not seem to be one. The problem is not epistemic but logical or conceptual. In short, Hegel is identifying a paradox that is inherent to the notion of sufficient ground itself. This notion is defined in such a way that it allows for this paradoxical state of affairs to arise. Hegel believes the concern is particularly acute in the normative domain. That it is wrong to steal is a sufficient reason for not doing so. That it is necessary to preserve one's life is a sufficient reason for doing so. Since a sufficient reason is decisive, the result is that both actions are necessary. Yet only one can be performed.

The possibility that there might be multiple, even opposed, sufficient grounds seems not to have been considered a particularly threatening one by rationalist metaphysicians. In all likelihood, they would agree that it leads to exactly the absurdities Hegel identifies. Yet Hegel and the rationalists draw different implications from the possibility of such absurd scenarios. For the rationalists, the implication is that we must stipulate from the outset that there can only ever be one sufficient cause, perhaps by laying down as axiomatic that God would not allow anything of the sort. For Hegel, this is ad hoc, especially in the context of a theory of

[26] Kim (1993).

the categories. In this context, no such *deus ex machina* is permissible. Instead, the correct implication to draw is that we must proceed to consider a new category that solves the problems of the old. More specifically, we must embrace a new and different conception of a ground that ensures sufficiency while avoiding the problems of multiplicity or opposition discussed earlier.

Surprisingly, Hegel finds inspiration for this approach in Leibniz himself, who he was always careful to distinguish from the thinkers of the Leibniz–Wolff school. Hegel attributes to Leibniz a solution that rejects efficient causes in favor of final causes: "[B]y 'sufficient ground' Leibniz understood one that sufficed also for this unity and comprehended, therefore, not just causes but final causes" (WdL 11: 293/SoL 388). An efficient cause is the sufficient ground of some effect distinct from itself. This opens up the possibility of multiple, even of conflicting, sufficient grounds: a contradiction in terms. Yet (internal) teleology helps us avoid this problem. Here, the form of teleology in question is not the external form, which obtains when some entity has as its purpose the promotion of some other entity distinct from itself: for example, rainfall for the sake of crop growth so that humans can have food to eat. Instead, we are here concerned with the internal variety of purposiveness, which is when something exists for the sake of itself: for example, the constitution of an organism existing for the purpose of preserving the organism's continued existence. The reason Hegel believes that internal teleology can resolve the problems with the PSR is that it allows us to see something (an organism) as its own sufficient ground. Since in the organic case a thing's sufficient ground is not distinct from itself, there is no possibility of there being multiple grounds, or opposed ones. It is through allowing a type of self-grounding characteristic of the living that we forestall the problem of multiple, conflicting grounds. Yet there is a sense in which any such solution would be premature at this stage. Teleology will not enter the argument until well after the Doctrine of Essence in the Doctrine of the Concept.

5.3 Applications: Dialetheism, Hylomorphism and Modality

Often, resistance to dialetheism is based on the suspicion that it is fundamentally anti-intellectual, stymieing our most basic efforts to understand the world. To embrace true contradictions is to embrace chaos, and therefore to renounce inquiry. Yet to Hegel and his followers, nothing could be further than the truth. Accepting true contradictions promises to enrich our understanding of the world immeasurably, and in nearly all its aspects: especially its indeterminate, dynamical and oppositional aspects. In this concluding section, I want to consider two additional areas in which Hegel thought rejecting traditional logic could yield results: hylomorphic metaphysics (form and matter) and modality (necessity, possibility and actuality). My discussion here in this concluding section is much more speculative than in previous ones, since the connection between Hegel's views on contradiction and on these other topics is mostly implicit in the text.

As we saw, Hegel maintains that traditional logic is ill-suited to metaphysics and must be overhauled if the latter is to make progress. This is reflected in Hegel's Aristotle interpretation. Hegel accuses Aristotle of lacking a logic sufficiently rigorous to accommodate his justly celebrated metaphysics. The following passages are representative:

> Aristotle is thus the originator of the logic of the understanding; its forms only concern the relationship of finite to finite, and in them the truth cannot be grasped. But it must be remarked that Aristotle's philosophy is not by any means founded on this relationship of the understanding; thus it must not be thought that it is in accordance with these syllogisms that Aristotle has thought. *If Aristotle did so, he would not be the speculative philosopher that we have recognized him to be; none of his propositions could have been laid down, and he could not have made any step forward, if he had kept to the forms of this ordinary logic.* (VGP: "Aristotle 4. The Logic," italics mine)
>
> Although this accomplishment [in logic] brings Aristotle great honour, *by no means is it the forms of syllogistic inference at the level of understanding or at the level generally of finite thinking that he employed in his genuine philosophical investigations.* (EL § 183 Z, italics mine)

In light of this peculiar feature of Hegel's Aristotle interpretation, it is noteworthy that the Doctrine of Essence includes not only Hegel's most trenchant critique of traditional logic but also his most extensive engagement with the figure he regards as the greatest metaphysician: Aristotle. What, though, might these two parts – one at the very beginning and the other at the end – have to do with one another? Hegel's provocative suggestion seems to be the following. Rejecting the professedly Aristotelian logical theory of the tradition is a prerequisite to appreciating what is most profound in Aristotle's own metaphysics. In other words, the critique of the formal logic of the tradition given at the outset prepares the way for the reappropriation of Aristotle's metaphysics at the close. Why, though, might the traditional formal logic constitute an impediment to that metaphysics?

Here, I speculate that the law of noncontradiction in its traditional form is incompatible with central doctrines of Aristotelian metaphysics:

for example, hylomorphism. In order to see that this is so, consider form and matter, the central categories of Aristotle's metaphysics and also the ones treated by Hegel in the Doctrine of Essence.[27] It is easy to understand why Hegel would have thought they require a rejection of the law of noncontradiction. Whatever else they might happen to be, the two are opposites in Hegel's technical sense of the term. Where there is opposition, there is true contradiction.

Let us now see why form and matter are opposites in this technical sense and therefore counterexample to the law of noncontradiction. In the first place, each is defined as what the other is not. Yet they are also (logically, conceptually) inseparable from one another. If that is so, then there is an important sense in which they are identical, aspects of a single structure. For Hegel, then, each is both itself and what it is not. It is therefore unsurprising that the Doctrine of Essence should begin by rejecting the laws of identity and noncontradiction and then proceed to consider form and matter. Aristotle's hylomorphism is a position we can embrace when we pass beyond the law of noncontradiction Aristotle himself thought fundamental.

Similarly, consider *energeia, Wirklichkeit,* the process of actualizing a form in matter: for example, an acorn maturing into an oak. As Hegel tells us in his lectures, Aristotle had arrived at this notion by making an amendment to the Heraclitian idea of becoming (VGP: "Aristotle: Physics"). Aristotle had argued that there is no such thing as a process of becoming-as-such but only becoming some particular type of thing or other: for example, an oak. As a process of becoming, *energeia* is a unity of being and nothing, though of being and not-being some particular type of thing. Just as something coming to be or ceasing to be both is and is not, something coming to be or ceasing to be an oak tree both is and is not an oak tree. This aspect of Heraclitus' view has survived the transition to Aristotle's teleological framework, and it remains one of the main examples of dialetheia or true contradiction to this day. Again, the placement of actuality in the text is significant here, and for much the same reason as before.

In addition to treating the laws of logic, the Doctrine of Essence also treats modal notions (possibility, actuality, necessity), and I here want to suggest that these two areas of Hegel's thought are also closely connected. Hegel's most characteristic doctrine in the area of modality is

---

[27] Cf. Priest (1976: Ch. 1 "Gluons and their Wicked Ways").

his "actualism."[28] This is the claim that all possible states of affairs are grounded in actual ones. If it is possible for a plant to fall ill, then that is a possibility which is grounded in actual facts about the plant's nature. Traditionally, the scope of possibilities was thought to be much broader, and not delimited in this way. Anything is possible that does not involve a logical contradiction, and this means there are many possibilities that are not grounded in actual states of affairs. It is technically possible that a plant should turn into an opera singer and perform an aria, even though this is a possibility in no way provided for by actual facts about the plant's nature.

Whether we agree with Hegel's actualism or not, it should be clear that it follows rather directly from his critique of traditional logic. For Hegel, the law of noncontradiction is just the negative version of the law of identity. Moreover, the law of identity is false. Nothing is self-identical in the strict sense, or noncontradictory. Everything is both self-identical and self-external. For this reason, Hegel denies that the logical criterion for being possible is ever met. He considers this a reduction of the traditional definition of possibility.

5.4   Conclusion: Hegel on the Laws of Logic

In this chapter, we considered the first part of Hegel's critical reconstruction of logic-conventionally-so-called: in particular, his treatment of the traditional laws of logic (noncontradiction, identity, excluded middle). These were, for Hegel and his contemporaries, classically logical topics and would continue to be widely recognized as such. In order to grasp the nature Hegel's innovation over tradition, we might recall Jäsche's dismayed reaction to the newly emergent idealist logic.

As we saw, Jäsche situates Kant in a long tradition of thinkers for whom the laws of logic are, in some sense, self-evident. They do not need to be argued for on the basis of some more primitive set of principles. According to Jäsche, however, the idealists had broken with this tradition and attempted the impossible, an argument for the principles on which all argument depends. It is Fichte whom Jäsche has in mind, alluding to the idea that the laws of identity and noncontradiction can be shown to emerge from self-consciousness and consciousness of objects. However, Hegel would soon follow suit, attempting to found these laws on a foundation

---

[28] See Zambrana (2019) and also Redding (2019c). By "actualism" Redding means the anti-Lewisian doctrine, something slightly different than my topic here.

liberated from any reference to self-consciousness: a "primordial" ontology in which logic's laws and materials find their primitive precursors.

In closing, I reiterate that Hegel's treatment has both constructive and destructive phases, though my presentation has been somewhat lopsided in favor of the latter.

On the one hand, the perspective on the tradition's laws that Hegel favors depicts each of them as self-undermining, though this would not necessarily set them apart from any other principles found in the logic. An extreme instance of this destruction of tradition can be found in Hegel's rejection of the laws of identity and noncontradiction.

On the other hand, Hegel has provided these laws with a firmer basis than they traditionally received, namely, a deduction of them from more fundamental principles that bypasses the need for an appeal to reason's self-reflection. The laws of identity and noncontradiction, we learn, possess a basis in the procession of ontological categories: in particular, the movement from nonrelational being ("is") to its relational equivalent identity ("A is A"). Hence, if it is true that such laws cannot claim unrestricted validity, it is no less true that they are beholden to Hegel's logic for the restricted validity that they do have.

I have defended an account of why the laws of logic emerge when they do in Hegel's *Logic*, and this account will be useful in orienting us toward what lies ahead. The laws of logic emerged at this phase of the logic, Doctrine of Essence, because it is here that we first encounter anything as complex as the form of the proposition (*Satz*). However, the laws of logic represent only one of traditional logic's central topics. We have not yet considered the trio that are most central to it: concept, judgment and syllogism. We now turn to Hegel's attempt to criticize and reconstruct the traditional logical teachings on these thought forms, mindful that here too he will need to avoid vicious circularity. This is the next phase of Hegel's attempt to resolve the logocentric predicament.

CHAPTER 6

Mediated Immediacy: Concept, Judgment and Syllogism

In this chapter, I reconstruct Hegel's theory of concept, judgment and syllogism. These are topics traditionally treated in logic, but Hegel adopts a different approach to them. As we have seen, Kant and the Aristotelian tradition regarded these as forms of thinking. They were the constitutive norms of the faculty of thought discoverable through a process of abstraction from thought's sensibly given matter. This is a psychological, though not "psychologistic," approach in Frege's sense. Though centered on thought's self-reflection, it is not intended to reduce the normative to the descriptive. However, Hegel objects that this approach renders the justification of these principles "empirical," a brute fact, and in a way that is hypocritical for a field based on the primacy of rational argument.

For Hegel, we ought to be able to legitimate the use of these materials through some type of argument. Hegel will claim as he has before that this can be achieved only by deducing these forms from the most primitive category, Being. In this way, concept, judgment and syllogism take on the status of forms of being. While it is common for Hegel scholars to insist that these are forms of being and thinking alike, I argue for a slightly different version of this point. Prospectively they are forms of being (and not of thinking), while only retrospectively they are forms of thinking (and being).

By proceeding in this way, Hegel inverts the order of priority Kant laid down between the theory of the categories and formal logic. Whereas Kant derived his categories from the forms of judgment, Hegel begins with a theory of the categories derived on a formal-logic-independent basis. He derives them from being, meaning his theory of the categories is ontological rather than one in transcendental philosophy.

Hence, this ontological theory of the categories is then available to be appealed to in a theory of concept, judgment and syllogism. Because concept, judgment and syllogism derive from Hegel's ontological categories, they are argued for, rather than treated as brute facts of (intellectual) experience. In consequence of being "sublated" forms of being, concept, judgment and syllogism are not "empty forms" in need of filling by sense experience. They are, rather, contentful in their own right, though just how this is so will need to be explained.

By inverting the order of priority between the theory of the categories and formal logic, Hegel is able to achieve something Kant arguably did not. As we have seen, Hegel objects that Kant's derivation of the categories was merely "empirical" (continent). This was because the table of logical forms of judgment on which it was based was merely "empirical" as well. We have already considered the way Hegel proposes to prove the necessity of his preferred table of categories. Now, however, we are in a position to see that Hegel proposes to do so for his preferred table of forms of judgment and inference as well. The inversion of the order of priority Kant laid down between (formal) logic and category theory not only makes possible a derivation of the categories but, on this basis, allows for a derivation of formal logic. The doubled, interconnected problem of incompleteness for Kant's categories and forms finds its counterpart in a doubled, interconnected solution in Hegel's inverted account.

Hegel's scheme of ontological categories, once deduced on a formal-logic-independent basis, furnishes the basis for an account of the forms of judgment and inference. Briefly, the theory of the categories provided in Being and Essence furnishes a master argument that I will call the argument for "mediated immediacy." This master argument is then cycled through once more when we reach the forms of judgment and syllogism. This is not question-begging but simple application. As forms of the Concept, judgment and syllogism must respect the argument that represents its proof. While I will not go through every step of Hegel's deduction of the form of judgment and syllogism, I do claim to have identified the strategy behind that argument.

This is an ambitious agenda and will need to confront the main obstacle to attempts to argue for the laws and materials of logic: vicious circularity. How can Hegel argue for concept, judgment and inference, as well as provide an account of their necessary forms, without already employing them?

I have already argued that the dialectic constitutes a non–formal logical method of argument. It does not make syllogistic arguments for claims, put forward as judgments or propositions. Nor even does it adhere to as minimal a logical principle as the law of noncontradiction. Showing that the dialectic was non–formal logical in this way was important to the project of Chapter 5: understanding Hegel's critical reconstruction of the laws of logic (identity, noncontradiction, ground). There, it was crucial to see that the ontological categories of the Doctrine of Being are more primitive than those from the Doctrine of Essence. Indeed, it is only in the latter that the form of the proposition (*Satz*) appears, inasmuch as it is here that the two-place relations first arise.

In this chapter, however, we are interested in Hegel's account of the forms of thinking, concept, judgment and inference, which appear in his Subjective Logic. Hence, solving the bootstrapping problem will require arguing for these forms in terms that do not presuppose them. This is equivalent to deducing concept, judgment and syllogism from the onto-logical categories that make up the Objective Logic. In addition to arguing that the dialectic, in its earliest employment, proceeds nonpropositionally and nonsyllogistically, I have also argued that the subject matter of the Objective Logic need not be considered conceptual, at least not if this mean having any philosophically ambitious or controversial theory of what concepts are.

However, as we will now see, the prospect of arguing from a preconcep-tual standpoint is made less daunting by the fact that Hegel views concepts as having a fairly rich structure: more specifically, a triadic structure. As is well known, Hegel's theory of concepts – or, better, the Concept – differs from Kant's in the following respect: It treats the singular items to which concepts apply as constituents of them, rather than as furnished by a separate faculty of sensible intuition. Since the capacity to subordi-nate or be subordinated by other concepts is also internal to them, we derive from this a triadic structure. Less important than the details of this structure itself, which we will discuss presently, is the implication for solv-ing the bootstrapping problem that the logocentric predicament involves. Hegel can argue for the concept in nonconceptual terms if he can invoke only nontriadic structures that do not yet have the triadic structure of the Concept. These nontriadic structures, it turns out, just are those from the Objective Logic: more specifically, the monadic or nonrelational struc-tures from the Doctrine of Being and the dyadic or relational ones from the Doctrine of Essence. As we will see, Hegel's terms for these structures are immediacy and mediation.

As I have mentioned before, I will depict the problems that afflict these structures as more primitive than contradiction, in the logical sense: pro-tocontradiction, arising internal to a concept rather than between a subject and predicate, or a judgment and its denial. Only now, however, are we in a position to unfold the different forms of protocontradiction: primarily, a type of regress and a type of inversion or oscillation.

Hegel does not use the terms monadic and dyadic, nonrelational and relational, one-place and two-place but, rather, "immediate" and "mediated." When Hegel provides an overview of the structure of the work in his *Encyclopedia,* he aligns the categories of Being with immediacy and those of Essence with mediation. He further claims that the categories of the Concept are both immediate and mediated. Here is the way he sets out the structure:

1. The doctrine of being
2. The doctrine of essence
3. The doctrine of the concept and the idea

   That is, into the doctrine of thought

1. In its immediacy – the concept-in-itself
2. In its reflection and mediation – the being-for-itself and the shining [Schein] of the concept
3. In its having returned back into itself and in its developed being-with-itself – the concept in-and-for-itself. (EL § 83)

In schematic overview, his argument for "mediated immediacy," then, is that neither of these two category types, Immediate or mediated, Being or Essence, suffices on its own. Rather they must be combined in a third category type, the mediated immediacy of the Concept.

I now turn to a brief summary of the argument it will be our task to reconstruct, the argument for the structure Hegel calls mediated immediacy.

In the first division of the *Logic* (the Doctrine of Being), Hegel will consider the categories of "immediacy" (*Unmittelbarkeit*). These are nonrelational or, as I will sometimes put it, monadic categories. In other words, they characterize a thing as capable of being what it is independent of its relations to other things. Each such category is considered singly and is meant to be sufficient unto itself. Quantity and quality are two examples of such categories. Hegel argues that such categories exhibit a problem he calls "passing into another" (*Ubergehen in Anderes*). The problem is that these nonrelational categories turn out to be relational after all. They seem to characterize the thing in question in nonrelational terms. Yet it then turns out that these things, so defined, can be what they are only because of their relations to others.

In the second (the Doctrine of Essence), Hegel will consider the categories of "mediation" (*Vermittlung*). These are explicitly relational categories. They characterize a thing as being what it is because of its dependence on something further, something independent of it. These categories come in pairs, ones in which there is asymmetric dependence of one term on the other. I mean pairs in which the first term depends on the second to be what it is without there being a corresponding type of dependence in the other direction. For example, the effect depends on the cause, though not vice versa, the grounded upon the ground, the whole on the parts and so on. Yet these categories exhibit a problem Hegel calls "shining into another" (*Scheinen in Anderes*). The one-way relation of dependence they purport to identify turns out on closer inspection to be a complex form of interdependence.

In the third (the Doctrine of the Concept), Hegel will consider categories involving both "mediation" and "immediacy" at once ("*sich als das durch und mit sich selbst Vermittelte und hiermit zugleich als das wahrhaft Unmittelbare erweist*") (EL § 83 + Z). As before, they characterize a thing as mediated, dependent upon another to be what it is. Unlike before, however, this proves compatible with immediacy, since the other on which the thing depends is none other than itself in a different guise. At least initially, these categories come in trios. The main example is the structure Hegel calls "the Concept." Hegel's example of such a structure is the triadic one made up of the genus animal, the species horse and then, finally, the individual, this horse. For reasons I will go into below, these categories solve the problems of "shining into another" and "passing intro another." Hegel calls the solution "development" (*Entwicklung*), a term whose associations with the organic he readily exploits.[1]

Admittedly, this broad-brush characterization of Being and Essence does not fit well with Hegel's claim that "there is nothing in heaven or nature or spirit or anywhere else that does not contain just as much immediacy as mediation, so that both these determinations prove to be unseparated and inseparable and the opposition between them nothing real" (WdL 21: 54/SoL 46). This means it is incorrect to describe the categories of Being as *purely* immediate and those of Essence as *purely* mediated. Unfortunately, Hegel at least appears to do so in remarks such as the one from the *Encyclopedia* § 83, creating a tension with the "nothing in heaven …" claim.

In my view, this is no contradiction, since Hegel is telling us only what the categories *purport* to be. He is leaving open the possibility that each one's claim to immediacy or mediation will not be upheld.

Some readers will be taken aback by the way in which I use the terms immediacy and mediation, since it is more common in the literature to find

---

[1] One interpreter who discusses something like this argument is de Boer (2010b: 59–68), who treats the movement from Being to Essence to Concept in her book. For de Boer, Being and Essence fail to "synthetically unite opposites," something only the Concept can do.

immediacy and mediation understood epistemologically: more specifically, in terms of Kant's distinction between the intuitions of sensibility and the concepts of the understanding. In keeping with the interpretative orientation I have advocated throughout, I regard this as a less fundamental version of the distinction. On this version, the distinction concerns whether our relationship to objects is mediated by concepts or immediate (direct) in the way sensible intuition is.

However, I contend that this is simply a local epistemological application of the global metaphysical distinction between immediacy (directness) and mediation (indirectness). All these terms inherently refer to is the condition of being related to something else via an intermediary or else in some more direct way. This represents a key instance of Hegel reframing epistemological questions from the critical philosophy in metaphysical terms. Yet it also displays his anti-Kantian conviction that it is the latter that a radically self-critical form of thought would prioritize. I agree that there is no absolute distinction between metaphysics and epistemology in Hegel or any idealist, for that matter. However, the distinction is legitimate to draw in light of the way I have advocated we see the interrelation between these areas. I have proposed that we refer them to prospective and retrospective orientations on the logic. It is also legitimate to draw in the dialectical context, since Hegel is often debating opponents who do not yet occupy the standpoint that thinking and being are one.

This chapter falls into four parts. In the first, I situate my account in relation to a debate in the recent literature between Jim Kreines and Robert Stern. In the second, I consider the categories of immediacy (Being) and the problem of passing into another. In the third, I consider the categories of mediation (Essence) and the problem of shining into another. In the fourth, I consider the Concept – the first category to unite immediacy and mediation – and show that it resolves the problems with the categories in the previous divisions, doing so through a process Hegel calls development.

6.1 Hegel and Conceptual Realism: Kreines and Stern[2]

Hegel defends an account of the nature of reality as "the Concept," and some recent authors equate that account of reality with a position in metaphysics they call "conceptual realism."[3] For these interpreters, Hegel is a conceptual realist because he is a realist rather than a nominalist about

---

[2] I here follow Knappik (2016), who also poses this question.
[3] Knappik (2016) even goes so far as to call this "the consensus view."

universals. He is a figure for whom universals are "in the world," rather than convenient heuristics or fictions. Moreover, Hegel is said to follow the Aristotelian tradition in viewing universals as immanent within the things that instantiate them. For this reason, he rejects a familiar Platonic conception of universals as transcending the things that instantiate them. Finally, Hegel is taken to view these immanent universals as prescribing to entities, especially teleologically organized entities such as artifacts and organisms, the kind to which they belong. As a result, these immanent universals have a crucial metaphysical role in constituting entities as the distinctive kinds of entities they are and making them behave in the characteristic ways that they do. However, they also play a crucial epistemological role in our attempts to explain these facets of such entities.

Though agreed that Hegel is a conceptual realist, these interpreters disagree about how he defends that view.[4] I will consider and reject the two main proposals from the recent literature, before turning to a third. In my view, Hegel's justification is furnished by his theory of the categories. That theory yields an argument that runs as follows: Conceiving of reality as the Concept solves the two broad types of problem afflicting any other conception of reality.

6.1.1   "Nothing but a Presupposed Fact of the Kantian Philosophy": Hegel and Kant's "Analytic/Regressive" Method

In recent work, Robert Stern (2009, 2016) has argued that Hegel defends his "conceptual realism" through a method of argument similar to the so-called "analytic/regressive" one from Kant's critical philosophy. In other words, Stern thinks Hegel defends his "conceptual realism" on the grounds that this metaphysical doctrine is uniquely well suited to explain the possibility of synthetic a priori knowledge, particularly in the natural-scientific domain.

As far as I know, however, there is only a single passage from the *Logic* in which Hegel explicitly discusses what Kant called the "the analytic/regressive" strategy of argument. Stern does not consider this passage, but I will argue that it raises both exegetical and philosophical problems for his interpretation (EL § 40 A). Kant's "analytic/regressive" strategy of argument presupposes that the natural sciences, at least, give us synthetic a priori knowledge. Yet Hegel denounces this presupposition as illegitimate: "nothing but a presupposed fact [of] the Kantian philosophy."

---

[4] See the exchange between Kreines (2016) and Stern (2016) in a recent issue of the *Hegel Bulletin*.

For Hegel, this presupposition is illegitimate because it begs the question against the Humean skeptic. The Humean skeptic can at least grant that we appear to have such knowledge: "[T]he fact that … universality and necessity [synthetic a priori knowledge – JM] are found in knowing is not disputed by Humean skepticism" (EL § 40 A). Unlike Kant, however, the Humean skeptic regards the appearance that we have such knowledge as misleading, a product of unreliable (or perhaps even error-prone) mechanisms in the human mind. For example, such a skeptic can agree that we *appear* to have knowledge of universal laws of nature. Yet she need not agree to the further claim that we actually do have such knowledge. This appearance, she would say, is misleading, a product of the fallacious inference that what has held true in all observed instances must hold true in all possible instances.

For Hegel, only the claim that we appear to possess synthetic a priori knowledge furnishes a truly neutral starting point for the debate between Kant and Hume. Once reframed in this way, however, the debate cannot be adjudicated in Kant's favor. As an explanation of the fact that we do, in fact, possess synthetic a priori knowledge, Kant's explanation may be preferable. From a certain perspective, any explanation would be, since the Humean view, denying that there is any fact standing in need of explanation, gives none. As explanations of the fact that we merely appear to have such knowledge, though, the two are on all fours with one another. Hence Hegel's central criticism of Kant: Compared to the Humean skeptic, Kant has "merely put forward a different explanation of [the same] fact."

Interestingly, Hegel does not appear to take seriously the possibility of arguing from the premise that we have synthetic a priori knowledge in mathematics. Like the early analytic critics of Kant, Hegel rejects the claim that mathematical truths are synthetic at all, let alone synthetic a priori. He thinks they are analytic. Hegel's position is developed through a detailed and painstaking critique of Kant's own. In the first division of the *Logic*, Hegel expends considerable effort attempting to show that Kant's examples (for example 7+5=12) do not support his claim that such truths are synthetic (WdL 21: 198/SoL 172).

As I will interpret it, Hegel's presuppositionless approach to deriving the categories will not presuppose that we are in possession of synthetic a priori knowledge. In this regard, it will not beg the question against the Humean skeptic. However, even a presuppositionless investigation of the fundamental concepts Hegel calls categories presupposes something not all opponents would grant. It presupposes that these fundamental concepts are of philosophical interest. Hence, it could be rejected by a radical empiricist who attempts to reduce all of human thought to the one stem of our cognitive power Kant called sensibility and is doubtful that the other, understanding, has any significant role. Since the Humean skeptic is presumably one such radical empiricist, we appear to be back where we started. This alternative starting point may still beg the question against the Humean after all, even if not for exactly the same reason as before.

Fortunately, Hegel has a response to such an opponent. In the introductory materials to the *Science of Logic*, Hegel responds to a critic in a way that is relevant to the present dispute. Hegel chooses as his system's first principle the concept of being, but this critic rejects Hegel's decision to begin from a first principle that is conceptual rather than one that is nonconceptual, or purely sensible in character (WdL 21: 55/SoL 47). This critic can agree with part of Hegel's case for beginning in this way. He or she can concede that such a first principle is presupposed by all other candidate concepts: the concept of the "I" (Fichte), "substance" (Spinoza), "Indifference" (Schelling) and so on. Minimally, all are concepts of things that "are" and so presuppose some antecedent grasp of the concept of "being." Relative to these further concepts, then, the concept of being has priority. However, this critic points out that such a first principle, since it is a concept, will not necessarily be presupposed by a nonconceptual or sensible first principle: for example, the empiricist's impressions of which all ideas are mere copies. Relative to the concept of being, then, and, indeed, all others, the sensible takes precedence, at least on this empiricist view.

In response, Hegel concedes that the *Logic*, taken in isolation, begs the question against such a radical empiricist opponent but argues that it does not do so when it is understood to function in concert with the opening arguments of the *Phenomenology*, a work described here as an introduction to the philosophical system whose first part is set forth in the *Logic* (WdL 21: 55/SoL 47). In Hegel's view, the opening arguments of the *Phenomenology*, particularly the argument of "Sense-Certainty," refute this radical empiricist opponent by revealing his proposed first principle to be untenable. At least when he reprises this argument in the introduction to the lesser *Logic*, Hegel emphasizes one point in particular (EL § 20 A). As Hegel reminds us, the protagonist of sense-certainty, as soon as he is called upon to report what he knows in language, must employ demonstrative/indexical concepts such as "this," "here" and "now." Yet the inherent generality of these concepts betrays the protagonist's intention of referring to the particular-qua-particular that sense perception is supposed to yield. At least in this version of the argument, the outcome seems to be the following. If there is such a thing as the nonconceptual particular-qua-particular, then it is epistemically irrelevant, and the protagonist seems to be forced to acknowledge some role for the conceptual in reporting what he knows.

Less important than the complex details of this famous argument, and the many difficult issues it raises, is its bearing on our understanding of the larger strategy Hegel will adopt in responding to an empiricist critic. This is a strategy employed in defense of his system as a whole, rather than any particular part of it. This strategy is as follows. The explicitly conceptual starting point of the *Logic*, though not one initially shared by a radical empiricist who regards sense experience as wholly nonconceptual, may be one he can be compelled to take up by the prior argument of the *Phenomenology*, which reveals this conception of sense experience to be impoverished. We will return to the question of the nature of Hegel's strategy in responding to such a critic later.

6.1.2   Does the Logic Seek the Unconditioned? Hegel and the Argument from Kant's Standpoint of Reason

In a recent book, Jim Kreines (2015) argues that Hegel defends an account of reality as "the Concept" by adapting an argument from Kant's Transcendental Dialectic. Hegel agrees with Kant that human reason seeks the unconditioned. He also agrees that the way in which rationalist metaphysics does so is unsuccessful since it gives rise to antinomies. Yet Hegel departs from Kant in proposing that knowledge of the unconditioned might also be achievable by a different (and more promising) metaphysical view: conceptual realism.

In my view, this argument is question-begging in a way Hegel would find objectionable. In Kreines' reconstruction of the argument, Hegel presupposes that reason seeks the unconditioned. However, we should recognize that a conception of ultimate reality as the unconditioned has (at least) two components:

1. a distinction (at least a notional one) between the unconditioned and something further, the conditioned; and
2. a relation between the two: Usually they are related as explicans and explanandum or else by means of some subspecies of this relation, for example cause and effect.

Accepting this two-component definition is to accept a conception of ultimate reality as "mediated." A category pair such as unconditioned–conditioned is found in any such conception. So too is a relation between the categories in the pair, such as the explicans–explicandum relation. Unsurprisingly, then, virtually all of the types of unconditioned that Kant recognizes in the antinomies *also* appear among the "mediated" definitions of the Absolute, given in the Doctrine of Essence: cause–effect, part–whole, ground–grounded, substance–accident and so on – indeed, even the conditioning–conditioned relation itself.

Ultimately, the presupposition that ultimate reality is the unconditioned, implying the presupposition that it is mediated, begs the question against an opponent who conceives of ultimate reality as immediate. On this alternative conception, it is not that there is something (even notionally) distinct from ultimate reality that it explains. Rather, in the most basic case, it earns its status, as it were, by default – because it is all that there is. In other cases, it does so because, though it is not all that there is, it can be what it is independent of its relations to anything else, explanatory or otherwise. By endorsing a conception of the Absolute as the unconditioned, Hegel would beg the question against numerous figures from the history, especially the early history, of philosophy. The main such figure that Hegel identifies is Parmenides, but there are others. Hegel's category-theoretic argument for conceptual realism will avoid begging the question in this way. It will begin by positing for analysis a more basic conception of reality as "immediate." Only once this conception has been refuted will it turn to an alternative conception of reality as "mediated."

A second reason for doubting that Hegel's argument in the *Logic* presupposes the standpoint of reason is that this standpoint may be a result of the argument rather than a presupposition of it. Instead of beginning with the standpoint of reason, the *Logic* may well begin with a version of the standpoint of sense experience considered in its first division, the Doctrine of Being. Interpreted in this way, the *Logic* would then proceed to the standpoint of understanding, considered in the second division, the Doctrine of Essence. Hegel gives this description of the overarching structure of the *Logic* in the following description of the transition from the first division (Being) to the second (Essence):

> Sensoriness's thoughtlessness, i.e. of taking everything limited and finite to be a being, passes over into the understanding's stubbornness, i.e. of grasping it as something identical with itself, something not contradicting itself in itself. (EL § 113 A)

Here, Hegel describes the categories from the Doctrine of Being as characteristic of the standpoint of sense experience and also as afflicted by its main limitation: "thoughtlessness." He then describes the categories from the Doctrine of Essence as characteristic of the standpoint of understanding and as afflicted by its main limitation: "stubbornness." Presumably, the categories considered in the Doctrine of the Concept, the standpoint of reason, will surmount these limitations.

At first, it may seem utterly impossible that the Doctrine of Being could be the standpoint of sense experience, and for a simple reason. It treats categories or concepts rather than the nonconceptual representations that might be thought to figure in sense experience. However, Hegel seems to maintain that the Doctrine of Being embodies not just any version of the standpoint of sense experience but *a conceptually articulate version of it*. For Hegel, this is possible because the categories considered in this division, particularly the categories of quantity and quality, serve to constitute the image of the world sense experience presents. As Hegel explains:

> The immediate sensory consciousness, insofar as its behavior involves thinking, is chiefly limited to the abstract determinations of quality and quantity. This sensory consciousness is usually regarded as the most concrete and thus also the richest. It is so, however, only in terms of its material, whereas it is in fact the poorest and most abstract consciousness with respect to the content of its thoughts. (EL § 85 Z)

The categories considered in this division are particularly well suited to inform sense experience's image of the world because they are categories of the immediate. Sense experience is immediate, though not necessarily for a more familiar reason given by Kant in the first critique and occasionally reprised by Hegel himself. On this first conception, sense experience is immediate because it puts us in touch with the object in a relatively direct or unmediated way. It does not place a further layer of mental representations, concepts, between us and the object. In the present context, however, Hegel is claiming that sense experience is immediate for a less familiar reason. For Hegel, it is characteristic of sense experience to present us with a world of objects that are immediate in the sense that they are independent of their relations to anything else distinct from themselves: "side-by-side ... connected only by the bare also" (EL § 20 A). Hegel argues for this claim indirectly by observing that sense experience cannot present anything richer in structure than this "side-by-side" unless it enlists the aid of another faculty: understanding. Only through the work of the understanding, and, in particular, a form of intellectual reflection subsequent to sense experience, do we encounter mediation in the form of relationships between objects, for example causal relationships.

> Representation here meets with the *understanding* which differs from the former only in that it posits relationships of the universal and the particular or of cause and effect, etc. It thus establishes relations of necessity among the isolated determinations of representation, while representation leaves them standing *side-by-side* in its indeterminate space, connected only by the bare *also*. (EL § 20 A)

With this background in place, it becomes easier to see how the categories we have considered, categories of the immediate, serve to articulate sense experience's image of the world as immediate, the category of the finite will describe such objects as having definite limits that set it apart from others. The categories of quality will describe objects as having features they can have independently of their relations to anything distinct from themselves. The category of quantity will describe (groups of) objects as having such features.

Significantly, Hegel does not so far as I know draw this association anywhere outside of the *Encyclopedia*. I mean the association between Being, Essence and Concept, on the one hand, and sensibility, understanding and reason, on the other. This suggests that the latter is dispensable from the perspective of the *Logic*'s argument.

Yet in all cases, these categories will fail to fulfill their appointed aim of describing the object as immediate, meaning sense experience's image of the world as immediate will be fatally undermined. If the categories presented in the Doctrine of Being express (a conceptually articulate version of) the standpoint of sense experience, then Hegel's critique of these categories will be a critique of this standpoint. Yet understanding the critique of the standpoint of sense experience Hegel advances will require us to take account of an important historical source of inspiration for it: ancient skepticism. Chiefly relevant to Hegel's critique of sense experience is the ancient skeptic's opposition to a dogma of modern, Humean skepticism: the conviction that sense experience alone is the "true."

> Humean skepticism ... must be clearly distinguished from Greek scepticism. Humean scepticism makes the truth of the empirical, of feeling and intuition its foundation, and from there contests the universal determinations and laws on the grounds that they lack justification through sensory perception. Ancient scepticism was so far removed from making feeling or intuition the principle of truth that to the contrary it turned first and foremost against the sensory. (EL § 39 A)

By claiming that the Humean skeptic regards sense experience as alone the "true," Hegel means to refer to the Humean's claim that we are only justified in assenting to the contingent truths sense experience yields:

for example, truths concerning constant conjunction. According to this Humean, we have no rational justification for assenting to the allegedly universal and necessary valid truths that go beyond what is given to us in sense experience: for example, truths concerning necessary connection. In essence, then, the Humean's skepticism is skepticism about the possibility of synthetic a priori knowledge.

For Hegel, this Humean insistence that sense experience is alone the "true" leaves open the possibility that sense experience may fail to be "true" in another sense emphasized by the ancient skeptics. Insofar as he wants to articulate his position, the modern Humean skeptic must offer some account of the content of sense experience. Admittedly, this account may have been successfully purged of more controversial categories: for instance, causality. Yet this leaves open the possibility that such an account nevertheless draws on another more basic set of categories: quantity, quality and the finite. As we have just seen, Hegel maintains that the standpoint of sense experience is pervaded by such categories. Indeed, he proposes to treat this standpoint through a critique of the categories constituting it. From Hegel's perspective, there is an opening for a critique of modern Humean skepticism inspired by ancient skeptical strategies of argument. As Hegel will show, even the more basic categories informing sense experience, as the modern skeptic conceives of it, nevertheless give rise to contradictions. Hegel does not mean that such a skeptic will necessarily regard the senses as providing veridical representations of the so-called "external world." Clearly, Humean skepticism is not incompatible with some version or other of "external world skepticism" (in fact, they are often thought of as closely associated). Sense experience, though "true" in Hume's sense, will be "untrue" in a sense emphasized by the ancient skeptical tradition as Hegel interprets its legacy.

In mounting this critique of (a conceptually articulate version of) the standpoint of sense experience, however, Hegel departs from the ancient skeptics in one crucial but decisive respect. For Hegel, contradictions in the categories, once identified, need not simply issue in a rejection of the categories in question. Any such outcome would only result in aporia, leaving us unsure how to proceed. Fortunately, Hegel maintains that these contradictions can be resolved, yielding a new set of categories that are not afflicted by (the same) contradiction. Hence, the critique issues not in aporia but, rather, in the forward progress of the dialectic. At that point, the process begins again. As we have seen, however, a critique of a certain set of categories is a critique of the standpoint they serve to express. Hence, Hegel's departure from the ancient skeptical approach to criticizing the categories also implies a different approach to the critique of these standpoints. In particular, the standpoint of sense experience will not simply be renounced. It will be renounced in favor of other successor standpoints that are more advanced: the standpoints of understanding and reason.

As before, the *Logic*'s critique of modern Humean skepticism, inspired by ancient skepticism, presupposes that sense experience tacitly draws upon the fundamental concepts Hegel calls categories. Once more, then, this presupposition might seem to beg the question against an especially radical empiricist who rejects any role for the conceptual in sense experience. As we have seen, Hegel responds to radical empiricist critics of the *Logic* project by arguing that the *Logic* is meant to function in concert with the *Phenomenology*. Fortunately, the more detailed account we have given of the *Logic*'s critique of Humean skepticism has the potential to enrich our understanding of how the two works function in concert. Putting the present account together with the previous one, we arrive at the following account of the division of labor between the two works. The *Logic* will critique the specific set of categories, or concepts, informing sense experience (quality, quantity, the finite), eliciting from the moderate empiricist a recognition that a richer set of categories are required (causality, substance and so on). Yet it can only do so once the opening arguments of the *Phenomenology* have elicited from such an opponent the admission from a more radical empiricist that sense experience is informed by some categories.

* * *

As I will reconstruct the argument for defining the Absolute as the Concept, it presupposes neither that we are in possession of synthetic a priori knowledge nor that reason necessarily seeks the unconditioned. As we have seen, neither starting point is in keeping with Hegel's ideal of a presuppositionless method of argument. Both beg the question against opponents Hegel wishes to convince (the Humean radical empiricist as well as the Parmenidean metaphysician who defines the Absolute as immediate).

Instead, the strategy of argument Hegel employs presupposes a different aspect of Kant's critical project, his interest in deriving the fundamental concepts Hegel calls categories. The strategy I reconstruct allows Hegel to avoid begging the question against these opponents and enable him to respond to them convincingly.

A consistently presuppositionless approach requires that we begin with categories of the immediate, rather than those of mediation. This is because the appointed task of the former set of categories is a prerequisite to the task their successors will perform. These categories of the immediate simply describe a "first." Their successors, the categories of mediation, will need to do this and something additional. They will need to both describe a "first" and then relate it to a "second."

6.2   Being: Immediacy

My aim in this section is to reconstruct Hegel's critique of the categories of immediacy, categories such as quality and quantity. These categories describe things as immediate or unmediated: capable of being what they are independent of their relation to anything else that is distinct from them. Hegel will seek to show that these categories are self-undermining. They turn out to entail that the things in question are mediated instead, a problem Hegel calls "passing into another" (EL § 84).

Before proceeding, I distinguish between two broad ways in which a category could describe things as immediate. On the first, which I call "exclusivity," the thing in question is immediate because it is the only thing that there is. This is true of Being and Nothing. As indeterminate, neither has a specific feature or property that could be used to distinguish it from anything else. Hence, each is (or is meant to be) the only thing. It is for this reason that their indistinguishability is such a problem. It may be that something similar is meant to be true of Becoming as well. Obviously this form of immediacy is central to monism and to the anti-Hegelian thinkers mentioned at the beginning of the logic: Parmenides and Spinoza.

We have already discussed this opening argument, so I will focus instead on a second form of immediacy. On this second, which I call "preeminence," the thing in question is immediate *not* because it is the only thing but rather because it is, as it were, of the first rank among all of the things. In particular, it alone possesses its determination, the specific feature or property that makes it the thing that it is independent of its relations to any other things. This is the form of immediacy Hegel evaluates in his treatment of the categories of quality and those of quantity. Each of these treatments follows a similar course. The initial appearance of immediacy gives way to mediation, not only by another but by an infinite series of others. There are "bad infinites" in both the qualitative and quantitative domains.

Though I will not dwell on the point, these developments suggest a connection between the two forms of immediacy. Infinite regresses are the form the aspiration to "exclusivity" takes within the domain of "preeminence." Infinity, as a sum whose parts are prior to the whole, stands in for the infinite, as a totality or whole prior to its parts (if it has any). Ultimately, neither succeeds.

Because both critiques follow a similar trajectory, I will simply focus on quality. Hegel defines a quality as a "determination [a specific feature or property – JM] that is identical with a thing's being" (EL § 61). A quality is identical with a thing's being in the sense that the thing would cease to be the particular thing that it is if it lost that quality. If the color red is defined by a certain qualitative characteristic, then the loss of that characteristic could lead it to cease being that color. Of course, there are cases in which a thing can remain the thing it is even when it loses a certain feature, but then this feature will not be a quality in Hegel's sense of the term. Hegel calls such features properties, rather than qualities, and deems them irrelevant at this early stage in the *Logic*. They become relevant when we turn to relational categories. Here, however, we are concerned with what he thinks of as a more basic phenomenon.

Prima facie, the category of quality characterizes things as immediate. A thing is what it is in virtue of its own quality. Therefore, a thing characterized in terms of its quality should be capable of being what it is independent of its relations to anything distinct from it. However, matters are more complex. Hegel argues that this characterization of things as immediate turns out to inevitably entail characterizing them as mediated. Hegel's explanation of why this contradiction arises invokes the famed Spinozist dictum so important to all of the German Idealists: "omnis determinatio est negatio" (WdL 21: 1010/SoL 87; EL § 91 + Z). As a "determination," a quality is necessarily some specific feature of a thing, one among (actual or possible) others. If that is so, then, it seems, a quality can be the specific feature that it is only insofar as it is not another. In terms of the Spinozist dictum, a quality can be the "determination" that it is only if it is not some other quality, defined as its "negation." Yet if this is so, then an important implication follows for the thing that bears this quality, that is, the thing that can be the distinctive thing it is only by virtue of bearing this quality. It follows that this qualified thing can be the determinate thing that it is only insofar it is not another thing, one defined as the negation of the first because it does not bear the original quality. If that is so, then a thing, defined in terms of quality, fails to be immediate. It is mediated, because it can be what it is only by virtue of standing in a certain relation to something distinct from it.

Occasionally, Hegel also describes this problem as one of indeterminacy. Defined as something (=a thing with a quality), a thing is the determinate thing it is by virtue of not being an other, something else defined as its negation (=a thing lacking the original quality). However, there is an equally valid argument for the reverse attribution. Relative to this other, it is the first thing that is the negation and the other that is the original something. But if so, then it seems the original something has ceded its status to the other. Once we recognize that the statuses of something and other are relative, Hegel argues, it becomes hard to say which is which: "Both are determined as something as well as other: thus they are the same and there is as yet no distinction present in them" (WdL 21: 106/SoL 91). Hence, the categories of something and other have failed to allow us to fix the status of one item as the determinate something that it is and that of the other item as its negation.

Determinacy must be introduced somehow, and Hegel maintains that the only way this can occur is for it to be introduced by an external observer. The result is that determinacy becomes observer-relative in a sense that is objectionable. For Hegel, rendering determinacy observer-relative is a nonsolution, since it only pushes the problem of indeterminacy back a level. As Hegel explains, the observer may attempt to fix the identities of the original something and its other as the determinate entities they are through ostensive definition, deeming one "this," or "A," and the other "that," or "B" (WdL 21: 105/SoL 91). If the items are ostensively defined, as "this" and "that" or "A" and "B" then the determination of which is which reflects nothing more than the observer's choice of a starting point, a choice that is completely arbitrary. In other words, the opposite choice could always be made, either by this particular observer or some other. Hence, indeterminacy remains.

We now turn to the final instance of the problem: an infinite regress. Hegel has two explanations for why this problem arises, one less complex and the other more so (EL § 95; WdL 21: 130–131/SoL 114). The less complex explanation is simply that each determinate thing will have to have its determinacy fixed by another. That other, in turn, must have its determinacy fixed by a third other, and so on, ad infinitum. Why can two not fix one another's determinacy, forming a closed system? Because that is what the dialectic of something and other showed was impossible. The result in that case is indeterminacy.

6.3 Essence: Mediation

Let us now attempt to understand how the categories of mediation will remedy the defect in categories of immediacy. As we have seen, Hegel maintains that the nonrelational categories turn out to be relational after all. They seem to define the thing in question as capable of being what it is, independent of its relation to anything else. Yet it then turns out that these things, so defined, can be what they were only because of their relations to others. Hence, we must make a virtue of a necessity. Hegel proposes that we introduce a relational set of categories, ones that characterize the thing as capable of being what it is in relation to something else. Such categories will describe a thing as dependent on something else that is independent of it.

Hegel uses a metaphor to describe these categories: "shining into another" (EL § 161). In this metaphor, a light source shines and the light it emits is the other into which it shines. The two are related as source and product. Hence, the categories from the Doctrine of Essence exhibit "shining into another." They do so by defining a thing in such a way that it is mediated and can only be what it is by virtue of its relation to another. An effect is an effect because of its cause, something grounded because of its ground, a manifestation because of the force its manifests, a whole because of the parts making it up and so on. Hegel is especially clear on this point in the lectures. As he argues, the categories of Essence are relational:

> Thought determinations in the logic of the essence are purely relative. Ground has meaning only by reference to existence, cause only by reference to effect, and so on. No such category is any longer purely independent of the other, but each is marked by its reflection within the other, by its reference to the other. (LL 129/)

Michael Wolff captures the point well, when he says of the Doctrine of Essence: "[I]t deals only with correlative determinations that, like appearance and essence, occur in pairs and relate to one another in what Hegel calls a relation of 'reflection'" (2012: 91).

What, then, is the problem afflicting these characterizations of things as mediated?[5] For Hegel, the problem concerns the form of argument used to justify conceiving of things in relational terms. More specifically, the problem afflicts this particular conception of what conceiving of things in relational terms entails. Suppose we argue that one thing is what it is because of its dependence on another that does not depend on it. For Hegel, this form of argument self-undermines, since it turns out to entail dependence in the other direction. Recall that, in Hegel's analogy, the light depends on the light source, rather than the reverse. This form of argument seems capable of being put to an alternative and equally legitimate use, for the

---

[5] Knappik (2016) discusses related problems from the Doctrine of Essence.

second is no less dependent on the first, though perhaps not for exactly the same reason. Light requires a light source, but it is no less true that something cannot be a light source without ever emitting light. This dependence is not attributable to any mysterious backward causal relation between the light emitted and the light source. Rather, the dependence is conceptual, since it is only relative to the light (actually or possibly) emitted that the light source can legitimately be defined as a light source at all. Similarly, it is only relative to some (actual or possible) effect that a cause can be a cause, only relative to something (actually or possibly) grounded that a ground can be a ground, only relative to an (actual or possible) manifestation that a force is a force and so on. If formerly it seemed that the light depended on the light source, now it seems that the reverse is the case. We seem to be at an impasse. One and the same general form of argument can be used to justify the attribution and the reverse attribution.

A caveat. Occasionally, the new use found for an original form of argument is not to effect a *full* reversal of the original attribution but simply a *partial* one. For instance, the objector who maintains that a light source is defined relative to emitted light could concede that emitted light is defined relative to a light source as well, since anything emitted must be emitted from something.

Hitherto, shining into another has seemed to be Hegel's name for a solution to the earlier problem of passing into another. Yet for complex reasons I will simply gloss over here, it is also thought by Hegel to be an appropriate name for a new problem this proposed solution creates.

In the next section, I will briefly consider an example of the problem Hegel identifies with definitions of the Absolute as mediated, shining into another.

Let us now turn to a straightforward example of the problem afflicting categories from the Doctrine of Essence, categories that characterize things in relational terms (as mediated). A clear example of this problem is found in Hegel's discussion of the category pair "whole and parts." As Hegel writes, we seem to oscillate between considering the whole to have priority over the parts and the parts to have priority over the whole.

> There is a passage from the whole to the parts and from the parts to the whole, and in the one [the whole or the part] the opposition to the other is forgotten since each is taken as a self-standing concrete existence, the one time the whole, the other time the parts. Or since the parts are supposed to subsist in … the whole and the whole to consist of [*bestehen aus*] the one time the one, the other time the other is the subsisting [*Bestehende*] and the other is each time the unessential. (EL § 136 A)

Here, Hegel offers a complementary description of the problem he calls shining into another. Any argument we give for the priority of the whole over the parts will succeed only on one condition. It will succeed only on the condition that we suppress (or "forget") some additional facet of its relationship to the parts ("opposition to the other"), a facet that is difficult to reconcile with its alleged priority over them. The same is true for arguments for the priority of the parts over the whole.

Importantly, Hegel denies that the relational categories of part and whole from the second division (essence) apply to organisms. Only with a richer set of categories that become available in the third division (the concept) will we be capable of grasping the distinctive relation between part and whole characteristics of living beings. At this stage, there can only be asymmetrical dependence relations between the parts and the whole. At most, then, there can be a mechanical relationship between the two. In an organism, however, there is *mutual* dependence between the parts and the whole. We will revisit this point later.

Let us attempt to see how this dynamic might arise by examining an argument for the priority of the whole over the parts. At first, the whole seems prior, since it is independent of the parts. The whole can certainly survive the loss of any particular part. It can even survive the loss of any subset of its parts, or the set of all its parts, provided the subset or whole set is eventually replaced. The whole endures, even as the parts do not.

Yet this very argument, when pressed further, turns out to reveal an important respect in which it is the parts and not the whole that are prior. By uncovering the true extent of the whole's independence of the parts, the argument has revealed the limits of this independence. True, a whole may be independent of any particular part or set of parts (complete or incomplete). Still, it cannot survive the loss of any and all parts whatsoever. Without any parts at all, it would not be. Hence, the whole may be independent of any particular part or (sub)set of parts. However, it is not independent of parts as such.

If that is so, then it may seem that the parts are independent of the whole and can subsist outside of it. Hegel confronts this claim with a dilemma. If we claim the parts can subsist outside the whole, then, it seems, we will have thereby ceased to conceive of these parts as parts at all. After all, the concept of the parts is an inherently relational concept. Parts are always parts of some (actual or possible) whole. This is not to say that we are not permitted to conceive of the parts in some other (nonrelational) way and then assert their independence of the whole – their independent status in relation to it. Rather than conceive of them as parts, we might conceive of these items as having some other defining (nonrelational) properties. These independently subsisting items might be conceived of as atoms, for example. However, once we conceive of them in this way, we are effectively conceding that it is not as parts at all that they earn their title to be considered independent. It is as bearers of some other (nonrelational) property that they do so.

Hence, we seem destined to revert to the first position. Once we concede that parts imply a (real or possible) whole of which they are constituent parts, then it would seem that the parts cannot subsist independent of the whole. It is relative to the concept of a (real or possible) whole that some set of things gain their entitlement to be considered parts. At this point, we seem driven back to arguing for a conception of the whole as that on which the parts depend, at which point the process of oscillation begins again.

It would be interesting to ask if there is something inherent in the nature of relations (metaphysical, logical, social or otherwise) that makes such processes of inversion likely. Not every relation is symmetrical. If I am your parent, this does not entail that you are mine. However, every relation between one term and a second can always be viewed from the reverse direction, namely, as a relation between the second term and the first. The road from Athens to Thebes is also the road from Thebes to Athens; relationality is a two-way street.[6] In terms of our present example, if I am a parent of yours, then you are necessarily a child of mine, because that is just the same relation viewed from the reverse direction. Like all relations, then, the dependence relation, though not necessarily symmetrical in any simple sense, will be two-sided. And, Hegel argues, this renders it vulnerable to a distinctive kind of reversal or inversion.

6.4 Concept: Mediated Immediacy

In the Doctrine of the Concept, we turn to a set of categories that characterize the thing as both immediate and mediated at once. As in the Doctrine of Essence, the thing is mediated, since it is what it is by virtue of its relationship to something else that is distinct from it. At this stage, however, the form of mediation in question is compatible with immediacy for the following reason. In a sense, this further thing by which the thing is mediated is nothing distinct from itself at all. Rather, it is simply the thing itself, albeit in a different form. If this is so, then it follows that the

---

[6] I here follow Descombes (2014), who makes this feature of relations a theme.

thing's mediation by another is, at the same time, mediation by itself. It is therefore immediate, independent of anything distinct from itself.

Described at this level of generality, Hegel's idea of something both mediated and immediate may seem to be a contradiction in terms. We must consider this new definition in greater detail if we are to dispel the impression that it is simply incoherent.

In the Doctrine of Essence, things were mediated, whereas in the Doctrine of the Concept things are both mediated and immediate at once. In order to clarify the difference between these two forms of mediation, Hegel introduces yet another metaphor. He distinguishes between the shining into another, found in the Doctrine of Essence, and a different process he calls "development," found in the Doctrine of the Concept.

> The way the concept proceeds is no longer passing over or shining in an other. It is instead development since what are differentiated are at the same time immediately posited as identical with one another and with the whole, each being the determinacy that it is as a free being ... of the whole concept. (EL § 161)
>
> Passing over into an other is the dialectical process in the sphere of being and the process of shining in an other within the sphere of essence. The movement of the concept is, by contrast, the development, by means of which that alone is posited that is already on hand in itself. (EL § 161 Z)

We will now proceed to examine the two forms of mediation in greater detail by comparing shining into another and development.

Chiefly important in this passage is Hegel's claim that the form of mediation called shining into another involves a fairly stark distinction between a thing and the other to which it relates. Returning to Hegel's metaphor, there is a clear distinction between the light source and the light. In this way, the possibility of deeming one and not the other independent is (allegedly) preserved. It is the light source that is independent rather than the light.

By contrast, the form of mediation Hegel calls development involves a less stark distinction between the thing in question and the other to which it relates. In order to illustrate why this is so, Hegel asks us to consider a paradigmatic case of development: the processes of growth and maturation that occur in the realm of organic life (EL § 161 Z). As before, there is mediation. Like the light and the light source, the plant can be understood only in relation to the seed. Yet the form of mediation differs for the following reason: While the light is distinct from the light source, the plant is just the seed at a later stage of its development. For Hegel, the two are identical, because the plant has a single nature or essence, one that is manifested at all phases in the process of its development, though perhaps most fully realized at the end (EL § 161 + Z). The term *Entwicklung* has a connotation Hegel may be drawing on in this passage: It connotes the uncoiling or unfolding of something. Hence, there is also immediacy. The plant's dependence on the seed is self-dependence. In that sense, it is independent of anything alien.

Having concluded his discussion of an illustration from the sphere of organic life, Hegel concludes that the form of mediation found in the realm of development is a form of immediacy as well. Since both are the same thing, this type of mediation is just the thing's mediation with itself. Hence, this type of mediation is immediacy, because the relation that the thing stands in to another is really just a relation it stands in to itself. Of course, this immediacy differs from an earlier, simpler form in that it is compatible with a degree of differentiation between the Absolute and its other. In the Doctrine of Being, by contrast, immediacy often took a different form: It existed without differentiation, since the thing (typically) had no other at all.

By describing such a complex structure in detail, Hegel seems to have succeeded in showing that a definition of the Absolute in terms of the Concept would not be incoherent, at least. However, he must now actually argue for such a definition. Since defining the Absolute in this way means defining it as undergoing development, in Hegel's sense, arguing for this definition can only mean explaining why development solves the problems to which shining into another and passing into another gave rise. We can briefly anticipate how it will do so by reflecting further on this metaphor, though more is required to argue for the claim.

Development will need to solve the main problem with shining into another. This problem, recall, arose in the following way. Initially, relations are conceived in such a way that one term is dependent upon the other, rather than the reverse. Yet it then seemed that there was dependence in the reverse direction as well. Development remedies this problem through a new conception of relations that does justice to their "two-sided" character. In these relations, the dependency of one on the other is acknowledged to coexist with – even to imply or entail – dependence of the other on the one, though the dependencies need not be of the same kind. The plant depends upon the seed in one sense. The plant was produced by it. Yet the seed depends on the plant in another. The plant is its telos.

Development also remedies the problem of passing into another. That problem, recall, arose when characterizing things in nonrelational terms turned out to entail doing so in relational ones. Yet development reveals these to be capable of coherently coexisting. The seed can be understood only in relation to something (notionally) distinct, the plant. Yet in another sense it is unrelated to anything distinct from itself, since that to which it relates is just itself in a different guise.

Crucially, the most extreme version of this problem also does not arise: the infinite regress. We can anticipate the form Hegel's solution will take by recalling that seed and plant are repeating phases in a life-cycle: seeds grow into plants, plants produce seeds, and the cycle begins again. In this way, Hegel is able to halt any regress that might arise by showing that the terms in a structure that exhibits "development" form a closed system: Each refers to the next until the first is reached once more and the circle is complete.

Yet the metaphor also reveals the limitations of Hegel's solution to the problem posed by passing into another. Clearly, there is a perspective we can take on seed and plant that will reveal something resembling an infinite regress. After all, we can ask where the seed came from, and then ask of that seed where it came from, and so on and so forth. There are organicist versions of the cosmological argument. Hence, Hegel's solution cannot be to deny that there is a perspective on reality that will reveal the regress to be present. It must instead be to deny that this perspective exhausts the nature of reality and, moreover, to offer an alternative that reveals a region of reality in which the regress is halted.

Especially as we prepare to consider specific examples of the definitions of the Absolute from this division, it is crucial to stress that development is only a metaphor. It is not literally true of every category or definition of the Absolute in the Doctrine of the Concept that it characterizes things as undergoing the form of development characteristic of living organisms. It is clearly true of one such definition that appears as the *Logic* draws to a close ("Life," the first form of the Idea). In other cases, it is less clear.

The first definition of the Absolute as both immediate and mediated is the Concept. In defending his definition of the Absolute as the Concept, Hegel contests a common-sense understanding of concepts as self-standing individuals, each of which is capable of being understood on its own, apart from its relations to other concepts. Actually, Hegel argues, every small-c concept, in that ordinary sense, belongs to a tripartite holistic structure he calls the Concept, a structure in which no one element type can be understood apart from the other two. This structure comprises three basic types of element: universal, particular and individual. We will consider the definitions of these element types in greater detail presently. For now, however, Hegel's examples of universal, particular and individual are helpful to consult: the concept of an animal (a "genus"), the concept of a horse (a "species") and, finally, this particular horse (the "individual"). "The horse is first an animal. and that is its universality. It then has its determinateness, which is its particularity – the species horse. Its particularity steps forth as the species of the genus. But third it is *this* horse, the singular subject" (LL 180).

Even if the Concept must contain each type of element, it does not follow that it need contain any specific number of each type of element. It might well contain any number of elements of the different types. In the case of one element type (individual), it might well contain zero tokens of that type. Not all universal or particular concepts need have individual instances. Every ghost may be a spirit, but there may be no such beings. Yet, as I argue, the element-type individual remains an irreducible component of the Concepts for the following reason. Every universal or particular concept must be *capable* of having individual instances.

Concerning the Concept, Hegel will make an argument we will spend the remainder of the chapter reconstructing. For Hegel, the structure of the Concept is holistic: None of these types of element can be understood apart from its (actual or possible) association with elements of the other two types (step 1). Moreover, Hegel draws from this the rather striking conclusion that each element type is identical with the other two (step 2). But then, Hegel argues, each element, owing to its identity with the other two, must also be identical with the whole, understood as the full triad (conclusion).

As we will see, this three-step argument is crucial to Hegel's overarching aims in the *Logic*, as they have been described here. It will be used to show that in the Doctrine of the Concept there is "development," rather than the "passing into another" that occurred in the Doctrine of Being or the "shining into another" in the Doctrine of Essence. In this way, Hegel can claim to have shown that a category type characterizing things as both immediate and mediated, rather than as either alone, succeeds where the other two types failed.

Begin with Step 1 of Hegel's argument: the claim that each element type must be understood in relation to the other two.

In order to construct an argument for this claim, we can begin by attempting to define each element type in isolation. We will then seek to show that these definitions always tacitly make reference to the other two element types. Defined accurately, each element type necessarily stands in some (actual or possible) relation to the other two.

It is relatively easy to understand why the element types universal and particular cannot be understood in isolation. Suppose we ask what makes a specific universal concept, such as the concept of an animal, the concept that it is. We might plausibly answer that it is a certain (characteristically broad) scope of application that this concept has. This definition of a concept might seem to stand on its own, but it does not. After all, the specific scope of application of this concept must (at least partly) be defined in terms of the less general (particular) concepts subordinated to the more general one and coordinated with one another. For surely the scope of the more general concept, animal, is such that it includes the less general concepts it subordinates to itself – concepts such as horse, mammal and so on. They, at least, fall within its scope, whatever else does. We will soon have more to say about what else does.

Similarly, these less general (particular) concepts can be understood only when they are related to the more general (universal) concepts to which they are subordinate. Once more, suppose we ask what makes a particular concept, such as horse, the concept that it is. Once more, we answer that is a certain scope of application, a certain characteristically restricted scope of application. Here, too, it might seem that this definition is free-standing, but by now we know better than to assume this is so. Whatever else defines it, the scope of this concept is itself partially defined by the broader scope of the more general concept to which it is subordinate. Whatever else it includes, the scope of the concept mammal must admit of being characterized a restricted range of the scope of the concept animal. We could also say that the scope of a less general concept that is *subordinate* to a more general one is defined relative to the other less general concepts with which this less general one is *coordinate*. Hence, the scope of the concept mammal would leave off where the scope of the concept bird begins, and so on and so forth. Once we ask how many further such less general concepts there must be, a role for the more general concept emerges. For the more general concept delimits the class of further less general concepts coordinated with any given one. Hence, defining one less general concept in relation to those with which it is coordinated amounts to defining it in terms of the more general one after all. This proposal too amounts to interdefining particular and universal. Of course, this is not to rule out that its scope must also admit of being defined in an alternative way, as we will soon see.

Universal concepts and particular concepts must be understood in relation to one another, since the scope characteristic of each can be understood only in relation to the scope characteristic of the other. Yet the inability of universal and particular to stand on their own becomes clear as soon as we ask about the nature of this scope itself, the scope in terms of which both are (inter)defined. Ultimately, there can be no scope without at least one (actual or possible) thing that would be included in it: an individual. Hence, Hegel insists that alongside universal and particular concepts, there must be individuals.

Of course, Hegel should not be understood to be claiming that every concept, in fact, has individual instances, such that those which fail to do so, for example concepts of fictional entities, are not concepts. Rather, Hegel is claiming that a concept, to be a concept, must be capable of having instances. The question of whether a given concept has instances may not always receive an affirmative answer. However, the question is always apt.

The element types universal and particular require the element type individual. Why, though, does the element type individual require those of universal and particular? Here, Hegel's answer relies on the Spinozist dictum he has used throughout the *Logic*: "*omnis determinatio est negatio.*" The concept of the individual can only be the determinate concept that it is in relation to other concepts that it is not, namely, its negations. At this point, however, we appear to have two distinct choices of which concepts to select as the negations. Hegel is intent on opting for one rather than the other.

On the one hand, we can define the concept of an individual as the determinate concept that it is by relating it to a second concept, the concept of another individual that the first is not. "This" over "here" can be defined in opposition to "that" over "there." This definition of the concept of an individual would require no recourse to the second and third concepts of a universal and a particular.

As Hegel makes clear, however, this route should not be taken: "[T]hey are … not singulars that just exist next to each other" (WdL 12: 52/SoL 549). For Hegel, this is essentially a new version of the same unpromising route that was already tried in the Doctrine of Being: "[A] plurality of this kind belongs to being." Hence, conceiving of individuality in this way results in "passing into another," a dynamic in which the concept of the particular can no longer serve as a definition of the Absolute. We can easily imagine Hegel giving the same arguments he did earlier. As before, there is a problem of indeterminacy: relative to "that," the first "this" is "that," and so the two seem to have exchanged their roles.

The alternative Hegel favors is to define the concept of an individual as the determinate concept that it is by relating it to the further concept of a universal that this individual instantiates. Or, rather, to two further such concepts, since Hegel believes there are always at least two: the one more general, the other less so. Henceforth, the concept of the individual is interdefined with these two further concepts, the concept of the universal and the concept of the particular. It is the instantiating and they are the initiated. It is "this horse" (animal) and they are "horse" and "animal." As Hegel also says, this view is accommodated well by the traditional idea that the individual is the subject in which the universal and particular inhere. In defining the individual, we are referred beyond it to the particular and the universal.

This comes at a cost, however. It entails that the concept of an individual cannot truly function on its own without the concepts of universal and particular. On this view, one never simply deploys the single concept "this" but, rather, always tacitly employs the triad "this horse" ("animal").

Unfortunately, Hegel does not elaborate on this part of his argument. It would be interesting to consider whether this claim wins support from the argument of "Sense-Certainty" in the *Phenomenology* though Hegel does not do so here. Briefly summarized, that argument showed that the use of demonstrative/indexical concepts in isolation results in indeterminate reference. Across different uses or even in one and the same use, terms such as "this" can refer to virtually anything. It would be interesting to ask how the use of these demonstrative/indexical concepts in conjunction with other more general ones might mitigate the problem of indeterminacy: "this" "horse" (animal) cannot refer to just anything, though some indeterminacy will still be present.

To sum up, each element of the Concept, each of the subconcepts that make up the Concept, must be understood in relation to the others. The individual is that which is subsumable under the universal and the particular. The particular is that capable of subsuming the individual and is subsumable under the general. The general is that capable of subsuming both.

Once we see that this is so, however, we are in a position to see that step 1 implies step 2 straightaway. If all element types must be understood in relation to one another, then all element types are identical with one another. To be sure, there is a sense in which they differ. We have the individual (subsumable by the universal and particular), the particular (capable of subsuming the individual and subsumable under the universal) and, finally, the universal (capable of subsuming both). Yet there is another in which they are identical, a sense revealed when we remove the parentheses. All are instances of the same tripartite structure examined from a different angle. In each case, we are simply alighting on a different one of the three elements, but the other two are always tacitly present. As Hegel himself puts it, "each of the moments is the whole that it is, and each is posited as an undivided unity with it" (EL § 160).

This holist claim is only true of the element types. It is not necessarily true of the tokens Hegel selects as examples of each element type. Universal, particular and individual are identical, for the reason just given. However, animal, horse and *this* horse are not. (It might, however, be true of the full extensions of the element types, i.e. all of the tokens falling under them.)

It follows directly that each element type is identical not only with the others but also with the whole triad. Each is identical with the next, and each is identical with both others. However, the whole is just all three. Hence, each is identical with the whole. This is simply to reiterate the conclusion we just reached: Each element is simply the same tripartite structure (the whole) considered from different sides.

* * *

The foregoing discussion positions us to understand how Hegel concludes that development solves the problems of shining into another and passing into another.

Development solves the problem of shining into another in a simple way. It rejects the conception of relations that gives rise to this problem. Henceforth, relations will not involve dependence of one term on another that is independent. Rather, they will involve interdependence, though often of a complex kind. The dependence of one term on the other will entail dependence of the other on it. However, the forms of dependence may differ in each direction.

Development solves the problem of passing into another. That problem arises for a characterization of things in nonrelational terms, as capable of being what they are independent of their relations to other things. That characterization turned out to entail that these things can be what they are only in virtue of their relations to other things. Now, however, there is more to the story. We have arrived at a stage at which these two characterizations can be reconciled. There will be a sense in which things can be what they are only because of their relations to others: The three components of the concept get their identities from their relations to one another. However, there will also be a sense in which things can be what they are independent of their relations to other things that are independent of them: Because these components are all identical, their dependence on one another is really just self-dependence and, in this sense, compatible with independence of a kind.

Development solves the problem of passing into another, because it avoids the problem of a regress. Since "all determination is negation," each constituent of the concept can be what it is only when considered in relation to the other two. However, there is no threat of infinite regress here, since, at least from a certain perspective, the three form a closed system in which we are constantly referred back to the term with which we began, rather than beyond it to yet another term. This closed system does not halt the regress by replacing the infinite series. However, it does so by existing alongside it and offering us a different perspective on the same phenomena.

6.5 Judgment and Syllogism (Inference)

In this final section, I briefly consider the account of the forms of judgment and inference that Hegel develops on the basis of his account of the Concept. I only consider the account of judgment and inference briefly because I think it adds little to Hegel's account of the Concept. This is best illustrated by contrasting Hegel's account of judgment and inference with a received one. Judgments are often thought of as combinations of concepts, and syllogisms as combinations of judgments. Certainly, this is the way Kant understands them. Yet Hegel rejects this approach, arguing instead that judgment and inference are simply further instances of the Concept. Odd as it may sound, there is a sense in which judgments and syllogisms contain only one concept, the Concept.[7] The reason Hegel prefers this unusual view is that it gives him a method of deriving the forms of judgment and inference that Kant lacked. In this way, he will succeed where Kant and the Aristotelian tradition before him failed.

Because Hegel's treatments of judgment and inference parallel one another almost perfectly, I will abbreviate the discussion further by focusing only on the former.

As I have said, Hegel's judgments do not combine two or more concepts at all. They each employ a single concept, though one of a distinctive type: "*the* Concept."

> The judgment is customarily regarded as a combination of concepts and, indeed, diverse sorts of concepts. What is right in this construal is this, that the concept forms the presupposition of the judgment and makes its appearance in the judgment in the form of the difference. But it is wrong to

---

[7] As he writes, "to regard the syllogism as merely consisting of three judgments is a [merely – JM] formalistic view" (WdL 12: 95/SoL 592).

speak of diverse sorts of concepts, for the concept, although concrete, is still essentially one and the moments contained in it are not to be considered as diverse sorts. Moreover, it is equally false to speak of a combination of the sides of the judgment since … (EL § 166 Z)

However, it is nevertheless also true that a Hegelian judgment is articulate, even if its parts are not themselves self-standing or independent. How can this be? The answer becomes clear when we recall that the Concept has parts as well. If a judgment is little more than the Concept in a different form, then its parts will be the Concept's parts. More specifically, they will be its three components ("moments"): universal, particular and individual.

Putting all of this together, we can say the following. Rather than combine two distinct concepts, a Hegelian judgment simply reconfigures the three component parts of *the* Concept, universal, particular and individual. When one judges "this horse is an animal," one is not combining three separate concepts in the way that Kant might have thought. According to Hegel's theory of the Concept, the three components, this, horse and animal, were not separate to begin with but interdependent components of a larger whole. Yet to know that a judgment reconfigures the moments of the concept is not yet to explain how it does so. What are the specific ways?

Because the Concept is defined as the structure in which these three moments are identical, the typical relation between them asserted in a judgment is one of identity. This means that Hegel regards identity as the fundamental case, not predication. Hegel does not deny that judgment admits of being understood in terms of the distinction between subject and predicate. Yet he does treat predication as a special case of identity, and indeed a defective one. Hence, Hegel treats what would seem to be obvious cases of the "is of predication," "the rose is red," as cases of the "is" of identity.

Ultimately, then, Hegel sides with ordinary language against traditional logic. In ordinary life, we have one word for the is of identity and that of predication. From a logical point of view, this can seem confused – as if surface grammar is misleading us about deep logical form. For Hegel, however, the two are modes of the same relation, identity. However, there is a much more profound reason than ordinary language. It is that identity is the relational form of the nonrelational category of being from which all further ones derive. Hence there is a fundamental continuity between all of these disparate forms of it.

If judgment simply reconfigures the components of the Concept, then how does it reconfigure them? Originally, as parts of the concept, these

components are configured in such a way that they are (a) defined in relation to one another, (b) identical with one another and (c) identical with
the whole. If that is so, then, we can conclude that the forms of judgment will simply be so many new forms in which the identity between
the Concept's moments can manifest itself. What, though, are these new
forms of the Concept's identity? Once again, answering this question
requires that we reflect more deeply on the nature of the identity relation
between the Concept's three moments. Here, it is important to realize that
the three components of the Concept are not just identical but are so in
such a way that they perform a certain important function. That function
is to resolve two broad types of problem that afflicted the two other broad
types of definition of the Absolute. These are the problems of passing into
another and shining into another, problems afflicting definitions of the
Absolute as immediate and as mediated respectively.

If that is so, then we have a basis for identifying the different forms
of judgment as the plurality of different forms of the Concept's identity.
These will be forms of judgement that identify in different ways, each of
which is more or less successful at fulfilling the constitutive function of
this identity: resolving the problems of passing into another and shining into another. In other words, the forms of judgment will be forms of
conceptual identity correlative with the two broad types of definition of
the Absolute which gave rise to these problems. These are the two type
definitions of the Absolute found in the Doctrines of Being and Essence.
As Hegel makes clear, the distinction between Being, essence and concept
is the basic principle of his derivation of the forms of judgment. It is what
enables him to avoid a derivation that is arbitrary:

> [W]e initially obtain three main species of judgment, which correspond
> to the stages of being, essence, and concept. The second of these main
> species is then doubled in turn, corresponding to the character of essence
> as the stage of difference [*Differenz*]. The inner ground of this systematic
> [character] of the judgment is to be sought in the fact that, since the
> concept is the ideal unity of being and essence, its unfolding, as it comes
> about in the judgment, also has to reproduce initially these two stages in a
> transformation [*Umbildung*] that conforms to the concept, while it itself,
> the concept, demonstrates itself to be the determining factor for the genu-
> ine judgment. The various species of judgment are to be considered, not
> as standing next to one another with the same value but instead as form-
> ing a sequence of stages, whose differences rest upon the logical meaning
> of the predicate. (EL § 171 Z)

Here, I will not go through the details of Hegel's deduction but merely
limit myself to a broad remark concerning how it proceeds. Drawing on

the above-cited passages, I simply want to note that it cycles through the same argument that brought us from Being to Essence to the Concept.

In other words, it considers forms of judgment that are associated with either Being or Essence and are therefore expressive of a conception of the Absolute as either immediate or mediated. It rejects these forms of judgment on the grounds that they raise versions of the problems Hegel called "passing into another" and "shining into another." Then, it settles on a form of judgement associated with the Concept that combines immediacy and mediation, thus solving these problems.

I earlier proposed that the argument for mediated immediacy is in a certain sense the master argument of Hegel's logic; however, it is only now that we are in a position to see why this is the case. There are two main reasons. In the first place, the argument for mediated immediacy does provide for the deduction of the Concept from the categories of traditional ontology, boldly inverting the order of priority between the subject matter of general and transcendental logic in Kant's critical philosophy. However, the master argument also provides for the deduction of the forms of judgment and inference, which Kant was content to simply take over from the tradition. The argument for mediated immediacy may not exhaust Hegel's attempt to resolve the logocentric predicament. However, it does bear most of the weight.

CHAPTER 7

Conclusion
A Circle of Circles: Analysis, Synthesis, Dialectic

7.1   Self-Comprehension and Self-Opacity

At the outset, we considered Hegel's critique of the logic of the Aristotelian tradition, as well as of Kant's transcendental logic. As we saw, these critiques have a parallel structure. According to Hegel, Aristotelian logic and Kant's transcendental logic are what we might call *non-self-comprehending sciences*. They comprehend their subject matter but not themselves. This is the devil's bargain that Hegel thinks all nonultimate forms of logic make. Knowledge of the object comes at the cost of self-opacity. Because transcendental logic is reliant on traditional logic, its problems are compounded by those of the latter.

How, though, are these rival sciences self-opaque? Hegel's answer is that they are so in a much straightforward sense than might at first be apparent. At the very basis of these sciences lie certain fundamental claims about our psychological faculties and their constitutive norms, claims testified to by a form of intellectual experience. Though by no means arbitrary, these beliefs are insufficiently well-grounded. They are the basis on which so much in these sciences is proven but are also claims these sciences cannot themselves prove. Hence, these sciences will be answerable to other sources of justification, whatever exactly those might be. For this reason, these sciences cannot be the ultimate in the way they have traditionally claimed to be. They are vulnerable to criticism, especially from the direction of a science that can comprehend those aspects of themselves that they cannot.

Incidentally, this is not a problem confined to the philosophical tradition. A more recent example of failure to self-comprehend might be logical positivism, a theory whose principle of verification is (notoriously) not itself verifiable. We might also consider forms of utilitarianism, which are, in Williams' terms, "self-effacing," those holding that we, in fact, maximize utility when we do not self-consciously attempt to maximize utility.

236

Here, Hegel hopes to succeed where his predecessors failed, offering a science that will differ from Aristotle's and Kant's in being a *self-comprehending science*. It will not just comprehend its subject matter but also itself. I want to focus on just one facet of this claim, namely, Hegel's idea that the account of the capacity upon which his science depends, and the norms internal to it, will be proven true in the course of the science itself. Hence, Hegelian science will not be answerable to either of these other sciences, which do not achieve this feat. Rather, they will be answerable to Hegel's science, inasmuch as they are forced to assume what Hegel alone can argue for in a sufficiently rigorous way. Where the deliverances of the capacity's self-reflection, "the facts of consciousness," contradict those of Hegel's dialectic, a method of proof and demonstration, then the former must give way. Although I lack the space to discuss it in sufficient detail, I do want to briefly outline how Hegel's *Science of Logic* achieves this feat of self-comprehension.

7.2 From the Concept to the Idea: (Finite) Knowledge

Commentators on the *Logic* vary widely in their views of when, exactly, in the course of its argument the (knowing) subject becomes an explicit topic. Straightaway in the Doctrine of Being? Only in the Doctrine of Essence? Or only in the Doctrine of the Concept?[1] My atypical view, which I will not defend in detail, holds that this development does not occur until even later in the *Logic*. More specifically, it occurs in the penultimate section of the Doctrine of the Concept: the discussion of Cognition (theoretical and practical), both forms of what Hegel calls the Idea.

In and of itself, the use of this terminology is both suggestive and provocative from a Kantian point of view. Kant had been concerned with whether we could have cognition of the unconditioned, or an Idea: the soul, the world-whole, God. Here, Hegel suggests the unexplored possibility that cognition is itself the unconditioned, or an Idea – even cognition in its finite, inadequate form. Such cognition does not have the unconditioned as its subject matter, inasmuch as it is ordinary scientific knowledge or right action. Yet it instantiates the unconditioned in its structure, the

---

[1] Longuenesse (2007: 39–40) treats the transition from the Doctrine of Being to that of Essence as marking, in effect, a Copernican turn away from precritical metaphysics and toward a recognizably Kantian form of idealism, albeit without the thing-in-itself, whereas an interpreter like Pinkard (2002: 249) locates this development in the transition from Essence to the Concept. Pippin (2018), if I understand him correctly, appears to think that something like Kantian apperception is present all throughout – even entering into the argument.

intimate relationship between subject and object it realizes. This is part of what I mean in suggesting that the turn to the subject at the close of the logic is not Kant's Copernican turn. The knowing subject, even in its most humble guise, figures here in a different way. It is as the source of conditions on the possibility of knowledge, but the Absolute. It is the paradigm of a structure that traditional metaphysics had sought in the form of substance or Being but never in the form of the knowing subject. The search for something other than the searcher herself concludes with the realization that it is the searcher herself who is sought.

Yet while this is a momentous development, I regard the argument of the *Logic* up to this point as devoid of any significant reference to the knower or thinker. There are three types of case that may appear to constitute exceptions but do not. The first, which we have already discussed, comes in the form of appeals to "facts of consciousness." These can be found in the prefatory materials and afford the reader a preliminary acquaintance with certain truths about the mind that are central to Hegel's theory. However, Hegel always insists that this appeal to fact is provisional and is meant to be supplemented by a proof later. The second type is Hegel's many descriptions of his own science. In the preliminary parts, he describes it as the science of the Idea in the pure element of thinking, of the Concept in its immediacy, and of thought determinations and so on. I have argued that the final self-characterization is no less premature than the others, which are widely acknowledged to me. As regards the third type, there are examples Hegel uses for illustrative purposes. In Hegel's definitions of categories such as form, matter and so on, he gives psychological or epistemological illustrations. Yet they appear alongside others that are biological, theological, political, economic. At issue is something much more general of which all of these are just so many specific instances. It is sometimes said that these further examples are for the sake of subjectivity, but there is no evidence I know of that Hegel means to privilege one class of illustrations over the others.

Most often, the turn toward the knowing subject is said to occur earlier in the *Logic*, in the transition from the Doctrine of Essence to the Doctrine of the Concept, the Objective to the Subjective Logic. As Hegel explains, the Objective Logic (Being and Essence) is his settling of accounts with precritical metaphysics. That is why we find showcased there attempts to know the unconditioned without taking account of the nature and limits of our cognitive power: "The objective logic thus takes the place rather of the former *metaphysics* which was supposed to be the scientific edifice of the world as constructed by *thoughts* alone" (WdL 21: 48–49/SoL 42).

Similarly, Hegel describes the Subjective Logic in terms that suggest it is broadly Kantian in inspiration, the Concept being something like Kant's transcendental unity of apperception (WdL 12: 18–19/SoL 515). If the *Logic* is a purified version of the history of philosophy, then the transition appears to have the following significance. The transition from Objective to Subjective Logic, Being and Essence to the Concept, would seem to be a version of Kant's Copernican Revolution in philosophy. In this transition, Hegel would seem to follow Kant in rejecting precritical metaphysics' attempt to know things-in-themselves. He appears to do so in favor of an alternative model that takes account of the role of the knowing subject in laying down conditions on the possibility of experience.

In my view, the appearance of such a transition is misleading, and I follow the many who have argued the Concept cannot be equated with any version of the transcendental subject. On this view, the Concept is a more generic structure than any found in the realms of nature or spirit (self-consciousness).[2] The transcendental subject may be an example of the Concept, but not every Concept is a transcendental subject. It is for this reason that Hegel uses examples to illustrate it that have nothing to do with subjectivity in the sense of early modern philosophy, let alone subjectivity as Kant conceived of it in the Transcendental Deduction.

The tripartite structure of universal, particular and individual has both spiritual and nonspiritual instantiations. The animal kingdom, as well as its species and their members, constitute one instance, but so too do the I-concept, all those beings using it to self-refer, and, finally, all of the representations they self-ascribe. In the former natural case, entities bear this tripartite structure without being conscious that they do so, whereas in the latter spiritual case they do so precisely by being conscious that they do. Yet in the logic we are abstracting from this difference between nature and spirit and focusing only the underlying logico-metaphysical scaffolding of both.

Moreover, Hegel is fairly clear that the precise sense in which the Subjective Logic is "subjective" is an older Aristotelian one, having little to do with the sense Descartes would later give the term when he used it to refer to the knowing subject: "Similarly, the individual has the meaning of being the subject, the foundation which contains the genus and species in itself and is itself substantial" (EL § 164). The subject in this older sense is simply that-which-underlies in general but not necessarily that-which-underlies our conscious states. In Hegel's terms, the subject is the individual, for example "this horse," that the particular and universal

---

[2] See, among others, Houlgate (2006: 139), Knappik (2016) and Tolley (2019a).

concepts, for example "animal" and "horse," are said to be "in." This is what Aristotle claims is true of particular substances in the *Categories*, and it is the basis of his claim that they are what is truly real. Particular substances are that which everything is said to be "in," whereas other things, like the universals so central to Plato and his followers, cannot be what is truly real since they are simply said "of" substances.

This also, I think, helps explain why Hegel goes on to define the Idea as the subject-object (WdL 12: 176/SoL 673). Life is a version of the Idea, a subject-object, even though living things need not be self-conscious (WdL 12: 179/SoL 676). They are subjects set over and against objects, not because they are knowers but because they cope with their environments in ways intended to preserve themselves. There is a certain reflexive relation to self in these organic processes: for example, living things self-nourish, self-repair, reproduce themselves. However, this is not necessarily the reflexivity of self-consciousness, found where I ascribe mental representations to myself or form intentions upon which I myself will act. Of course, finite cognition, the other version of the Idea, does involve this broadly Kantian form of subjectivity, that of the knowing and acting subject. However, the Aristotelian sense of subjectivity emerges earlier in the dialectic than does the Cartesian, suggesting the former has a certain priority over the latter.

If this is correct, then subjectivity must enter at a later point than in the transition from the Doctrine of Essence to that of the Concept, and the only real candidate is the section on the Idea of Cognition, since nothing before that point treats subjectivity. There, Hegel considers a definition of the Absolute as finite cognition, theoretical and practical. Both are finite because they presuppose a distinction between the knowing and acting subject, on the one hand, and the objective world it seeks to know or act in, on the other. In both cases, I have yet to achieve a certain type of concord between thought and reality, "truth" in the theoretical domain and "goodness" in the practical.

For our purposes, the important point is that the argument of the *Logic* has vindicated a certain account of cognition whose status was previously uncertain. This is important because, as we saw, the conception of cognition Hegel appeals to in the Prefatory materials is not itself supported by rigorous argument. It is not that the thought of thinking was unavailable to us in any way, but that it was not available in the way Hegel's rigorous method of argument requires. It is, instead, based on an appeal to "facts of consciousness" and other less rigorous methods of verification. The most noteworthy feature of Hegel's account of cognition is the distinction between sensible experience, on the one hand, and conceptual thought, on the other. There are many further distinctions, between sensibility, representation and intuition, on the one hand, and understanding and reason, on the other. Yet for our purposes it is just the broad dichotomy between sensibility and thought that matters.

Crucially, this distinction is entailed by the finitude of cognition. We are dependent on affection by an independently given object, and sensibility is the mode in which we are affected. To be sure, Hegel's case for a definition of the Absolute as finite cognition is more extensive. In reverse order, working backward from finite cognition, the components of that case are as follows. It first involves his claim that finite cognition is a higher form of the Absolute Idea or subject-object than life. It also involves the broader claim that the Absolute Idea, or subject-object, in general, living or non-, represents a more advanced definition of the Absolute than either the Subjective or Objective Concept alone. Then there is Hegel's general case for a definition of the Absolute as the Concept and his case against those from Being and Essence.

Ultimately, the assumption Hegel makes at the outset of the logic concerning our cognitive power is only substantiated once we reach the end, something that I think explains well why Hegel only invokes his psychological theory glancingly throughout the logic. The argument of the logic has brought us to the conclusion that the Absolute is (finite) cognition. Yet as the qualifier finite makes clear, this cannot be the highest standpoint reached. As we will soon see, there is an even more dramatic respect in which the end of the logic returns us to the beginning. Finite cognition is not the most advanced form reached. That distinction belongs to the form of thinking we have been engaged in throughout the logic. We have been engaged in this form of thought in an implicit way through the logic but will now become an explicit topic of reflection in the logic at its close.

One clear sign of this is the reemergence of language integral to Hegel's famed "instrument" objection to Kant's critical philosophy (WdL 12: 51/ SoL 751). As we saw earlier, Hegel rejects the traditional conception of our cognitive power as a tool or instrument. In particular, he deems this assumption inadmissible for the purposes of (speculative) logic. Yet he now reprises this claim, not at the outset of the logic, as before, but at its close. Why? The reason is that the rejection of an instrumental conception of thought is not in any straightforward sense a prerequisite for speculative logic. It is, more accurately, its concluding achievement. The definitive rejection of instrumentalism about cognition is achieved in the transition from finite to Absolute cognition. In hindsight, the earlier rejection appears to have only been provisional.

7.3 From Finite to Absolute Knowledge: Aristotle Again

In the Idea of cognition, Hegel makes a stunningly simple argument for the claim that *all finite cognition is defective as cognition*.[3] Since this encompasses virtually all ordinary instances of natural-scientific and mathematical knowledge, it follows that they are defective too. What is more, philosophy has often sought to emulate these methods, meaning it is implicated as well. Spinoza's *more geometrico* is a clear case of this, and one deeply important for Hegel (EL § 229 Z). We are here in the sphere of finite cognition, meaning we presuppose that the subject of knowledge and the object known are distinct (WdL 12: 201/SoL 698). This form of knowledge is achieved through the use of concepts by the knowing subject in conjunction with the sensible intuitions produced in her by the object known. Yet as Hegel also proceeds to explain, this process of knowledge formation through the cooperation of conceptual and nonconceptual components can occur in one of two ways: analysis and synthesis.

In analysis, we begin with the particulars that are presented to us in sensible intuition.[4] We then form universal concepts of them using Locke's method from the essay of comparing the particulars, abstracting from the differences between them and reflecting on the similarities (Hegel draws the parallel in an addition, EL § 227 Z). Yet according to Hegel no such method can yield satisfying results. This method always runs into the same problem. We are always limited by the finite size of the sample from which we begin. There could always be further instances that undermine the classificatory scheme we have formed by reflecting on previous instances. They could reveal what we have called "plus" as "qwus" or "blue" "grue."[5] Here, Hegel is just reminding us of the problem of induction as he so often has before. A further problem arises once we recall the normative dimension of the Hegelian Concept. In Hegel, giving the concept of a thing is not just giving the necessary and sufficient conditions that a thing need meet to be considered an instance of its kind. It is also giving an account of what it is to be an exemplary or good instance of that kind. If that is so, however, then the method of analysis may lead us astray. Averaging across all of the instances encountered so far will not necessarily tell us what it is to be a good one. After all, good instances may be rare, and bad ones

---

[3] I have benefited in this section from consulting the discussion of Hegel's critique of analytic cognition in Werner (2018).

[4] "This activity thus consists in dissolving the given concrete dimension, individuating its differences, and giving them the form of abstract universality" (EL § 227; cf. WdL 12: 203/SoL 700).

[5] See Goodman (1973) and Kripke (1982).

common. For this reason, analysis may not just yield a different result than the desired one but the opposite result (WdL 12: 214/SoL 712).

Because of these problems with analysis, we turn to a different method, synthesis, which moves in the opposite direction. Unlike analysis, synthesis begins from universal concepts possessed by the knowing subject and attempts on this basis to achieve knowledge of the particular objects presented by sensible intuition: "The advance from the universal to the particular characteristic of the concept constitutes the basis and the possibility of a synthetic science" (WdL 12: 215/SoL 713). Here, Hegel may partly be thinking of the method of division from Plato's *Sophist*. This is the method employed by Socrates and his interlocutors when they try to figure out what defines somebody as a true philosopher rather than a mere sophist. Using this method, we begin from a general concept, animal, and then divide it into various subconcepts, rational and nonrational, proceeding in the same way until we arrive at the particular we want to classify: the sophist himself, as opposed to the philosopher. We then cast a backward glance up the Porphyrean tree, each node of which gives us a concept that the definition of our particular will need to cite (the intension, as opposed to the extension). For Hegel, the problem with this approach is its arbitrariness. We simply have too many choices as to how to divide the concept with which we begin.[6] Because the manner in which we divide is not dictated by the concept from which we start we must simply choose one. Should we start by dividing the rational from the nonrational, the mammals from the reptiles, something else? Here, Hegel's claim is not that we fail to make the correct choice but that even where we do our victory will be a hollow one. If we do choose to divide a certain way and our choice is not random, then it must be because we are already anticipating the result we want to achieve. For example, we know that the sophist is a type of animal already, which is why we start by dividing into animals and non-. That means that even in the best case, the method of division can only be a way of calling to mind and organizing knowledge we already have, not of acquiring new knowledge.

Admittedly, it would be legitimate to wonder if Hegel's critique of this unusual method from an obscure Platonic dialogue can really constitute a critique of all nonphilosophical knowledge. After all, it is not clear that nonphilosophers use this method. Yet it seems to me that Hegel has a response to this worry. He thinks that the synthetic method encompasses much else besides Plato's approach in the *Sophist*. It is applied in

---

[6] Werner (2018: "Hegel on the Porphyrean Tree").

mathematical proofs such as those of the theorems of geometry, syllogistic arguments and other much less exotic forms of knowledge acquisition than that described in Plato. In all cases, Hegel thinks, we only succeed because we already know what we claim to be discovering for the first time. Disappointingly, his explanations of why this is so in the less exotic cases are underdeveloped, but it is not difficult to fill in the details. When we prove geometrical theorems, such as the Pythagorean, no line we draw tells us what the next ought to be. How, then, do we know which one to draw? We must, as it were, anticipate the end result, and work our way back to where we currently are. Yet if we are doing this, we must already know what we are attempting to prove. It is for this reason that Hegel objects to modeling philosophical arguments on mathematical proofs. Yet the syllogistic arguments made by more traditional philosophers are no better in this regard. No premise tells us what the next ought to be, and we must supply it ourselves. How, though, do we know which one to supply? Again, we must be looking ahead to the desired conclusion, working our way back from there to where we currently are.

For Hegel, we avoid these problems only when we abandon the methods of knowledge acquisition he calls analysis and synthesis, both of which combine concept and intuition. We must turn to the method of philosophy, whose medium is pure conceptual thought without intuition. Using the same term he did in the prefatory material, Hegel describes philosophy as the abandonment of presuppositions: in particular, we might add, the presuppositions of analysis and synthesis (WdL 12: 244–245/SoL 743–744). In other words, his logic not only commences with the renunciation of unexamined assumptions but culminates in the realization that this approach to knowledge acquisition is superior to all others. Once we reach this stage, we ask not whether some concept is "correct," whether it corresponds with an object represented in sensible intuition. Instead we ask whether it is "true," whether it corresponds with itself. Being is what simply is. Yet if that is so, then it is Nothing. And so on. Another way to put the point would be that Hegel regards the dialectic as a more rigorous method of operating with concepts than analysis or synthesis. That is because the dialectic need not rely on sense experience, which introduces an element of arbitrariness.

For Hegel, this method will not fall prey to the problems afflicting analysis or synthesis. We do not need to worry about the finite size of our sample. After all, there is no sample. There is no sensible component to our knowledge from which a sample would be drawn. Nor need we worry about the fact that the concept from which we start does not divide itself or tell us which principle to use for the division. It self-divides, serving as the principle of its own division. Beginning with Being, the dialectic leads us all of its necessary forms: quantity, quality, Identity and the rest. This is not one path among others, arbitrarily selected. It is the only one that can be taken, given this starting point and this method of progression.

This alternative method is not just one being recommended to us for future occasions but the one we have been employing all along. If the *Logic* culminates in an account of the type of knowledge achieved in speculative logic, then it has succeeded in comprehending itself. This is a type of reflexivity different from that with which Fichte thought philosophy should begin, the self-consciousness of the knowing subject. It is instead the reflexivity that comes at the end of philosophy, when we achieve that rare thing, a theory that not only explains its subject matter but itself.[7] As we have seen, Aristotelian and transcendental logic failed to self-comprehend, but Hegel's has succeeded where they failed. It can therefore claim to be ultimate in a way they are not.

As we have seen before, Hegel's relationship to the Aristotelian tradition is ambivalent. Hegel rejects the logic of Aristotle, denouncing it as the logic of the understanding. Yet he only does so because he is such an ardent admirer of another part of Aristotle's legacy, his metaphysics. For Hegel, the former is an impediment to the latter. As we saw earlier, Hegel quips that Aristotle would not have reached his most "speculative" insights if all he had been doing was constructing syllogistic arguments. Even as he takes an important step beyond the logic of Aristotle, then, Hegel pays tribute to his metaphysics.

In an addition to the main text, Hegel famously describes the Absolute Idea of the *Science of Logic* as the God of Aristotle's *Metaphysics*, thought-thinking-itself (EL § 236 Z). The passage is extremely well known and has been extensively discussed. Yet approaching Hegel's tribute to Aristotle in terms of a problem in philosophical logic, the problem of self-comprehension, allows us to see it in a new and distinctive light. At least part of what Hegel is claiming by describing his *Logic* as thought-thinking-itself is that it is self-comprehending in a way earlier logics are not. With the achievement of this form of self-comprehension, Hegel's *Logic* comes to an end. Yet it is only now that it can truly begin.

---

[7] This idea of a self-comprehending theory has an afterlife in Critical Theory. See Horkheimer's "Traditional and Critical Theory" (1972), as well as the discussion of this idea in Geuss (1981).

7.4   Conclusion: Prospect and Retrospect

Having clarified the place of the thinker in Hegel's *Logic*, I conclude my effort to explain the place of logic-conventionally-so-called in this work. Logic-conventionally-so-called presupposes the capacity conceptual thought and inquires into the "constitutive" laws of this power. Hegel, by contrast, considers its laws and materials, and only at the close turns to the power. This marks the close of Hegel's effort to resolve the logocentric predicament.

As we have repeatedly seen, the most basic laws and materials of formal logic, effectively unquestioned in the tradition, receive from Hegel a critique and reconstruction. This requires a method of argument that does not already rely on the laws and materials of formal logic, and this Hegel finds in his dialectical method. Operating below the level of syllogistic inference, judgment or even of the concept (in any technical sense of that term), this method is also innocent of even such elementary principles as the laws of identity and noncontradiction. It relies on more primitive precursors of them. I mean versions of these laws in which the problems whose resolution spurs rational progress are *sui generis*, nonformalizable.

As we further saw, in discussing Hegel's treatment of the laws of logic, it is a "primordial" ontology that forms the basis for Hegel's critical reconstruction of logic. Hence, the famed opening sections of Hegel's logic, though argument-based and not a product of mystical intuition, move in a medium that is prepredicative and noninferential. What is more, the contentfulness of this discourse is secured by a rehabilitated version of the ontological proof, which furnishes Hegel with the idea of concepts that are necessarily nonempty.

Hegel begins his critical reconstruction of formal logic with its laws. The deductive interrelations between these laws reveal themselves when their "primordial" category-theoretic substructure is unveiled. Being can serve as the monadic or nonrelational precursor to formal logic's most basic proposition, Being's dyadic or relational equivalent as expressed in the law of Identity. While securing for each law the measure of validity it can legitimately claim, this more probing approach will undercut each one's claim to be unconditionally valid.

Hegel will next turn to thought's most fundamental materials: concept, judgment and syllogism. Here too he will show how the tripartite structure, which all three share, emerges from a more fundamental source. A theory of the categories, undertaken on a non–formal logical basis, provides the basis for formal logic. Hence, the order of priority between the two is the reverse of what Kant saw it as being. Here too the risk of vicious circularity must be avoided, and this is achieved through the use of a method of argument that identifies and resolves problems emerging at a lower level of logical complexity than the one we eventually reach. More specifically, these are problems existing on a monadic (nonrelational) or dyadic (relational) level, problems of regress and inversion. In Hegel's terms, they are problems arising at the standpoints of Being and Essence, immediacy and mediation, respectively.

The very argument that will bring us from Being and Essence to the Concept bring us from the most primitive forms of judgment and inference to those which fulfill their potential. Hence the argument for mediated immediacy is Hegel's master argument. It provides the key not only to conceptuality but to deriving the forms of judgment and inference Kant and the tradition simply assumed.

* * *

I have throughout sought to address the main obstacle to the success of Hegel's project, vicious circularity; however, this obstacle has many faces, and there is, I think, one other that I would like to address here at the close.

As I have indicated obliquely throughout, there is an important difference between the prospective and retrospective perspectives that a reader can take on Hegel's *Logic*. Among other things, the former does not rely upon formal logic, whereas the latter does. More accurately, the former does not rely on these resources for the purposes of argument, though it may do so in some other way: for example, as illustrative "facts of consciousness." While it would be legitimate to conclude, in retrospect, that the logic has considered the Concept, the Idea, thought determinations, and so on, none of these designations of the logic's subject matter can be presupposed the outset. I have therefore felt justified in referring to the opening parts of the logic as general and special metaphysics, ontology and theology, a theory of the categories and a version of the ontological proof. I have proposed that Hegel, in effect, recasts these areas of philosophy as the default for thinking, in something like the way logic had traditionally been.

However, it could be argued that the turn to the standpoint of the knowing subject, effected in the Subjective Logic, reacts back upon the earlier Objective one, revoking its standing as metaphysics (general and special). This would, in effect, constitute a Hegelian version of Kant's "Copernican turn." It would also severely curtail the sense in which these earlier portions of the logic constitute a replacement for earlier metaphysics. What can be said in the face of this challenge to my attempt to depict Hegel as rehabilitating traditional forms of metaphysics and as wary of even the most radical versions of transcendental idealism?

I restrict myself to one line of response and attempt to address this interpretive counterargument from the perspective of the philosophical problem that interests me: the logocentric predicament. There may be some type of dependence of earlier on later, Objective Logic on Subjective, clarified in the murky final section of Hegel's *Logic* ("the Absolute Idea"). However, it is the dependence of the later on the earlier, presented to us at every step along the way, that takes precedence in my account. This is not just a dependence that reflects the order of exposition but a dependence in the order of argument. This suggests to me that, whatever the precise nature of the dependence of the earlier on the later, it cannot be perfectly symmetrical with the dependence of the later on the earlier. In particular, the earlier "premises" must retain their independence, regardless of the ways in which they are further fortified or better illuminated by the later "conclusion." Only in this way can the earlier material provide an independent source of support for the later, and not introduce vicious circularity into the whole. Without a basis in something even notionally independent, the conclusion would undercut the premises on which it is based. It would fail to self-comprehend in the way I have argued it must if it is to move beyond the impasses of logic in the Kantian and Scholastic-Aristotelian traditions.

Works Cited

Al-Azm, S. 1972. *The Origins of KantOriArguments in the Antinomies*. Oxford: Clarendon Press.

Alznauer, M. 2016. "Hegel's Theory of Normativity." *Journal of the American Philosophical Association*. Vol. 2, Issue 2. pp. 196–211.

Ameriks, K. 1985. "Hegel's Critique of Kant's Theoretical Philosophy." *Philosophy and Phenomenological Research*. Vol. 46, Issue 1. pp. 1–35.

Ameriks, K. 2000. *Kant and the Fate of Autonomy: Problems in the Appropriation of the Critical Philosophy*. Cambridge: Cambridge University Press.

Anscombe, G. E. M. 1975. "The First Person." In: Gutenplan, S. D. ed. *Mind and Language*. Oxford: Oxford University Press. pp. 45–65.

Aristotle. 1984. *The Complete Works of Aristotle: The Revised Oxford Translation*. 2 vols. Ed. Barnes, J. Princeton: Princeton University Press.

Arndt, A., Iber, C., and Kruck, G. (eds.). 2006. *Hegels Lehre vom Begriff, Urteil und Schluss*. Berlin: Akademie Verlag.

Beiser, F. 1987. *The Fate of Reason: German Philosophy from Kant to Fichte*. Cambridge, MA: Harvard University Press.

Beiser, F. 2005. *Hegel*. London: Routledge.

Boghossian, P. 2000. "Knowledge of Logic." In: Boghossian, P. and Peacocke, C. eds. *New Essays on the A Priori*. Oxford: Oxford University Press. pp. 229–254.

Bordignon, M. 2017. "Hegel: A Dialetheist? Truth and Contradiction in Hegel's Logic." *Hegel Bulletin*. Published Online September 11.

Bowman, B. 2013. *Hegel and the Metaphysics of Absolute Negativity*. New York: Cambridge University Press.

Boyle, M. 2020. "Kant on Logic and the Laws of the Understanding." In: Miguens, S. ed. *Logical Aliens*. Cambridge, MA: Harvard University Press. pp. 118–144.

Brandom, R. 1994. *Making It Explicit: Reasoning Representing and Discursive Commitment*. Cambridge, MA: Harvard University Press.

Brandom, R. 2002. *Tales of the Mighty Dead: Historical Essays in the Metaphysics of Intentionality*. Cambridge, MA: Harvard University Press.

Bristow, W. 2007. *Hegel and the Transformation of Philosophical Critique*. New York: Oxford.

Burbidge, J. 2006. *The Logic of Hegel's Logic*. Peterborough, Ontario: Broadview Press.

Burbidge, J. 2014. "Hegel's Logic as Metaphysics." *Hegel Bulletin*. Vol. 35, Issue 1. pp. 100–115.

Carroll, L. 1895. "What the Tortoise Said to Achilles." *Mind*. Vol. 104, Issue 416. pp. 691–693.

Cassirer, E. 1981. Trans. Haden, J. *Kant's Life and Thought*. New Haven, CT: Yale University Press.

Chalmers, D. 2020. "Idealism and the Philosophy of Mind." In: Seager, W. ed. *The Routledge Companion to Panpsychism*. New York: Routledge. pp. 353–374.

Cohen, H. 1885. *Kants Theorie der Erfahrung*. 2nd ed. Berlin: Dümmler.

Conant, J. 1991. "The Search for Logically Alien Thought: Descartes, Kant, Frege and the *Tractatus*." *Philosophical Topics*. Vol. 20, Issue 1. pp. 115–180.

Crary, A. and Read, R. 2000. *The New Wittgenstein*. London: Routledge.

de Boer, K. 2010a. "Hegel's Account of Contradiction in the *Science of Logic* Reconsidered." *Journal for the History of Philosophy*. Vol. 48, Issue 3. pp. 345–373.

de Boer, K. 2010b. *On Hegel: The Sway of the Negative*. New York: Palgrave Macmillan.

de Boer, K. 2011. "Transformations of Transcendental Philosophy: Wolff, Kant, and Hegel." *Bulletin of the Hegel Society of Great Britain*. Vol. 32, Issue 1–2. pp. 50–79.

Deleuze, G. 1994. Trans. Patton, P. *Difference and Repetition*. New York: Columbia University Press.

Deleuze, G. and Guattari, F. 1987. Trans. Massumi, B. *A Thousand Plateaus: Capitalism and Schizophrenia*. Minnesota: University of Minnesota Press.

Derrida, J. 1996. Trans. Spivak, G. *Of Grammatology*. Baltimore: Johns Hopkins University Press.

Descombes, V. 2014. Trans. Schwartz, S. *The Institutions of Meaning*. Cambridge, MA: Harvard University Press.

Doz, A. 1987. *La logique de Hegel et les problèmes traditionnels de l'ontologie*. Paris: Vrin.

Dummett, M. 1991. *The Logical Basis of Metaphysics*. Cambridge, MA: Harvard University Press.

Düsing, K. 2009. *Das Seiende und das Göttliche Denken. Hegels Auseinandersetzung mit der Antiken ersten Philosophie*. Paderborn: Brill.

Dyck, C. 2016. "The Priority of Judging: Kant on Wolff's General Logic." *Estudos Kantianos*. Vol. 4, Issue 2. pp. 99–118.

Edgar, S. 2010. "Hermann Cohen." Last revised September 17, 2015. *Stanford Encyclopedia of Philosophy*. https://plato.stanford.edu/entries/cohen/

Engels, F. 1947. Trans. Burns, E. *Anti-Dühring. Herr Eugen Dühring's Revolution in Science*. Moscow: Progress Publishers.

Ficara, E. 2015. "Contrariety and Contradiction: Hegel and the Berliner Neo-Aristotelismus." *Hegel-Studien*. Vol. 49. pp. 39–55.

Ficara, E. 2016. "Hegel on the Interplay between Logic and Metaphysics." In: de Laurentiis, A. ed. *Hegel and Metaphysics*. Berlin/New York: De Gruyter. pp. 109–118.

Ficara, E. 2020a. *The Form of Truth: Hegel's Philosophical Logic*. Berlin: De Gruyter.

Ficara, E. 2020b. "Hegel and Priest on Revising Logic." In: Baskent, C. and Ferguson, T. eds. *Graham Priest on Dialetheism and Paraconsistency*, Outstanding Contributions to Logic Series. Cham, Switzerland: Springer. pp. 59–71.

Fichte, I. H. (ed.). 1971. *Fichtes Werke*. Berlin: De Gruyter.

Fichte, J. G. 1794–5. *Wissenschaftslehre*. In: Fichte, I. H. ed. (1971). Vol. 1/ 1982. Ed. and Trans. Heath, J. and Lachs, P. *Science of Knowledge*. Cambridge: Cambridge University Press.

Franks, P. 2005. *All or Nothing: Systematicity, Transcendental Arguments, and Skepticism in German Idealism*. Cambridge, MA: Harvard University Press.

Frede, M. 1987. *Essays in Ancient Philosophy*. Minneapolis: Minnesota University Press.

Frege, G. 1892. "On Concept and Object." Reprinted in G. Frege. 1984. *Collected Papers on Mathematics, Logic, and Philosophy*. Ed. McGuinness, B. F. Oxford: Basil Blackwell. pp. 182–194.

Frege, G. 1980. *Foundations of Arithmetic*. Trans. Austin, J. L. 2nd rev. ed. Evanston: Northwestern University Press.

Frege, G. 1984. *Collected Papers on Mathematics, Logic, and Philosophy*. Ed. McGuinness, B. F. Oxford: Basil Blackwell.

Fulda, H. F. 1965. *Das Problem einer Einleitung in Hegels Wissenschaft der Logik*. Frankfurt am Main: Vittorio Klostermann.

Gadamer, H.-G. 1976. Trans. Smith, P. C. *Hegel's Dialectic: Five Hermeneutical Studies*. New Haven: Yale University Press.

Geuss, R. 1981. *The Idea of a Critical Theory: Habermas and the Frankfurt School*. Cambridge: Cambridge University Press.

Goodman, N. 1973. *Fact, Fiction, Forecast*. Indianapolis: Hackett.

Gottlieb, P. 2019. "Aristotle on Non-Contradiction." *Stanford Encyclopedia of Philosophy*. First published 2007. plato.stanford.edu/entries/Aristotle-noncontradiction

Grier, M. 2001. *Kant's Doctrine of Transcendental Illusion*. New York: Cambridge University Press.

Grünbaum, A. 1967. *Modern Science and Zeno's Paradoxes*, Middletown, CT: Wesleyan University Press.

Guyer, P. 1993. "Thought and Being: Hegel's Critique of Kant." In: Beiser, F. ed. *Cambridge Companion to Hegel*. New York: Cambridge University Press. pp. 171–210.

Habermas, J. 1971. Trans. Shapiro, J. *Knowledge and Human Interests*. Boston: Beacon.

Hahn, S. 2007. *Contradiction in Motion: Hegel's Organic Concept of Life and Value*. Ithaca: Cornell University Press.

Hanna, R. 1986. "From an Ontological Point of View: Hegel's Critique of the Common Logic." *The Review of Metaphysics*. Vol. 44, Issue 2. pp. 305–338.

Harrelson, K. 2009. *The Ontological Argument from Descartes to Hegel*. Amherst, NY: Humanity Books.

Hatfield, G. 2003. "What Were Kant's Aims in the Deduction?" *Philosophical Topics*. Vol. 31, Issue 1. pp. 165–198.

Hegel, G. W. F. 1968. *Gesammelte Werke, Deutsche Forschungsgemeinschaft*. Hamburg: Meiner.

Hegel, G. W. F. 2001a. *Enzyklopädie der philosophischen Wissenschaften im Grundrisse Teil 1: Logik. Werke*. Vol. 13. Hamburg: F. Meiner/2010. Ed. and Trans. Brinkmann, K. and Dahlstrom, D. O. *Encyclopedia of the Philosophical Sciences in Outline: Part 1, Science of Logic*. New York: Cambridge University Press.

Hegel, G. W. F. 2001b. Transcribed by Hegel, K. Ed. Rameil, U. and Lucas, H. C. *Vorlesungen über die Logik, Berlin 1831*. Hamburg: Meiner/2008. Trans. Butler, C. *Lectures on Logic, Berlin, 1831*. Bloomington: Indiana University Press.

Hegel, G. W. F. 2016/2020.*Vorlesungen über die Geschichte der Philosophie. Werke*. Vol. 30, 1–2. Hamburg: F. Meiner/1995. Trans. Haldane, E. S. and Simson, F. H. *Lectures on the History of Philosophy*. 3 vols. Lincoln: University of Nebraska Press.

Hegel, G. W. F. 1984/1978/1981.*Wissenschaft der Logik. Werke*. Vols. 21, 11, 12. Hamburg: F. Meiner/2010. Trans. di Giovanni, G. *Hegel's Science of Logic*. Cambridge: Cambridge University Press.

Heidegger, M. 1969. *Identity and Difference*. Trans. Stambaugh, J. New York: Harper & Row.

Heidegger, M. 1984. Trans. Heim, M. *The Metaphysical Foundations of Logic*. Bloomington: Indiana University Press.

Heidegger, M. 2009. Trans. Gregory, W. T. and Unna, Y. *Martin Heidegger: Logic as the Question Concerning the Essence of Language*. Albany, NY: State University of New York Press.

Heidegger, M. 2010. Trans. Sheehan, T. *Logic: The Question of Truth*. Bloomington: Indiana University Press.

Heis, J. 2018. "Neo-Kantianism." *Stanford Encyclopedia of Philosophy*. https://plato.stanford.edu/entries/neo-kantianism/

Henrich, D. 1960. *Der Ontologische Gottesbeweis: Sein Probleme und Sein Geschichte in der Neuzeit*. Tübingen: Mohr.

Henrich, D. 1965/66. "Hölderlin über Urteil und Sein. Eine Studie zur Entwicklungsgeschichte des Idealismus." *Hölderlin-Jahrbuch, Yearbook* 14. pp. 73–96.

Henrich, D. 1972. *Hegel Im Kontext*. Frankfurt am Main: Suhrkamp.

Henrich, D. 1997. Ed. Förster, E. *The Course of Remembrance: Essays on Hölderlin and Others*. Palo Alto: Stanford.

Henrich, D. 2001. Ed. and Trans. Pacini, D. S. *Between Kant and Hegel: Lectures on German Idealism*. Cambridge, MA: Harvard University Press.

Hölderlin, F. 1962. "Urteil und Sein." Band 4. *Sämtliche Werke*. 6 Bände. Stuttgart: Kohlhammer.

Horkheimer, M. 1972. Trans. O'Connell, M. J. et. al. "Traditional and Critical Theory." In: *Critical Theory: Selected Essays*. New York: Seabury. pp. 188–244.

Horstmann, R. P. 1990. *Wahrheit aus dem Begriff: Eine Einführung in Hegel.* Berlin: Anton Hain.

Horstmann, R. P. 1995. "What's Wrong with Kant's Categories, Professor Hegel?" In: Robinson, H. ed. *Proceedings of the Eighth International Kant Congress, Memphis 1995, Vol. I.* Milwaukee: Marquette University Press. pp. 1005–1015.

Houlgate, S. 1986. *Hegel, Nietzsche and the Critique of Metaphysics.* Cambridge: Cambridge University Press.

Houlgate, S. 2006. *The Opening of Hegel's Logic.* West Lafayette, IN: Purdue University Press.

Houlgate, S. 2011. "*Essence, Reflexion* and Immediacy in Hegel's Science of Logic." In: Houlgate, S. and Baur, M. eds. *A Companion to Hegel.* Oxford: Wiley-Blackwell. pp. 139–158.

Houlgate, S. 2016a. "Hegel, Kant and the Antinomies of Pure Reason." *Kant Yearbook.* Vol. 8, Issue 1. pp. 39–62.

Houlgate, S. 2016b. "Hegel's Critique of Kant." *Hegel-Jahrbuch.* Vol. 1. pp. 24–32.

Houlgate, S. 2019. "Hegel's Realm of Shadows: Logic as Metaphysics in Hegel's Science of Logic by Robert Pippin." *Journal for the History of Philosophy.* Vol. 57, Issue 4. pp. 765–766.

Husserl, E. 2013. Ed. Moran, D. *Logical Investigations Volume 2.* London: Routledge.

Hylton, P. 1993. *Russell, Idealism, and the Emergence of Analytic Philosophy.* Oxford: Clarendon.

Iber, C. 1990. *Metaphysik Absoluter Relationalität.* Berlin: De Gruyter. Reprint.

Iber, C. 2016. "Hegels Begriff der Reflexion als Kritik am traditionellen Wesens – und Reflexionsbegriff." In: Arndt, A. and Gruck, G. eds. *Hegels "Lehre vom Wesen."* Hegel-Jahrbuch Sonderband. Berlin: De Gruyter. pp. 21–34.

Inwood, M. J. 1983. *Hegel: Arguments of the Philosophers.* London: Routledge.

Jacobi, F. H. 1994. Ed. and trans. Di Giovanni, G. *The Main Philosophical Writings and the Novel Allwill.* Montreal and Kingston: McGill-Queen's University Press.

Kant, I. 1902–. *Kritik der Reinen Vernunft.* Ak. Vol. 3–4. Berlin: De Gruyter/1999. Ed. and Trans. Guyer, P. and Wood, A. *Critique of Pure Reason.* Cambridge: Cambridge University Press.

Kant, I. 1902–. "Jäsche Logik." Ak. Vol. 9. Berlin: De Gruyter/"Jäsche Logic." In: Michael Young, J. ed. *Kant's Lectures on Logic.* Cambridge: Cambridge University Press.

Kant, I. 1902–. *Prolegomena zu einer jeden künftigen Metaphysik.* Ak. Vol. 4. Berlin: De Gruyter/Ed. and Trans. Hatfield, G. *Prolegomena to Any Future Metaphysics.* Cambridge Texts in the History of Philosophy. New York: Cambridge University Press.

Kant, I. 1902–. *Immanuel Kant: Gesammelte Schriften.* 29 vols. Berlin: De Gruyter.

Kant, I. 2003. "On the Introduction of Negative Magnitudes into Philosophy." In: Walford, D. with Meerbote, R. eds. and trans. *Theoretical Philosophy 1755–70.* Cambridge: Cambridge University Press. pp. 203–243.

Kim, J. 1993. *Supervenience and Mind: Selected Philosophical Essays.* Cambridge: Cambridge University Press.

Kimi, I. 2018. *Thinking and Being.* Cambridge, MA: Harvard University Press.

Knappik, F. 2013. "Hegel on Consciousness, Self-Consciousness, and Idealism." *International Yearbook of German Idealism.* Vol. 11. pp. 145–168.

Knappik, F. 2016. "Hegel's Essentialism: Natural Kinds and the Metaphysics of Explanation in Hegel's Theory of 'the Concept.'" *European Journal of Philosophy.* Vol. 24, Issue 4. pp. 760–787.

Koch, A. F. 2000. "Sein – Nichts – Werden." In: Arndt, A. and Iber, C. eds. *Hegels Seinslogik. Interpretationen und Perspektiven.* Berlin: De Gruyter. pp. 140–158.

Koch, A. F. 2014. *Die Evolution des logischen Raumes: Aufsätze zu Hegels Nichtstandard-Metaphysik.* Tübingen: Mohr Siebeck.

Koch, A. F. 2018. "Das Sein: Erster Abschnitt, die Qualität." In: Quante, M. and Mooren, N. eds. *Kommentar zu Hegels Logik.* Hamburg: Felix Meiner Verlag. pp. 43–145.

Koch, A. F. 2019. "Robert Pippin on the Speculative Identity of Thinking and Being." *European Journal of Philosophy.* Vol. 27, Issue 4. pp. 1048–1054.

Kreines, J. 2006. "Hegel's Metaphysics: Changing the Debate." *Philosophy Compass.* Vol. 1. pp. 466–480.

Kreines, J. 2008. "Hegel: Metaphysics without Pre-Critical Monism." *Bulletin of the Hegel Society of Great Britain.* Vol. 29, Issue 1/2. pp. 48–70.

Kreines, J. 2015. *Reason in the World: Hegel's Metaphysics and Its Philosophical Appeal.* New York: Oxford University Press.

Kreines, J. 2016. "Fundamentality without Metaphysical Monism: Response to Critics of Reason in the World." *Hegel Bulletin.* Vol. 39, Issue 1. pp. 138–156. Published Online October 17.

Kripke, S. 1982. *Wittgenstein on Rules and Private Language.* Cambridge, MA: Harvard University Press.

Krohn, W. 1972. *Die Formale Logik in Hegels Wissenschafts der Logik.* München: C. Hanser.

Lau, C.-F. 2008. "The Aristotelian-Kantian and Hegelian Approaches to Categories." *The Owl of Minerva.* Vol. 40, Issue 1. pp. 77–114.

Leibniz, G.W. 1989. Trans. and ed. R. Ariew and D. Garber. *Philosophical Essays.* Indianapolis: Hackett.

Lewis, D. 2001. *On the Plurality of Worlds.* Revised ed. Oxford: Blackwell.

Locke, J. 2008. *An Essay Concerning Human Understanding.* New York: Oxford University Press.

Longuenesse, B. 2007. Trans. Simek, N. J. *Hegel's Critique of Metaphysics.* New York, NY: Cambridge University Press.

Longuenesse, B. 2013. "Kant and Hegel on the Moral Self" In: Emundts, D. ed. *Self, World and Art.* Berlin: De Gruyter. pp. 93–119.

Longuenesse, B. 2017. *I, Me, Mine: Back to Kant, and Back Again.* Oxford: Oxford University Press.

Lu-Adler, H. 2018. *Kant and the Science of Logic: A Historical and Philosophical Reconstruction.* New York: Oxford University Press.

Martin, C. G. 2012. *Ontologie der Selbstbestimmung: Eine Operationale Rekonstruktion von Hegels "Wissenschaft der Logik."* Tübingen: Mohr/Siebeck.

Martin, C. G. 2015. "Metaphysik als Logik." In: Urbich, J. and Zimmer, J. eds. *Metzler Handbuch Ontologie.* Berlin: Springer. pp. 126–138.

Martin, W. 2003. "Nothing More or Less than Logic: General Logic, Transcendental Philosophy, and Kant's Repudiation of Fichte's Wissenschatselhre." *Topoi.* Vol. 22, Issue 1. pp. 29–39.

McDowell, J. 1994. *Mind and World.* Cambridge, MA: Harvard University Press.

McDowell, J. 2009. *Having the World in View: Essays on Kant, Hegel, and Sellars.* Cambridge, MA: Harvard University Press.

McNulty, J. 2016. "Transcendental Philosophy and Intersubjectivity: Mutual Recognition as a Condition for the Possibility of Self-Consciousness in § 1–3 of Fichte's *Foundations of Natural Right.*" *European Journal of Philosophy.* Vol. 24, Issue 4. pp. 788–810.

Melichar, G. 2020. *Die Objektivität des Absoluten: Der ontologische Gottesbeweis in Hegels "Wissenschaft der Logik" im Spiegel der kantischen Kritik.* Collegium Metaphysicum 23. Tübingen: Mohr-Siebeck.

Meyer, T. 2017. "Hegels Wesenslogisches Kausalitätskapitel als Identitätstheorie der Kausalität." *Hegel-Studien* 51. Munich: F. Meiner Verlag. pp. 90–121.

Moss, G. 2020. *Hegel's Foundation Free Metaphysics: The Logic of Singularity.* New York: Routledge.

Nuzzo, A. 2016. "Hegel's Metaphysics. The Absence of the Metaphysical Subject in Hegel's *Science of Logic.*" In: de Laurentiis, A. ed. *Hegel and Metaphysics.* New York/Berlin: De Gruyter. pp. 119–135.

Nuzzo, A. 2018. "Determination, Determinability, and the Structure of Ens: Baumgarten's Ontology and Beyond." In: Fugate, D. and Hymers, J. eds. *Baumgarten and Kant on Metaphysics.* Oxford: Oxford University Press. pp. 23–41.

Peacocke, C. 2014. *The Mirror of the World: Subjects, Consciousness and Self-Consciousness.* Oxford: Oxford University Press.

Peacocke, C. 2019. *The Primacy of Metaphysics.* Oxford: Oxford University Press.

Pinkard, T. 1994. *Hegel's Phenomenology: The Sociality of Reason.* Cambridge: Cambridge University Press.

Pinkard, T. 2002. *German Philosophy 1760–1860: The Legacy of Idealism.* New York: Cambridge University Press.

Pinkard, T. 2017. *Does History Make Sense? Hegel on the Historical Shapes of Justice.* Cambridge, MA: Harvard University Press.

Pippin, R. 1989. *Hegel's Idealism: The Satisfactions of Self-Consciousness.* New York: Cambridge University Press.

Pippin, R. 2017. "Hegel on Logic as Metaphysics" In: Moyar, D. ed. *The Oxford Handbook of Hegel.* New York: Oxford University Press. pp. 199–219.

Pippin, R. 2018. *The Realm of Shadows: Metaphysics as Logic in Hegel's Science of Logic.* Chicago: University of Chicago Press.

Priest, G. 1976. *One: Being an Investigation into the Unity of Reality and of Its Parts, Including the Singular Object Which is Nothingness.* Oxford: Oxford University Press.

Priest, G. 1985. "Inconsistencies in Motion." *American Philosophical Quarterly.* Vol. 22, Issue 4. pp. 339–346.

Priest, G. 1989. "Dialectic and Dialethic." *Science and Society.* Vol. 53, Issue 4. pp. 388–415.

Priest, G. 1995. *Beyond the Limits of Thought.* Cambridge: Cambridge University Press.

Priest, G. 2006. *In Contradiction: A Study of the Transconsistent.* Reprint. Oxford: Oxford University Press.

Quine, W. V. O. 1948. "On What There Is." *Review of Metaphysics.* Vol. 2, Issue 5. pp. 21–38.

Quine, W. V. O. 1951. *Mathematical Logic.* Cambridge, MA: Harvard University Press.

Redding, P. 1991. "Hegel's Logic of Being and the Polarities of Pre-Socratic Thought." *The Monist.* Vol. 74, Issue 3. pp. 438–456.

Redding, P. 1996. *Hegel's Hermeneutics.* Ithaca: Cornell University Press.

Redding, P. 1997. "Georg Wilhelm Friedrich Hegel." Last revised August 4, 2015. *Stanford Encyclopedia of Philosophy.* http://plato.stanford.edu/entries/hegel

Redding, P. 2007. *Analytic Philosophy and the Return of Hegelian Thought.* New York: Cambridge University Press.

Redding, P. 2014. "The Role of Logic Commonly-So-Called in Hegel's *Science of Logic.*" *British Journal for the History of Philosophy.* Vol. 22, Issue 2. pp. 281–301.

Redding, P. 2015. "An Hegelian Solution to a Tangle of Problems Facing Brandom's Analytic Pragmatism." *British Journal for the History of Philosophy.* Vol. 23, Issue 4. pp. 657–680.

Redding. P. 2019a. "Hegel and the Tractarian Conception of Judgment." In: Mácha, J. and Berg, A. eds. *Wittgenstein and Hegel: Reevaluation of Difference.* Berlin: De Gruyter.

Redding, P. 2019b. "Hegel's Treatment of Predication Considered in the Light of a Logic for the Actual World." *Hegel Bulletin.* Vol. 40, Issue 1. pp. 51–73.

Redding, P. 2019c. "An Hegelian Actualist Alternative to Naturalism." In: Giladi, P. ed. *Responses to Naturalism: Critical Perspectives from Idealism and Pragmatism.* London: Routledge. pp. 120–143.

Redding, P. and Bubbio, P. 2014. "Hegel and the Ontological Argument for the Existence of God." *Religious Studies.* Vol. 50, Issue 4. pp. 161–181.

Reich, K. 1992. Trans. Kneller, J. and Losonsky, M. *The Completeness of Kant's Table of Judgments.* Palo Alto, CA: Stanford University Press.

Ricketts, T. 1985. "Frege, the Tractatus, and the Logocentric Predicament." *Nous.* Vol. 19, Issue 1. pp. 3–15.

Rödl, S. 2007. "Eliminating Externality." In Ameriks, K. and Stolzenberg, J. eds. *Metaphysik im Deutschen Idealismus/Metaphysics in German Idealism.* Vol. 5 of *Internationales Jahrbuch des Deutschen Idealismus/International Yearbook of German Idealism.* Berlin: De Gruyter. pp. 176–188.

Rödl, S. 2018. *Self-Consciousness and Objectivity: An Introduction to Absolute Idealism.* Cambridge, MA: Harvard University Press.

Rosen, M. 1982. *Hegel's Dialectic and Its Criticism*. Cambridge: Cambridge University Press.

Rosen, M. 1988. "From Vorstellung to Thought: Is a 'Non-Metaphysical' View of Hegel Possible?" In: Horstmann, R. P. and Henrich, D. eds. *Stuttgarter Hegelkongress 1987: Metaphysik nach Kant?* Stuttgart: Klett-Cotta. pp. 248–262.

Russell, B. 2015. *Principles of Mathematics*. Routledge Classics. Reprint. London: Routledge.

Schick, F. 2002. "Die Urteilslehre." In: Schick, F. and Koch, A. F. eds. *G.W.F. Hegel: Wissenschaft der Logik. Klassiker Auslegen,* Bd. 27. Berlin: Akademie Verlag. pp. 203–225.

Sedgwick, S. 1991. "Hegel's Strategy and Critique of Kant's Mathematical Antinomies." *History of Philosophy Quarterly*. Vol. 8, Issue 4. pp. 423–440.

Sedgwick, S. 2012. *Hegel's Critique of Kant: From Dichotomy to Identity*. New York: Oxford University Press.

Sorensen, R. 2005. *A Brief History of the Paradox: Philosophy and the Labyrinths of the Mind*. New York: Oxford.

Stern, R. 1990. *Hegel, Kant and the Structure of the Object*. New York: Routledge.

Stern, R. 2009. *Hegelian Metaphysics*. New York: Oxford University Press.

Stern, R. 2016. "Kreines on the Problem of Metaphysics in Kant and Hegel." *Hegel Bulletin*. Published Online October 17.

Stewart, J. 1996. *The Hegel Myths and Legends*. Evanston, IL: Northwestern University Press.

Taylor, C. 1975. *Hegel*. Cambridge: Cambridge University Press.

Thompson, M. 2008. *Life and Action: Elementary Structures of Practice and Practical Thought*. Cambridge, MA: Harvard University Press.

Tolley, C. 2006. "Kant on the Nature of Logical Laws." *Philosophical Topics*. Vol. 34, Issue 1. pp. 371–407.

Tolley, C. 2017. "The Relation between Logic and Ontology in Kant." In: Emundts, D. and Sedgwick, S. eds. *International Yearbook of German Idealism*, Vol. 12. Berlin: De Gruyter. pp. 75–98.

Tolley, C. 2019a. "The Subject in Hegel's Absolute Idea." *Hegel Bulletin*. Vol. 40, Issue 1. pp. 143–173.

Tolley, C. 2019b. "Hegel's Conception of Thinking in His Logics." In: Lapointe, S. ed. *Logic from Kant to Russell*. London: Routledge. pp. 73–101.

Varzi, A. 2009. "On the Interplay between Logic and Metaphysics." *Linguistic and Philosophical Investigations*. Vol. 8. pp. 13–36.

Weiss, L. 2018. "Ground in a Teleological Sense: Meta-grounding in Hegel's Science of Logic." Unpublished manuscript.

Werner, A. 2018. "Hegel on Kant's Analytic/Synthetic Distinction." *European Journal of Philosophy*. Vol. 26, Issue 1. pp. 502–524.

White Beck, L. 1978. "Did the Sage of Königsberg Have No Dreams?" In: White Beck, L. ed. *Essays on Kant and Hume*. New Haven, CT: Yale University Press. pp. 38–60.

Williams, R. 2017. *Hegel on the Proofs and the Personhood of God: Studies in Hegel's Logic and Philosophy of Religion*. New York: Oxford.

Winegar, R. 2016. "To Suspend Finitude Itself: Hegel's Reaction to Kant's First Antinomy." *Hegel Bulletin*. Vol. 37, Issue 1. pp. 81–103.

Wittgenstein, L. 2005. Trans. Pears, D. and McGuinness, B. *Tractatus Logico Philosophicus*. 2nd ed. New York: Routledge.

Wittgenstein, L. 2009. Ed. and Trans. Hacker, P. M. S. and Schulte, J. *Philosophical Investigations*. 4th ed. Oxford: Wiley-Blackwell.

Wolf, C. 2019. "The Province of Conceptual Reason: Hegel's Post-Kantian Rationalism." PhD dissertation, Marquette University. https://epublications .marquette.edu/dissertations_mu/873

Wolff, M. 1981. *Der Begriff des Widerspruchs. Eine Studie zur Dialektik Kant und Hegels*. Berlin: Hain.

Wolff, M. 1986. "Über Hegels Lehre vom Widerspruch." In: Henrich, D. ed. *Hegels Logik: Formation und Rekonstruktion*. Stuttgart: Klett-Cotta. pp. 107–128.

Wolff, M. 1995. *Die Vollständigkeit der kantischen Urteilstafel: Mit einem Essay über Frege's Begriffschrift*. Frankfurt am Main: V. Klostermann.

Wolff, M. 2013. "The Science of Logic." In: de Laurentiis, A. and Edwards, J. eds. *The Bloomsbury Companion to Hegel*. New York: Bloomsbury Press.

Zambrana, R. 2015. *Hegel's Theory of Intelligibility*. Chicago: University of Chicago Press.

Zambrana, R. 2019. "Actuality in Hegel and Marx." *Hegel Bulletin*. Vol. 40, Issue 1. pp. 74–91.

Index

9 781316 512562